FIRST WORLD, THIRD WORLD

First World, Third World

William Ryrie

First published 1995 by
MACMILLAN PRESS LTD
Houndmills, Basingstoke, Hampshire RG21 6XS
and London
Companies and representatives
throughout the world

ISBN 0–333–62314–2 hardcover
ISBN 0–333–65731–4 paperback

A catalogue record for this book is available
from the British Library.

10   9   8   7   6   5   4   3   2
04   03   02   01   00   99   98   97

Copy-edited and typeset by Povey-Edmondson
Okehampton and Rochdale, England

Printed and bound in Great Britain by
Antony Rowe Ltd
Chippenham, Wilsthire

Published in the United States of America 1995 by
ST. MARTIN'S PRESS, INC.,
Scholarly and Reference Division
175 Fifth Avenue, New York, N.Y. 10010

ISBN 0–312–15873–4 hardcover
ISBN 0–312–17279–6 paperback

Contents

List of Tables

List of Figures

Acknowledgements

This book was written in the year or so after I retired from the IFC (using a computer which was the senior staff's generous farewell gift). A number of people at the IFC and the World Bank have been immensely helpful with advice and information. I am especially grateful to Rita Bhagwati, my research assistant, without whose extraordinary diligence and tolerance of my unreasonable demands the book could not have been written. I am also grateful to Guy Pfeffermann, Nissim Ezekiel, Richard Frank and Will Kaffenberger, who all reviewed my material and offered me valuable counsel and guidance. Bob Solomon of the Brookings Institution in Washington, David Henderson of the Institut des Etudes Politiques in Paris and Ian Byatt, a former Treasury colleague, were generous with their time in reading and commenting on the draft. My son Alec, who was studying history at St Andrews University as I was writing, helped with perceptive comments. And my wife, Christine, not only helped me, month by month, in developing the project and discussing it at every stage, but corrected drafts, pointed out many flaws, and rescued me from innumerable tangles with the computer caused by my incompetence.

WILLIAM RYRIE

Introduction

International aid is in crisis. It is a crisis which has crept up over a number of years, but gradually, so that its full extent is not appreciated. There is presently much more confusion about the basic purposes and aims of international aid than ever before in the past half century. This is reflected in the fact that official aid is now under attack from an extraordinary number of directions.

There are those who see aid simply as a diversion of resources from more pressing needs at home – the "charity begins at home" school. On the other hand a vocal lobby complains that aid budgets are too small, and that the larger countries, in particular, are failing to meet UN targets for the percentage of GNP which should be devoted to aid. (Demands for more aid usually come from people who regard the amounts of debt owed by poor countries as evidence that they need more aid.)

From the political right and some academic economists comes the argument that aid simply does not work – meaning that it does not increase economic growth. Some indeed argue that aid must be positively harmful to poor countries because it conflicts with sound economics, causing distortions and misuse of resources and creating inefficiency through dependence on subsidy. On this view, at any rate in its extreme form, poor countries would be better off with no aid. On the other hand, many left-minded groups are vehemently opposed to the types of aid provided and the policies promoted by institutions such as the World Bank, precisely because they see mainstream economics as irrelevant to the problems of poor countries, and likely to result in the rich becoming richer and the poor poorer. Aid, on this view, should consist mainly of direct action to reduce poverty, by implication through redistribution rather than growth.

A general hostility to governments and big institutions sometimes unites critics of aid from both the right and the left. This is the source of the romantic proposal that all aid should be channelled through non-governmental organisations or NGOs. To those who hold this view, the fact that such organisations (no matter how unrepresentative they may be) operate locally and on a small scale rather than on large projects is positively welcome. At the same time, aid is increasingly under attack from people who are more concerned with the environment than with promoting economic development, and who see the two as in conflict, especially where big industrial or infrastructure projects are involved. Some of the environmental opponents of aid are nonetheless interventionist, willing to use the need of the less-developed countries as an opportunity to induce them to adopt better environmental policies than have generally been followed in the now-rich industrial world.

Again, there is a crescendo of attack on official aid programmes for supporting corrupt governments (and allowing aid itself to be used for corrupt purposes), governments which spend massive amounts on armaments and undemocratic governments which do not respect human rights. This appears sometimes as a general condemnation of Third World aid and sometimes as an argument for using aid to coerce recipient countries into more democratic behaviour. The tendency to think of "development" as consisting of promoting the political and social beliefs of donors (including, amongst other things, equality for women) has increased greatly in recent years.

In another part of the field, a battle goes on about the use of aid to support the commercial objectives of donor countries. Some see this as a diversion of aid from its proper purposes and others who would like to see more aid used to assist their own countries' export and investment interests.

And the whole debate takes place against the background of a profound change in economic policies in much of the Third World over the past ten years. Policies which allow market forces to operate more freely and encourage the private sector to play a leading role in economic growth are now widespread. International financial markets have been providing previously unheard-of amounts of private capital to a number of developing countries. The implications of these far-reaching changes should be a central issue in the current debate about aid, but so far they are not.

This immensely confused debate – most of which takes place in the First World rather than the Third – reflects a general disillusionment and cynicism about official aid. The confusion about objectives, and the consequent difficulty of assessing performance, must be one underlying reason for this disillusionment. Amongst the general public in First World countries, attitudes range from outright hostility on the part of voters as taxpayers, especially in the United States, to a passive indifference which simply accepts aid as part of the given order of things, an attitude which is more common in Europe. Neither attitude reflects any conviction that official aid achieves worth-while results.

Paradoxically, however, in the First World, the aid business thrives and grows. The numbers of people engaged in development and aid is now very large and continues to grow – in government departments and the large number of international development agencies of all kinds, including many in the UN family; in institutes and research organisations devoted to analysing the problems of poor countries in extraordinary detail; and in colleges and universities where the popularity of "development studies" seems still to be on the increase. Third World development has become a profession. The volume of literature produced annually on the subject in its many aspects is far beyond the ability of any one individual to keep abreast of.

I have become convinced that a new effort must be made to deal with this confusion and to bring more coherence and rationality to the whole subject. I start from a personal conviction that the effort to improve the lot of people in poor countries certainly deserves support in principle; but that we must be very clear about what we are trying to achieve and ruthlessly honest in assessing success and failure. We must also beware of the insidious dangers that lie in the self-satisfaction to be derived from doing good to the poor; and of the danger that the institutional interests of long-established development organisations and the career interests of those who work in them, may over-ride the essential aims of aid.

International aid has to be seen in the context of the overall relationship between the First and Third Worlds over the half-century since the end of World War II: indeed it has been a central theme in that evolving relationship. To understand the problems we confront now, it is important to look back over the whole of this period. It happens that this has been, more or less exactly, the period of my working life, although I have been directly involved in aid and development matters for only a part of it. A few words about my own experience of the Third World and development problems may shed light on what follows.

I am a child of the Third World – though of First World parents – born in Calcutta, India, in 1928. Until I was 15, home was a village some distance north of that city, where my father built a school to train Bengali teachers. My brother, sister and I played with the village children, speaking Bengali, while we were at home, but for the greater part of the year we were at school in Darjeeling, in the foothills of the Himalayas. It was then a beautiful wooded place, looking out, as it still does, on the magnificent Kanchenjunga, the third highest mountain in the world.

In adulthood I have more than once revisited these childhood places, in rural Bengal and in the mountains, to find both changed, but recognisable. In both cases, there has been a bewildering increase in the numbers of people, and at the same time a limited but perceptible improvement in their living conditions. Today the density of population in rural Bengal is almost overwhelming, but at the same time the evidence is everywhere of the agricultural advances which make it possible for this huge number of people to eat. As for Calcutta itself, the change from the elegant city I knew well as a boy in the early 1940s is very sad – a degree of squalor, deprivation and overpopulation I have not seen anywhere else.

The Second World War prolonged my childhood years in India – but for Hitler, we would have come home to Britain in 1940. Eventually my father managed to get berths for the family on a troopship returning to Britain in 1944. I then spent seven years at school and university in Edinburgh, Scotland, which is my home city, if I have one. But Asia still called and in the early 1950s I returned there for a year as a young army officer. My compulsory two years of service in the army offered the opportunity of a posting to Malaya, which I seized. More recently I have enjoyed the experience of returning to that country also, now part of Malaysia; but in this case the change is a total transformation – a stride forward in the wealth of the country and the standard of living of the people which makes it unrecognisable compared with 40 years ago.

After the army I joined the British Civil Service, not out of a vocation to be a civil servant, but with the sole intention of working in the Colonial Office, to which I succeeded in getting myself appointed. In 1956 I was offered a two-year secondment to an African colony. I chose Uganda and spent two wonderful years there, first in the capital, Entebbe, and then as an Assistant District Officer in the Northern Province. This was my first experience of Africa and the longest time I have ever spent on that continent. I have been back to East Africa many times since, but only once to Uganda, in 1993, when again I revisited the places I knew as a young man. The effects of years of war and the perverse policies especially of the dictator Idi Amin were still obvious. The Uganda of the mid-1990s, although it is now making slow progress, is in a condition which is, sadly, little or no better than that of the late 1950s.

My last four years in the Colonial Office were spent as a member of the International Relations Department. The United Nations was involving itself very much in the affairs of the countries which were still under colonial rule. I spent several months in New York at meetings of the General Assembly and the Trusteeship Council, working under the former Colonial Office official and Governor of Uganda, Sir Andrew Cohen, who then spoke for the UK on these matters in the UN. Cohen, an unusual and gifted man, was a realist and a liberal, who strongly believed in the need to conciliate the anti-colonial pressures in the United Nations.

But the times were changing fast. In the 1950s it was possible to believe that a career in the Colonial Office had a future, but not in the early 1960s. When Ghana, then known as the Gold Coast, became independent in 1957 – the first British colony in Africa to do so (apart from the Sudan, a special case) – expatriates working in Uganda speculated that that country might follow in 1970 or 1980. But to the perceptive it was clear that the old system was crumbling, and in fact the date of Uganda's independence was to be 1962. De Gaulle in French Africa and Harold Macmillan and his Colonial Secretary, Iain Macleod, in British Africa brought the two main European empires in Africa to an end in the early 1960s.

In 1962 I moved to Her Majesty's Treasury, and there I stayed for 20 years, on a variety of assignments, quite a number of them to do with international affairs of a financial and economic kind. In the 1960s, this did not involve many dealings with the Third World – I worked mainly on international currency matters and British dealings with the International Monetary Fund. But in the mid-1970s I was posted to Washington, where I spent four years as the British Treasury representative in the United States, as well as Board member and spokesman for Britain at both the IMF and the World Bank.

This job obviously involved close dealings with both of the main Bretton Woods institutions. I spent some time studying and reporting on the American economy. The British financial crisis of 1976, when the Labour government was forced by its own mismanagement of the economy to turn to the IMF for help, dominated my life for a couple of years. But over these four years I was also involved with the World Bank in its world-wide development role. The Bank was then under the leadership of Robert McNamara, whom I came to know well and admire, who expanded it vigorously and moved it into new fields. And I had some dealings with the International Finance Corporation, the private sector adjunct of the Bank, then a relatively small organisation.

There followed two years back in London in a senior position in the Treasury as one of the Second Permanent Secretaries, dealing with domestic affairs and particularly the state-owned or "nationalised" industries. In 1982 I moved to the Overseas Development Administration, the British aid agency, as Permanent Secretary, where I stayed until 1984. This job involved the management of the UK aid programme. The ODA's budget included both bilateral aid and British contributions to international organisations, including the European aid programme, as well as the World Bank and the UN specialised agencies. To do the job effectively, it was important to travel to the main countries receiving British aid, and I made a number of journeys to Africa and the Indian sub-continent.

In 1984 things changed again. The then President of the World Bank, Tom Clausen, asked me if I would come back to Washington to manage the International Finance Corporation. I was interested at once, because I had the feeling that the IFC's day had come. In the mid-1980s, the private sector was moving to the forefront of the development scene everywhere. Although the Corporation was small, it was the leading private-sector aid agency in the world and it had just been given a big capital increase to enable it to expand. At the IFC, I could expect to have all the advantages of operating as part of the World Bank Group, but also a large measure of operational independence. I accepted the job without hesitation.

There followed nine hard but immensely rewarding years. The job involved not only managing the IFC, its programmes and projects, its finances and its staff; dealing with its shareholders and clients, expanding its role; but also travelling to all parts of the Third World and thinking about the development challenge in the 1980s and 1990s. It involved working closely with the World Bank. All through my time at the IFC, the Third World was changing fast and I became increasingly convinced that the whole development task and challenge had to be seen in a new light. It is these thoughts and ideas which are the main theme of this book.

1 International Development, 1949–94

The phrase the "Third World" was invented in the early 1950s by the French sociologist Alfred Sauvy. The world, as he observed it in the immediate aftermath of the Second World War, was divided into two great blocs – the capitalist, democratic west and the communist east, the First and Second Worlds. But this classification was incomplete – it did not encompass the whole of mankind. There were also the poorer, backward countries of Asia, Africa and Latin America who were thus the Third World or "Tiers Monde", the French formal usage echoing the name of the third house of the French parliament of the *ancien regime*, the Tiers Etat.

It is a phrase which suggests a view of these countries, which now make up about three quarters of the population of the globe, as somehow outsiders on their own planet, and that way of thinking has persisted, even in the minds of Third World people. Sauvy's three-part classification would not readily suggest itself to anyone looking at the world anew today – the phrase "First World" is hardly ever used, and the "Second World" has all but disappeared. But the "Third World" is still very much with us, and to most people its defining characteristic is that it is poor. And so, many people assume, it will always be.

In fact, of course, the Third World, even when the phrase was first invented, was a varied group of countries with differing standards of living, and it has become much more variegated over the past half-century. What the Third World shared, with all its variety, was relative poverty and therefore a pre-occupation with trying to raise standards of living. So, for most of the second half of this century, governments and people in both the Third World and the First World have been concerned with the problem of "development". (The Second World, the former Communist Bloc, was involved only to a limited extent and for what appeared to be political and propaganda purposes.) However, with a few

1

striking exceptions, success in the battle with under-development
and poverty has been elusive, progress painfully slow.

The period immediately after the Second World War was one
of optimism and creativity rare in human history. It was in this
post-war atmosphere that the western democracies embarked on
an unprecedented effort to raise standards of living in poor
countries and alleviate poverty, partly through bilateral aid
programmes, directly from donor governments to the Third
World, and partly through the family of new international
organisations which appeared on the scene in the late 1940s. The
international development movement, which was to be a key part
of the relationship between the First and Third Worlds for the
next four decades, was launched.

The effort to promote economic development in poorer
countries, initiated by the western capitalist democracies soon
after the end of World War II, is something which distinguishes
the second half of our century from all previous periods of history.
It is important to understand how novel it was at that time. The
notion that richer countries, through their governments, should
accept responsibility for efforts to raise standards of living in
poorer countries would have seemed bizarre to most people in
previous periods. In fact, the idea that governments were
responsible for the economic well-being even of their own citizens,
through the "management" of the economy, was also fairly new.
The origins of development aid lay partly in the extension to the
international sphere of this new view of the responsibilities of
governments, and partly in the idealistic internationalism of the
immediate post-war period.

Since those heady, creative days, nearly half a century has
passed and much has changed. The aid movement was launched
in a mood of optimism, especially in the United States, which is
hard to appreciate in the atmosphere of the 1990s. Now it is all
too obvious that the movement has lost its sense of purpose and
direction. The mere passage of time is one factor in this –
institutional decay in the national and international organisations
concerned with aid and development. The ending of the Cold
War has changed the environment in which the development
movement has operated. The budgetary problems which most of
the richer countries now face is another factor. Popular cynicism
about the effectiveness of the whole effort is pervasive.

And there is another highly relevant factor. Aid was and is predominantly an activity of governments, and in recent years we have been witnessing a world-wide change in attitudes to governments and the functions they should or should not perform. The world-wide shift, over the past decade or so, towards market-based economic policies poses far-reaching questions for international aid and development which have been only partly recognised and confronted by practitioners in the field. So the basic questions about the aims of development and the purpose of international aid have to be asked again. We need to re-examine the record of the aid effort, which now covers nearly half a century, to see what it tells us about what can be achieved by the efforts of governments and international agencies to promote economic development, and what cannot. This book is an attempt to throw some light on these issues, based on my own involvement with them at various times and in various different capacities since the 1950s. Written by a First World person, it is naturally concerned to a considerable extent with what western countries can or should do, and therefore with "aid". But First World people should not fall into the trap of thinking that western aid has been the main factor in determining the success or failure of the development effort in the Third World. Aid is only part of the picture, to be considered in the context of the wider question of the overall progress in development by the Third World.

We can articulate the questions which demand attention now only if we understand how we arrived at the point where we stand in the mid-1990s. So I begin with an attempt to pick out the main strands of the story of international aid over the past four and a half decades. Later chapters suggest a broad assessment of the success or failure of the development effort, with some attempt to discern the historical reasons for both. This leads to the question of the nature of the development task now. I believe that, in the deeply changed environment in which we now live, it must be very different. And, before presenting my conclusions and some thoughts about the future, in Chapter 11, I shall offer some observations about the Bretton Woods institutions now and in the future, in the light of my experience of those institutions, particularly as head of the International Finance Corporation, the private-sector arm of the World Bank, for nine years.

* * *

If the international development effort is to be dated from any particular moment it should probably be the launching of President Truman's "Point Four Programme" in his inaugural address of January 1949. Speaking for a nation that was then by a huge margin the richest and most powerful in the world, he said:

> More than half the people of the world are living in conditions approaching misery . . . For the first time in history, humanity possesses the knowledge and skill to relieve the suffering of these people . . . I believe we should . . . in co-operation with other nations, foster capital investment in areas needing development . . . Democracy alone can supply the vitalising force to stir the peoples of the world into triumphant action, not only against their human oppressors, but also against their ancient enemies – hunger, misery and despair.

The aid effort in the early stages took the form mainly of "bilateral" aid by individual donor countries which could afford it. The United States, as we shall see, played a leading role, but the efforts of the European countries which had been on the winning side in the war were also very significant. But the launching of the international aid effort was also reflected in the creation of international mechanisms whose financial role was at first small but which became very influential as time went on. This was the origin of "multilateral" aid.

At the end of the Second World War, a new family of global organisations emerged, including the United Nations itself and its Specialised Agencies such as UNESCO, WHO and FAO. There were also the new world financial institutions which emerged from the conference held at Bretton Woods in New Hampshire in 1944, the International Monetary Fund and the World Bank. A great deal of ingenuity went into the creation of these institutions. The IMF was launched to promote international monetary stability and unfettered trade and payments, and was not primarily concerned with development or poverty, although later on it would become very much involved in the affairs of less developed countries. In its early years, the International Bank for

Reconstruction and Development (IBRD), the World Bank, focussed chiefly on post-war reconstruction in Europe and Japan; but in the 1950s and 1960s it moved on to become mainly concerned with development in poorer countries. The World Bank was founded on a simple ingenious formula that has continued to be its basis for half a century. Capital is provided by the governments of the richer countries (at first predominantly the United States – the US share in 1946 was 41 per cent of the total). However, most of this is contributed not in cash, but in the form of capital which could be called up if necessary. This "callable" capital costs the rich countries nothing (no call on it has ever been made), but provides a basis for the institution to borrow on keen terms in international financial markets. These funds can then be on-lent to countries which could not borrow for themselves on comparable terms. The IBRD money which is lent to developing countries, therefore, comes not from taxpayers but from the markets. This model was later copied in a number of regional development banks in Asia, Latin America and Africa.

In 1960 this IBRD lending was supplemented by the creation, within the World Bank Group, of the International Development Association (IDA) for very poor countries who could not afford to borrow even from the IBRD. The IDA provides credits repayable over very long periods at nominal interest rates (35 years at 1 per cent), terms which make them effectively grants. In contrast to IBRD loans, this type of aid requires donations from governments using tax-payers' money. Ever since then the IDA has been replenished every three years by new contributions from the donor countries.

When one considers the novelty of the whole idea, a remarkable aspect of the story of international aid is simply the scale of the effort. Table 1 and Figure 1 summarise the global flow of aid funds from the First World to the Third World over the four decades from 1950 to 1993.

As early as the first half of the 1950s the total flow of aid from the main industrial countries and the international organisations they supported averaged about $8 billion a year in terms of US dollars of 1987 value. By 1960–61 this had trebled in real terms to $24 billion; and over the next thirty years, to the beginning of the 1990s it more than doubled again in real terms to over $60 billion.

Table 1   Aid to Developing Countries (in constant 1987 US dollars: $ billions)

	1950–55*	1961	1971	1981	1991	1993
Net concessional aid	7.9	15.3	18.0	30.4	50.5	44.6
bilateral	–	15.9	14.9	21.1	36.9	31.5
multilateral	–	–0.5	3.1	9.3	13.6	13.2
Net official development finance	N.A.	24.0	23.4	53.7	63.2	55.4
bilateral	–	23.6	17.0	25.8	42.5	36.2
multilateral	–	0.4	6.4	27.9	20.7	19.2
*annual average						

Note: "Concessional aid" covers grants and loans at concessional interest rates. "Official development finance" includes concessional aid and also other loans provided for development purposes.

Source: OECD.

Table 2 Aid as a Percentage of Donor Country GNP

	1950–55	1960–61	1980–81	1992–93
United States	0.32	0.56	0.23	0.17
France	1.24	1.35	0.67	0.63
Germany	0.11	0.38	0.45	0.38
United Kingdom	0.42	0.56	0.39	0.31
Netherlands	0.27	0.38	1.01	0.84
Sweden	0.04	0.06	0.80	1.01
Japan	0.04	0.22	0.30	0.28
EU (combined 1993 members)	0.52	0.64	0.45	0.43
Total OECD countries (1993 members)	0.34	0.52	0.35	0.32

Note: The figures are based on net concessional aid only, but include contributions to international aid funds such as IDA.

Source: OECD.

Table 2 shows the main countries' contributions as a percentage of their own national incomes. The average for the industrial countries together (the members of the Organisation for Economic Co-operation and Development or OECD) was a little over one third of one per cent of those countries' GNP even as early at 1950, rose to a half of one per cent in 1960 and then fell

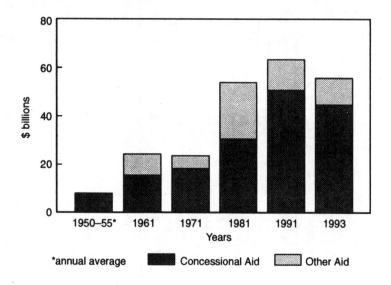

Figure 1   Aid to Developing Countries (in constant 1987 US dollars)

Table 3   Aid flows from Main Donor Countries in Real Terms (in constant 1987 US dollars: $ billions)

	1950–55*	1961	1971	1981	1991	1993
USA	4.50	10.26	7.73	7.23	9.69	7.86
Germany	0.15	1.24	1.82	3.98	5.93	5.63
France	2.01	3.06	2.67	5.22	6.44	6.40
United Kingdom	0.76	1.55	1.54	2.74	2.79	2.35
Japan	0.04	0.27	1.27	3.96	9.42	9.10
*annual average						

Source: OECD figures.

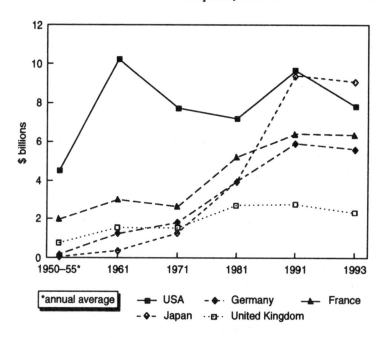

Figure 2　Aid Flows from Main Donors (in constant 1987 US dollars)

back to about a third, where it has remained ever since, although with significant variations between countries.

I should explain that I use the word "aid" here, and throughout the book, in its broad popular sense, that is, meaning any official funds provided for the purpose of economic development. In the aid business a distinction is properly made between "official development assistance" or ODA, meaning aid in the narrow sense of grants and soft loans, i.e. loans at concessional interest rates (or, strictly speaking, the concessional element of such loans); and aid in the wider sense of "official development finance" or ODF, which includes both ODA and finance provided for development on market-like terms, which the recipient countries could not themselves obtain from the markets. The distinction is, of course, important, but in common parlance "aid" refers to either or both. The figures include only official aid, not money provided by non-governmental or charitable organisations (known as NGOs). The total amounts provided by such bodies is now large – about $6 billion a year in 1993 – but there is a dearth of information about where it goes and for what purposes. A substantial part appears to go to disaster relief although many NGOs are also involved in small project financing.

Figure 2 and Table 3 show how the contributions of the main donors progressed in real terms over the years. In the early stages, the factor of American wealth was of course important. With Europe and Japan devastated by war, the US in 1950 accounted for about 63% of the GNP of the industrialised countries. US aid grew strongly at first – by 1961 it was over double the amounts of the early 1950s – but then weakened, falling in real terms over the next two decades and recovering to something like the levels of the early 1960s only at the beginning of the 1990s.. In 1960–61 the United States was providing 58 per cent of the total flow of concessional aid, an amount equal to 0.56 per cent of US GNP. By the early 1990s, the US was providing only 18.7 per cent of the total, corresponding to less than 0.2 per cent of American GNP.

At the same time, another remarkable aspect of the story was the strength of the European contribution, even in the early stages, and especially that of France. French aid levels were always high, exceeding the British both in absolute terms and as a percentage of GNP, but heavily focussed on French colonies and former colonies. German aid overtook the British in the 1970s and now runs at over double the UK rate. European aid, like the American, grew very fast in the first decade, up to the early 1960s, and then more slowly until the mid-1970s. But, unlike the American, it has continued to grow rapidly since the mid-70s, including aid through the instruments of the European Union, formerly the Community. From the 1970s onwards a significant part of European aid was provided through Community mechanisms, mainly under the successive Lomé Conventions (the first signed in 1975, the latest, Lomé IV, in 1989). The remarkable fact is that by 1980 the member countries of the EC, with a collective GNP only slightly larger than that of the United States, were already providing more than double the amount of aid coming from the United States, and by the early 1990s over two and a half times.

A number of smaller European countries, especially the Netherlands and the Nordic group, became significant aid donors in the 1960s and have out-performed all the larger countries except France in terms of aid as a percentage of their GNP over the period since then.

The Japanese contribution was naturally very small at the beginning of the period. Japan became a member of the OECD in 1964 and was keen to behave like a leading industrial power. Her economy was growing very fast in the 1960s, and Japanese aid rose sharply from the late 60s onwards. Expressed in dollars of the time, it was only slightly less than the American contribution in 1992 and has since exceeded it, making Japan the largest single aid donor in the world in dollar terms. This comparison is affected by the strong appreciation of the yen against the dollar in the late 1980s. As a fraction of Japanese GNP, aid rose to a third of one per cent in 1980, close to the OECD average, and has not changed much since then.

Where did this aid go? The distribution has changed over time, as Figure 3 and Table 4 show. In the early stages, the main area of concentration was Asia, followed by the middle east and north Africa. The middle east share fluctuated with changing politics, whereas that of Asia, after rising until the end of the 1960s, has declined sharply over the last two decades. Latin America has never been a major recipient of concessional aid, although some poorer countries in the region have. The main gainer since the beginning of the 1960s has been Sub-Saharan Africa. In 1960–61 Africa was getting only 9 per cent of the global aid flow, but by the beginning of the 1990s this had risen to over 30 per cent. By the end of the period we are looking at, Africa had become very much the priority for aid donors.

So much for the numbers. What were the motives which led donor governments to provide aid? They were of course mixed. Through the four-decade story, there appear to have been three main motives: humanitarian (or developmental), political, and commercial.

The origins of the international development movement lay in a combination of humanitarian and political concerns. Amongst the major donors, the humanitarian motive was probably at its

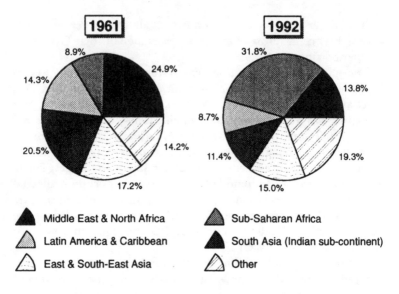

Figure 3   Regional Distribution of Aid*

Table 4   Regional Distribution of Aid* (per cent)

	1961	1971	1981	1992
Middle East & North Africa	24.9	8.3	14.2	13.8
Sub-Saharan Africa	8.9	18.4	27.5	31.8
Latin America & Caribbean	14.3	12.3	9.6	8.7
South Asia (Indian Sub-continent)	20.5	22.8	18.8	11.4
East & South-East Asia	17.2	23.7	12.7	15.0
Other	14.2	14.5	17.1	19.3
	100	100	100	100

*Based on net concessional aid in current US dollars.

Source: OECD.

strongest in the early days of the movement. As we look back from the cynical 1990s we should not underestimate the part played by idealistic motives at the start. At a time when American power and self-confidence were at a peak, the US displayed an optimism about what could be achieved through aid which seems naive now. It was no doubt influenced by the success of the Marshall Plan, where US generosity seemed to have paid off well. Within a few years Europe's economic regeneration had begun and that success seemed to have provided a basis for democracy in western Europe and stemmed advancing Soviet power.[1] Could not something similar be achieved in the less-developed world?

But, as the case of Marshall aid itself shows, from the very earliest days, political considerations played an important part. Truman's "Point Four Programme" was part of a wider vision of the post-war world, outlined in the speech. The first three points were support for the United Nations, continuation of the Marshall Plan and new defence arrangements which eventually emerged as NATO. Within a few years of the end of the war it had become clear that the post-war world was not, in fact, going to see an harmonious functioning of the new global institutions, but confrontation between world blocs. An important American motive for the Point Four Programme was a desire to contain communism by promoting prosperity, especially in countries around the fringe of the USSR; and as time went on Soviet activity in the Third World, especially in the middle east and Africa, strengthened this motivation. This became an important part of the environment in which the development movement evolved.

In the American case political factors, especially cold-war factors, became more dominant as time passed and eventually this resulted in an extraordinarily skewed distribution of American bilateral aid, based on Congressional views of priorities. Humanitarian motives have appeared to play a much smaller – indeed a minor part – in American aid in recent times. To illustrate the point, in 1991, one country, Egypt, received no less than 32 per cent of American aid and Israel, a relatively rich country, 8 per cent. These figures exclude military aid. Nicaragua and Honduras between them received another 4.6 per cent, while the whole of Sub-Saharan Africa got 3.6 and India 0.8 per cent.

Political considerations, although of a somewhat different kind, were important in Europe also. European governments shared cold-war motivations to some extent, but in the case of the colonial powers other motives were at work. The colonial empires of the victorious European powers appeared to stand intact in 1945, but they would be largely gone within twenty years. A desire to retain influence in former colonial territories was a factor in aid, particularly in the case of France. Indeed, much of this expenditure in former French colonies, and some of it in parts of the Third World which remained legally part of France, was in forms peculiar to the French system, which perhaps should not be included in aid statistics – expenditure on teachers, policemen and administrators, evidently aimed mainly at maximising the influence of France and French culture. French aid was and is focussed on Africa and they were also able to influence the direction of European Community aid towards Africa. The British aid effort was also concentrated to a considerable extent on former colonies, but was both smaller and of a different character.

Humanitarian motives seem now to be more alive in Europe than in the US, although very much mixed with political and commercial motives in the case of the larger donors. European aid programmes have generally given a good deal of priority – more than the American – to helping the poorest countries. And the smaller countries of northern Europe, the Netherlands and Scandinavia, still seem to be motivated primarily by humanitarian concerns.

In the case of Japan, whose aid programme now roughly equals the American in terms of current dollars, political motivations are more difficult for a westerner to discern or interpret. There would not appear to have been any strong cold-war motivation in Japan's case, but especially in the early days of Japanese aid a lot of effort was concentrated on building up Japanese political influence in neighbouring Asian countries, and supporting Japanese exports. In the 1980s, however, the growth of Japanese aid and the de-linking of aid from exports were partly a response to the objections of Japan's powerful trading partners to her persistent trade surplus. Under American and European pressure, Japan increased its share of IDA funding to 15.5 per cent of the total in 1984–85, as part of a deal which gave her the second position in the IMF and World Bank. Japanese aid, which was originally concentrated mainly on Asia, now contains a significant African component.

*   *   *

As the international development movement expanded in the decades after 1950, another trend emerged. Commercial considerations began to play an increasingly important part in aid policies and decisions. The movement had begun with a good deal of idealism, but business interests in the many donor countries became increasingly aware of the possibilities of using aid expenditures to further commercial objectives – financing exports or construction contracts for the benefit of companies in the donor countries, or providing a market for farm produce. This kind of influence generally runs a greater risk of diverting aid from its original and basic purpose than political pressures. The argument, seductive at first sight, has usually been that aid can serve a dual purpose, both contributing to development in poor countries and supporting commercial interests in the donor countries. In my period as Permanent Secretary of the British Overseas Development Administration, I started from a position of sympathy for the dual-purpose approach, but gradually came to the conclusion that the use of aid money to support exports usually meant that it did not effectively serve the purpose of development.

Unsurprisingly national bilateral programmes have been more prone than international aid to being corrupted by commercial objectives. Aid expenditure by individual governments is susceptible to pressures from companies in the donor country. International development organisations such as the World Bank are more able to avoid such pressures. For many years now, the aid programmes of most donor countries have included funds which are used supposedly for dual development-commercial purposes.

The British case is probably typical. The "Aid and Trade Provision" (ATP) was introduced in 1977 by a Labour Government, responding to pressures from industry for aid to be used to help them secure export contracts, and thus support employment at home, in competition with foreign firms that were said to be receiving such help from their own governments. The arrangements were extended by the Thatcher government in the 1980s. This part of the aid programme was (and is) spent on the initiative of the Department of Trade and Industry, reacting to requests from British firms. The British aid administration, the ODA, is required to give an opinion on the developmental value of the projects, but this usually has little influence: the fact is that when the commercial interest is acknowledged as legitimate, it tends to predominate. While the British government's aid policy is to give priority to the poorest countries, ATP allocations do not conform to this criterion at all. There have recently been some flagrant cases, such as the Pergau dam in Malaysia, where British aid was provided to a country whose standard of living was much too high for it to qualify for aid under the normal rules, to secure business for British companies in a questionable project as part of a deal involving the sale of armaments. If aid is used primarily for the purpose of supporting national exports, justified by the argument that other countries do it too, it becomes a pointless competition in subsidy and in the end wasteful for all countries which join in the game.

Many of the same objections apply, it must be said, to the practice of tying aid to the purchase of goods or services from the donor country, which has been common amongst donor countries since the beginning of the development movement. However, this, although undesirable, is more understandable. It may make the aid less than optimally efficient, but it does not generally pervert its purpose, as arrangements like the ATP are apt to do.

International efforts through the Development Assistance Committee of the OECD to regulate the use of aid in this way have had limited success. However, it is interesting that Japan, which had been one of the most blatant users of aid for commercial purposes, withdrew from this type of activity in the mid-1980s when it came under pressure to reduce its balance-of-payments surplus which was also driving the yen up against other currencies. The Overseas Economic Co-operation Fund or OECF, a Japanese agency which was originally created to provide subsidised finance in support of Japanese exports or Japanese private investment, now finances exports and investments from other countries also. But this is an exception: the widespread use of aid to support national commercial objectives continues to corrupt the process and encourage public cynicism about the whole activity.

Moreover, corruption of the more obvious kind, which is a danger with aid programmes generally, is particularly likely to occur where aid is linked to exports. Recipient countries and their ministers see through the whole thing easily and manipulate the donors for their own purposes, playing one off against another. I recall a minister of finance of Sri Lanka, when I was visiting on behalf of the ODA, telling me that he could "offer" us a particular dam for British aid and construction. He was not so crude as to ask for an inducement, but discussion with the British firms in the running for contracts made it clear that they knew who would take the decision and how to persuade him. British aid had been dragged into an unpleasant game in which it should never have been involved.

And of course we must recognise that aid has often been perverted by blatant corruption on the part of ministers and officials in recipient governments. In the nature of things this is a hidden part of the story which it is not possible to tell in detail. But the general fact can hardly be doubted. There can be no reasonable doubt that many people in power in Third World countries have succeeded in enriching themselves by taking a percentage of aid provided for projects in their countries. Estimates of the amounts involved have been put forward from time to time but are necessarily speculative. The indications seem to be that, although this kind of thing has no doubt occurred in many countries, it has been at its worst in Africa and in countries which have had governments with arbitrary powers whose activities are not open to public scrutiny.

In short, over the years since the international development movement was launched, powerful commercial interests have come to have an influence on it in most countries. Industry in donor countries has become a supporter of aid – or at least of certain kinds of aid – because it has acquired a vested interest in it. This, and corruption on the part of recipient governments has diverted a part of the aid effort away from its original and basic purpose – how significant a part, we really do not know.

The story of aid and development is also part of a wider story: the evolving relationship between the First and Third Worlds over the past four decades. The relationship went through several phases. The development movement was initiated at a time when a significant part of the Third World was still under colonial rule; and in the early stages western countries dominated the scene and there was little dialogue. But as time went on the Third World found its voice and in the 1960s an intense international debate developed, which was considerably influenced by the existence and activities of the Second World. For a number of years the Third World seemed to have a kind of institutional existence in the Non-Aligned Movement, launched at a conference at Bandung in Indonesia in 1955. Despite its title, the movement, which included Castro of Cuba and Tito of Yugoslavia, was more concerned with attacking the capitalist west than the communist east.

To begin with, this First World-Third World debate took place mainly in the United Nations. In the two decades after the War, the UN was transformed by the accession to membership of a large number of newly independent countries. Between 1945 and 1970, 56 such countries joined the membership, as the African empires of Britain, France and Belgium disappeared. The western industrial democracies found themselves in a minority in the General Assembly and other UN bodies. In the late 1950s and through the 1960s colonial issues were the dominant concern of the majority of members of the UN. The Trusteeship provisions of the UN Charter, which established a system of accountability for one group of colonies (mainly those which had changed hands after the First World War and had been under the League of Nations Mandate system) and a more general requirement in the Charter that colonial powers should provide certain information to the UN, provided a basis for debates on colonial questions.

In the 1960s and the 1970s the former colonial powers – and those, like Portugal, which continued to be colonial powers for some time – were increasingly forced on to the defensive in the international debate about economic development. This attack on the western countries took place against the background of the fight for independence of the colonial countries and was inevitably influenced by the emotions of that episode. Colonialism was frequently held to be the cause of economic backwardness in former colonial countries, an argument for which little supporting evidence could be produced and which ignored the fact that parts of the Third World which had never been under colonial rule, such as Ethiopia, had done no better than the ex-colonies, and worse than many of them. To this was added a general assault on the western capitalist democracies, who were said to be in control of the world economy, partly through multinational companies, and were therefore charged with responsibility for the poverty of the

Third World. The Leninist notion that imperialism and capitalism were in fact aspects of the same phenomenon was a powerful and appealing idea to the emerging Third World, and one which of course tarred the United States with the same brush as the colonial powers, and indeed made it even more a target of attack.

The USSR, always better at public relations than at economic performance, was highly successful for many years in escaping blame and in putting about the view that the problems of the poorer countries in the world were due to capitalist exploitation. In fact, the Communist bloc of countries made a very small contribution to the international development effort, consisting mainly of a few high-profile projects, carefully selected for political impact, and usually technically third-rate as it turned out. The demand for a "New International Economic Order", which was much talked of in the 1970s, also reflected the view that the capitalist west was to blame for poverty in the Third World and that an alternative world economic system could overcome these problems if only the richer countries would find the political will to introduce it. How exactly this was to be achieved, even if the "political will" had been there, was never convincingly explained.

An intellectual justification of sorts for this kind of approach appeared in the dependency theory which became popular especially in Latin America in the 1950s and 60s. This theory (one of whose main prophets was the Brazilian economist Fernando Henrique Cardoso, who 30 years later, with a very different philosophy, was to become President of Brazil) maintained that market domination by the major capitalist countries and corporations deprived poorer countries of the freedom to develop their economies except as the capitalist centres of power allowed. This dependency led to the populations of these countries becoming impoverished or "immiserated" like Marx's industrial proletariat. It was, in fact, a quasi-Marxist view of capitalism as a form of imperialism, and as basically in conflict with development. Under-development was not a stage prior to capitalism, but a consequence of the expansion of capitalism. This kind of thinking was one element in the demands for a New International Economic Order.

Much of the Third World's complaint about the world economic "system" centred around terms of trade and commodity prices in particular. A number of attempts were made to establish systems to protect primary exporting countries from the effects of fluctuations in commodity prices. However, what the commodity exporters were really pressing for was not schemes which merely evened out fluctuations, but sustained higher prices to raise incomes in the exporting countries. In hard reality, this could have been achieved only by regulating and limiting production, something which the producing countries were, with one major exception, unable to organise. The exception was of course OPEC, the oil producers' cartel, an area where production could be much more closely controlled by governments than in the case of most commodities and where the industrial powers were particularly vulnerable.

The early response of most of the western countries to this assault was conciliatory. A sense of guilt played a part in the process, particularly in the case of the former colonial powers, although in an economic sense there was very little for them to feel guilty about. During the 60s and 70s there was much discussion, in response to this Third World pressure, of schemes to regulate commodity prices. It was the age of UNCTAD, the United Nations Conference on Trade, Aid and Development, a gathering which took place in Geneva in 1964 and left a permanent secretariat in being, headed by Raul Prebisch of Argentina, one of the originators of the idea of the New International Economic Order. The conference approved a plan for "Supplementary Finance" to help developing countries deal with falls in export earnings, especially those due to weakening commodity prices.

This was very much in the spirit of the times. So was the "North-South" dialogue, an idea promoted by President Giscard d'Estaing of France, which became fashionable especially in Europe in the 1970s. People concerned about poverty hoped that talking to each other might produce new ideas for dealing with the problem, although, as became increasingly apparent, the real solutions were to be found only in sound economic policies. It was the time when it became mandatory to speak not of "under-developed" or "less-developed" but of "developing " countries, a term redolent of the political correctness and economic illusions of the time. (The notion of political correctness was of course invented later, but is precisely apt in this case.)

The political debate took place mainly in various organs of the United Nations. A contrast developed between the UN institutions and the so-called Bretton Woods institutions, the IMF and the World Bank, based in Washington, which operated in a less political atmosphere. This has to be attributed mainly to a difference in the way the institutions were constituted. The UN institutions operated on the basis of one-country-one-vote, although financial contributions were related to each country's size and wealth. In the Washington institutions, voting power was related to financial contributions. This realistic basis had the effect that the richer countries were willing to endow the Washington institutions with much more substantial resources, making them considerably more effective in practice. They were two different worlds. While the United Nations indulged in heated debate on matters such as the New International Economic Order, the World Bank was increasingly able to deploy significant and real resources for development. A number of the UN Specialised Agencies – WHO, FAO, UNESCO and others – which performed a useful role as providers of technical assistance for a time (and one, the UN Development Programme, still does) became highly politicised, which provoked the Americans and British to withdraw from UNESCO in 1983.

As time went on and the political demands in the UN became more shrill and insistent, the effect on attitudes in the richer countries turned gradually negative. For their part, the western countries tired of the attacks and began to forget their sense of guilt. UNCTADism, the demands for a new economic order and support for the dependency theory gradually faded. The economic problems which afflicted developing countries in the 1980s, especially the debt crisis in Latin America, had the effect of persuading the leaders of many countries to face and deal with hard realities and to resort less to rhetoric. By the early 1990s the climate had changed radically, but that is a part of the story we shall come to later.

* * *

However, there was one important area where the attack on the First World did raise valid issues. What impact were the trade policies of the industrialised countries having on the economies of the Third World? Were the efforts of the First World to help the Third World through aid being undermined by the barriers to their exports into the developed markets? Might developing countries have been better off with no aid, but open market access?

The subject has to be approached with a dash of realism. Aid is financed through national budgets, so that it forms a small part of the general burden of taxation which does not fall on any group in particular. Access to markets for developing country products, on the other hand, is likely to affect particular groups, sometimes painfully, so that they often fight hard to protect themselves. The resistance is wont to come from less well-off parts of the population who may take little interest in Third World development. So it is often easier for politicians to vote for aid than for market access and it is not altogether surprising if they end up taking positions which, from a developing country viewpoint, seem mutually contradictory.

It is also fair to add that the record of the Third World, as it has demanded access to developed markets, has not been exemplary in the opposite direction. It was often argued that it was appropriate for developing countries to protect "infant industries", while expecting the advanced countries to open their doors to their exports. But the infancy often became prolonged and, generally speaking, it was not until the 1980s that "import substitution" policies became discredited and developing countries began to see it as in their own interest to open up their markets.

That said, however, the record of the First World countries in this field is not one in which we can take great pride. There are no reliable estimates of the cost to developing countries of protectionism in the developed world, but it has clearly been substantial.

The easiest part of the question concerns the commodities produced in developing countries which are not in competition with any produced in industrial countries. Tropical products like coffee, cocoa and tea, and certain mineral products which do not occur in large amounts in the industrial countries, such as copper and bauxite, do not in practice compete seriously with industrial country products. Exports of many of these products brought great benefits to developing countries in the 1950s and 60s. This was followed by hardship when prices weakened in the 1970s, as supply grew faster than demand, and in some cases substitute products emerged; but generally speaking, there were few problems of access. An important exception, however, is the case of bananas, where the European system discriminates in favour of certain Third World countries and against others – an extraordinary intervention in international trade based on no European trading interest.

Products which do compete with First World output fall naturally into two categories: agricultural products and manufactures. Agriculture is the area of greatest distortion in world trade and this has had a considerable impact on developing countries. Systems of protection and subsidy have been operated by virtually all the rich industrial countries over the decades since World War II. The European Common Agricultural Policy is the most comprehensive system of agricultural protection in the world with probably the greatest impact on developing countries, although American and Japanese policies have also been damaging. The CAP maintains high prices for a variety of products produced in the Union (formerly the Community) by means of market intervention and a common external tariff, making it virtually impossible for an outsider to export products covered by the CAP to Europe. The Union also subsidises its own produce for export, thus driving down prices in external markets, including markets in a number of commodities which are important to Third World countries.

At the same time, it is characteristic of the European system that selected developing countries are given privileged access to the European market in the form of quota rights which can be very valuable to developing country exporters because, within their quotas, they can sell their products at the artificially high European prices. A classic case is sugar, a commodity which is most efficiently produced in the tropics (in cane form, rather than beet) but where the leading industrial countries, including the United States, have distorted the market in a way that denies the tropical producers their natural advantage. But the impact on developing countries differs widely: those who have quotas are able to sell a fixed quantity in Europe at a price which in the three years 1992–1994 averaged 52 US cents a kilogram. Those who do not may have to sell their output on the world market, where the price for the same three years averaged 23 cents per kilo.

There is no question that the effect of agricultural protection and subsidies by the industrial countries on the developing world has been damaging. Subsidised food exports to developing countries do provide consumers there with cheap food, but it is through the effect on agricultural producers in the Third World that the damage is done. Artificially depressing the prices of agricultural products in backward countries undermines the agricultural sector, driving people off the land and into the towns – precisely the effects that the subsidies are intended to avoid in the industrial countries, and effects that are in direct conflict with aims of aid programmes. To make matters worse, the European Community for a time in the late 1970s and early 1980s developed a programme of "food aid" which consisted of unloading some of the surpluses accumulated through market intervention, in poor countries, often in forms that were unsuitable from a dietary point of view. This programme was later modified.

A number of studies have suggested that if the Common Agricultural Policy were simply abolished the developing world's aggregate GNP would be higher by significant amounts, although the effect on individual countries would differ widely. Burniaux and Waelbroek concluded in 1985[2] that without the CAP, the income of developing countries as a whole would be 2.9 per cent higher. Latin America, where few countries have privileged access to the European market, would gain by almost 4 per cent of its national income, south-east Asia by 2.8 per cent, and even Africa, where most countries have European quotas for agricultural products, would gain by 1.8 per cent. According to this study, the only area that would lose from the abolition of the CAP, and that only marginally, is the Mediterranean.

However, the question of trade in manufactures is probably more important still. If serious economic development is to take place, Third World countries must move into the export of manufactures on a substantial scale, and this requires access to developed country markets. This in turn calls for industrial changes in the developed countries in sectors where Third World producers have become competitive. This adjustment is painful, especially when unemployment is high, and efforts to avoid that pain have been the main cause of the protectionist policies adopted by the developed countries.

Over the post-war period there has been remarkable progress in the lowering of tariffs in world trade in manufactures generally through successive GATT rounds. This kind of progress was particularly marked in the period up to about 1974, by when tariffs on manufactures had fallen on average from 40 per cent at the end of World War II to between 6 and 8 per cent, and the subsequent Tokyo and Uruguay rounds took this process further. Probably the main benefit of this went to the industrial countries themselves, but developing countries also benefited. Total imports of manufactures from the developing countries into the main industrial countries – the United States, Europe and Japan – have been rising steadily for some time, both in absolute terms and as a percentage of all imports of manufactures into these countries. More significantly, they have been rising as a percentage of the GNP of the importing countries. Between 1980 and 1990, imports of manufactures rose from 1.3 to 2.1 per cent of European Union GNP. In the case of the United States they nearly doubled from 1.3 to 2.5 per cent. Japanese imports of manufactures from developing countries are lower as a percentage of GNP, but have also risen – from 0.7 to 1.2 per cent during the 1980s. These figures do not in themselves tell us much about of the relative openness of these markets to developing countries' exports because they are influenced by a wide variety of factors affecting competitiveness. On the face of it, the United States would appear to be somewhat more open to developing country exports of manufactures than the others, but the US figures include imports from a number of richer – and highly competitive – developing countries in east Asia whereas Europe is more open, although in a selective way, to imports from a number of poor countries.

However, from the early 1970s onward, when economic conditions in the advanced countries were less favourable and unemployment was generally higher, a new protectionist trend emerged. It took the form, not of tariffs, but of discriminatory measures affecting particular sectors, mainly sectors where Third World competition was threatening jobs in the First World. These non-tariff barriers, quota limits of various kinds, have grown in number over the past two decades, and, although they have included a number of measures against Japanese exports to Europe and the United States, non-tariff barriers by developed countries have more impact on developing countries' exports than on trade amongst developed countries.[3] The barriers which have the greatest impact are in the field of textiles and clothing, where the Multi-fibre Arrangement, first introduced in 1974, has provided a comprehensive framework for restrictions on imports into developed countries.

It is more difficult to discern clearly the impact on the developing world of regional free trade arrangements amongst industrial countries, which have grown in number and importance in recent years. These arrangements, including the North American Free Trade Area and the European Union, do not generally involve putting up any new barriers against those outside each group; but they do, by their nature, involve discrimination in favour of members and against non-members. Developing countries are generally in the latter category – Mexico being a notable exception – although they too sometimes benefit from discriminatory measures in favour of some countries.

Such discriminatory measures are a feature of the European system. Europe maintains a generally higher level of protection than the United States but combines this with special measures to provide access for selected developing countries and products. The extraordinary mixture of such measures in Europe stems from conflicting pressures. There are pressures for protection from European producers threatened by Third World competition; and at the same time there are pressures to help particular poor countries, stemming partly from lobbies in European countries and partly from overseas governments which have friendly relations with European countries. The Lomé Conventions have been the framework for a complex set of trading arrangements with the ACP (Africa, Caribbean and Pacific) group of countries, most of them former colonies of European Union members; and there are special arrangements for other developing countries: for example, imports of textiles from Bangladesh, a very poor country, are favoured compared with those from Hong Kong and Singapore. Whether this selective manipulation in favour of certain countries is a desirable use of trade policy may be questioned.

It is easy – perhaps too easy – to conclude that more openness on the part of the main First World countries could have contributed very substantially to economic development in the Third World. Over the past half century, there has indeed been an inconsistency between the aid and trade policies of the First World. Estimates of the total long term effects of the removal of all trade barriers are difficult and uncertain, besides being politically naive, but it may well be true that open access to developed country markets would have contributed more to the development of those countries than all the aid which they have received. My conclusion is that, given the internal political pressures which governments have faced, the record, so far as trade in manufactures is concerned, is not a shameful one. The case of agriculture, however, is different. Political pressures from workers whose jobs are suddenly threatened by imports are understandable; but most of the structure of agricultural protection and subsidies, especially in Europe, was not created as a response to such threats from the developing world, and the use of subsidies, in particular, has been a means of invading world markets to the detriment of the interests of Third World countries, in direct contradiction of the declared purposes of aid policies.

* * *

In the last two decades of the international development movement, there has been a change of mood in the donor countries. In most of them, but particularly in the Anglo-Saxon countries, the idealism which characterised the movement in its early stages has declined and been replaced by a mixture of indifference, cynicism and outright hostility. In the United States each successive Administration since the 1970s has found it increasingly difficult to persuade the Congress to vote for aid programmes and voter pressures are generally hostile to foreign aid. In the American case a number of factors have contributed to this trend, including the general disenchantment with the world outside that followed from defeat in Vietnam, the change in attitudes to taxation, together with domestic budgetary pressures. American aid fell to less than 0.2 per cent of GNP, compared with 0.56 per cent in 1960, having declined by 25 per cent between 1992 and 1993. And voices have been heard in the new Republican Congress calling for aid to be abolished entirely, along with the American Agency for International Development. America, the initiator and leader of the movement in the post-war years, now seems to be abandoning the field.

In Britain things have not moved quite so far, but British aid, which also amounted to 0.56 per cent of GNP in 1960, now stands at 0.31 per cent. The aid programme now has only a handful of strong supporters in Parliament. Budgetary pressures and rising demands from the European Union for contributions to collective European aid are putting increasing pressure on Britain's bilateral aid programme.

France and Germany have maintained their programmes more effectively, despite budgetary pressures. French official development assistance was over one per cent of GNP in the 1950s. It fell to about 0.6 per cent in the 1970s and has remained in that area since then. German aid has declined slightly as a percentage of GNP over the past decade but in 1992 was still running at just under 0.4 per cent. It is probably fair to say that popular opinion plays a smaller part in determining the level of aid in these two countries. The main reason why France maintains a higher level of aid flow than the Anglo-Saxon countries has more to do with political and foreign policy objectives originating with the government than with popular support for the programme.

With aid budgets under pressure in a number of western countries, much of the burden has been moved to Japan, now the largest aid donor, in US dollar terms, accounting for 20 per cent of total aid to developing countries. However, decisions on this subject are largely left to the government and popular attitudes play little part.

At the same time, there are still countries where "aid-fatigue" and cynicism do not seem to prevail. In the Scandinavian countries and the Netherlands there continues to be a degree of support for the international development effort which surprises foreigners. The Netherlands and the Nordic countries have consistently exceeded the UN target of 0.7 per cent of GNP for official aid, although these countries have not been without their budgetary problems. However, in most of the larger developed countries there is a perceptible disenchantment with the aid effort. Hostility to the World Bank and its partner institutions extends well beyond the United States, and in fact is particularly strong in Europe.

And amongst the professionals of aid, there is widely perceived to be a "crisis". There is a general sense that the movement has lost its way. This is well illustrated in a recent British-American-Canadian report on *Crisis or Transition in Foreign Aid,*[4] which is not untypical of the genre today. The report rejects the notion of a "crisis", but, despite the eminence and expertise of the authors, it amply demonstrates the prevailing confusion by failing even to identify the problem. It is largely concerned with a description of the widely varying views to be found in the community of aid professionals around the world about the direction, purpose and priorities of aid in the 1990s. It is therefore hardly surprising that it offers no significant solutions or conclusions.

Why has this happened? Many factors seem to have contributed. Competing needs at home, at a time when most governments are fighting to control their budgets, contribute to the problem, but this simply confirms that for the electorates of many donor countries, although by no means all, aid is not a high priority. The commercialisation of aid has no doubt contributed to the mood of cynicism, as do frequent reports of the misuse of aid and of aid monies being stolen by corrupt officials and ministers in recipient countries, whether entirely true or not. In recent times the ending of the cold war has removed one motive for aid and added to the uncertainty about the purpose of the whole enterprise. Attempts by some groups to re-direct the effort towards new objectives, such as environmental concerns, equality for women or democracy, add to the confusion. There is much talk about poverty-reduction as a key objective, but views differ widely about what this should mean in practice.

But besides all this, there is an underlying factor which in my view is probably a more important reason for the current mood, namely a massive cynicism and disillusionment about what can be expected of aid. For as long as most people can remember, the Third World has been out there, apparently asking for money. It is hardly surprising that ordinary people in the First World assume that this is a permanent fact of life. As more aid is always needed, electorates in the richer countries have come to assume, whether they give the matter much thought or not, that aid does not achieve much. When the venture was new, it was not difficult to persuade electorates – and Americans in particular – to support an attack on world poverty. But four decades later it is difficult to overcome a general feeling that aid consists of pouring money into a bottomless pit, and simply does not achieve the results for which it is intended.

*   *   *

Behind these popular attitudes there lies a valid question which we cannot escape. What has the international development movement actually achieved? Many opinions are heard on the subject, some prejudiced and extreme, and it is important to form a balanced and fair view.

But if we are to start at the beginning, we should recognise that the question is worth considering only if the basic objective is worth while. Why should the First World care about standards of living or problems of poverty in the Third World? I, for one, start from the position that the original aim, as set out by President Truman in 1949, was an honourable one, and is still valid.

The basis of the international development effort is a dual conviction, part moral, part political. The moral conviction is that, just as each national community accepts some obligation to support its own weaker and less fortunate members, so the global community should acknowledge an obligation towards the less fortunate members of that wider community. There is no logic which could support the proposition that moral obligations towards the poor and weak stop at national boundaries. There are obligations which arise from our common humanity.

Admittedly the parallel with obligations to the disadvantaged in our own national communities is not a precise one. In the international arena the means by which these obligations can be discharged are very different. Both within national communities and internationally, the preferred way must be to help the weak and poor to help themselves – development rather than subsidy, aimed at independence not dependence. In fact, international development assistance generally has more this character than most programmes of support for the needy within national communities. In both cases there are groups who are unable to help themselves – in national communities, the aged and disabled who are recognised as needing direct support; and in some developing countries, people suffering from famine or war, who clearly need straightforward relief. But if aid which enables the needy to help themselves is the preferred approach, we should acknowledge that this is usually the aim of international aid. How successfully the aim has been achieved in practice is a point we shall come to.

But one must also enter three caveats, which are not always recognised by critics of aid. The first is that acknowledging a moral obligation towards less fortunate members of the human race does not mean accepting that richer countries in the First World are guilty of causing their poverty. In general there is no sound basis for arguing that this is so, although of course there are historical exceptions where the behaviour of individual First World countries and companies has done harm, sometimes lasting harm, to the Third World. There are also cases of the reverse. But the moral obligation I believe we should recognise does not rest on guilt.

The second caveat is that this is not about global egalitarianism. Some attacks on international aid assume that the objective is to equalise incomes world-wide – for example Lord Bauer in his book on *Equality, the Third World and Economic Delusion,*[5] devotes pages to demolishing this straw man. We shall come to the question of poverty and inequality within countries later, but an aim to equalise incomes between countries, even if a moral case could be made out for it, would be a fantasy.

A third caveat is that a moral obligation to help does not mean that outsiders should accept total responsibility for dealing with Third World poverty. On the contrary, the main responsibility rests with the people and governments of the countries concerned. It is not only mistaken but patronising to assume otherwise, and aid people must always beware of the danger of being patronising.

Besides the moral basis for the international development effort, the case for the aid effort rests on a political conviction: that we all stand to benefit from the greater stability and prosperity that should flow from successful economic development. The benefits which can follow, both for Third World people and First World, are many, including improved chances in the long run of democratic government.

The moral and political arguments for supporting aid aimed at development in the Third World are, I believe, sound and valid, subject to one overriding consideration. Everything depends on whether we can honestly believe that aid can and will *produce successful results in practice.* The difficult questions about the international development effort are not, in my view, about issues of principle, but about practicability. They are not about whether it is right to try, but about whether, after nearly half a century, we can be confident that we know how to achieve what we are aiming at. It is pointless for the protagonists and professionals of development, of whom I have now been one for some years, to complain about the growing cynicism and apathy of Western electorates if these electorates cannot be shown results. Voters have to be convinced that, as taxpayers, they are paying for something that works.

So what has the international development movement actually achieved in the past forty-five years? The next chapter attempts an answer.

2 Success or Failure?

By what test is the success or failure of the development effort to be judged? "Development" is one of the most over-used words in the English language, and has a number of meanings. I apologise to the reader for the frequency with which it inevitably appears in this book. What does it mean in this context of the Third World?

The convenient vagueness of the word allows people to stretch its meaning to include almost anything. There is a school which would use it to mean the achievement of a general well-being in the population and particularly the well-being of poor and disadvantaged groups. How this state of well-being is to be defined or measured is not always explained, but the argument offers opportunity for well-meaning people to add their own favourite ingredients to the soup. The availability of good educational and health services, as reflected in literacy rates, infant or child mortality rates and life expectancy may reasonably be regarded as measures of well-being and therefore of progress in development. But there are many other possibilities, such as the supply of potable water, average calorific intake, levels of pollution, the availability of electricity, or the number of telephones. It is suggested that not only the reduction of poverty but the achievement of greater equality, the reduction of discrimination against women and the handling of environmental problems should be treated as critical tests of developmental progress. Others, or sometimes the same people, would include progress towards democracy.

There is also a view, expounded, for example, in the 1994 *Human Development Report* of the UNDP,[1] which puts the emphasis heavily on "human" development in ways that may have little to do with standards of living. Human fulfilment, we are told, does not depend mainly on material wealth or income. Cultural and spiritual opportunities for self-expression and social tranquillity may be more important. No-one would dispute these points, which might be proclaimed from any pulpit, but should they be the concern of governments and official aid agencies, or do they belong to a different, more private sphere?

I take the position that the role of governments and aid agencies in this matter is to do the things which will raise income levels and so increase the choices available to people and their governments. The further one goes towards targeting specific social measures of well-being, let alone spiritual well-being, the greater the danger of thrusting outsiders' preferences and priorities onto the people of developing countries, of becoming paternalistic. The government of a country may have some justification for getting involved in some such choices, but outside aid agencies should be very cautious about it. After all, if these are appropriate aims for official development agencies, why should they confine themselves to poor countries? Why not a world development agency to promote human well-being in every country? The fact is that when countries become sufficiently rich they will not be likely to seek the help of aid agencies on matters like this. It is unacceptable for aid agencies to exploit the fact that countries are poor to impose alien values on them.

We avoid this kind of danger if we take the position that the main measure of "development" should be economic well-being as measured by average income per person. Gross National Product per capita is a general measure of the material standard of living. It is not a measure of the *quality* of life, and it is of course quite illogical to criticise it, as some do, for not being so; but rising incomes increase the choices available both to individuals and to the country as a whole which can certainly affect the quality of life. With rising income, a country has opportunities not only for greater consumption of goods and services by its population, but also other social advances, for example, better health and educational facilities or a safety net for the unemployed. Their choices may not always be what outsiders would prefer. And if it is argued that giving priority to raising income levels itself involves a value choice, the important point is that even this has to be the choice of the government and people of the country concerned and cannot be imposed from the outside.

So I make no apology for measuring the success or failure of the development effort mainly in terms of the growth of real GNP per head. This is also the most natural measure if one is taking a broad view and comparing the performance of countries and regions over time. At the same time, we should take some account of a few basic and uncontroversial social measures of progress, such as literacy and school enrolment, life expectancy and child mortality, measures which are also closely linked to economic advance. These points are particularly worth considering in cases where they present a picture different from the income-per-head statistics.

And we have to recognise the difficulty that the statistics we work with in Third World countries are even more questionable than in the First World. In many developing countries there can be significant income in non-monetary form, which the statistics of income per head do not capture. Market exchange rates often mean that figures in dollars do not accurately reflect the real purchasing power of incomes in local currencies. In an attempt to present a more accurate picture, the World Bank has recently produced estimates based on "purchasing power parities" or PPP. The poor, according to these numbers, are not as poor as the traditional numbers indicate. The PPP figures, which are also nothing more than approximations, give us a presumably truer picture of real incomes now, but they cast less doubt on the rates of growth and change over the years revealed by the traditional figures, and since they relate to recent years only they do not offer an alternative way of making long-term comparisons. So in the main there is no alternative to using the traditional figures as the main basis for discussion, while bearing their deficiencies in mind.

We must also remember that averages mislead. If there are extremes of wealth and poverty, as in Brazil, a relatively high average GNP per head may conceal the existence of wretched poverty. Chapter 5 contains some discussion of inequality and poverty.

So what can we tell from the record about the progress of development in the Third World over the past three or four decades in the sense of growth in standards of living? This is, of course, a different question from the achievements or failures of international aid. The evidence tells us that the main determinant of success or failure in development is the quality of the government of the developing country itself and the policies it follows. But aid has of course had its influence, benign or malign, which we must review.

Looking at the Third World as a whole, the picture is immensely
varied; but there has been overall progress as Figure 4 and Table 5
show. The average income per head of the people of the developing
world doubled between 1960 and 1980. It grew by 3 per cent a
year between 1960 and 1980 and then more slowly in the 1980s.
Over the same period, however, in the main industrial countries
average income more than doubled – it rose by 134 per cent – so
that GNP per head in the Third World, which stood at about 17
per cent of First World levels in 1960, had fallen to 15 per cent by
1990.

However, there were wide differences between regions in the
developing world, as the table shows. Latin America did fairly
well in the years 1960-80 and then badly in the 1980s. South Asia
(the Indian sub-continent) did poorly in the first period,
improving in the 1980s, while east and south-east Asia grew
strongly in the first period and then more strongly still. Africa's
performance in the first period was weak and in the second even
worse.

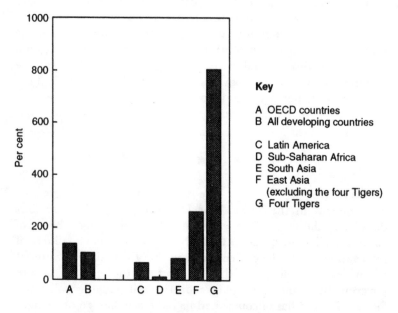

Figure 4   Growth of Income per Head (1960–92)

Table 5 Growth of Real Income per Head by Region

	GNP per capita (constant 1987 US$)		Total growth (per cent)	Average growth rate (per cent per annum)	
	1960	1992	1960–92	1960–80	1980–92
All developing countries	381	767	101	3.1	1.3
of which					
Latin America	1104	1799	63	2.9	−0.2
Sub-Saharan Africa	404	452	12	1.5	−0.8
South Asia	196	353	80	1.2	3.0
of which India	205	372	81	1.3	3.1
East Asia (excluding 4 Tigers)	122	433	255	4.0	5.7
of which China	79	320	305	4.6	7.8
Four Tigers	660	5954	802	7.1	7.5
OECD countries	7665	17894	134	3.2	2.3

Source: World Bank.

The most striking comparison is between developing countries generally and the four "Tigers" of east Asia – South Korea, Taiwan, Hong Kong and Singapore – which grew much faster than the rest and moved themselves out of the category of developing countries. These four were all unquestionably "Third World" countries in the years after World War II, with an average annual income per head in 1960 of $660 (measured in 1987 dollars); but over the three decades from 1960 to 1990 that income increased nine-fold, at a rate of 7.3 per cent a year, to nearly $6000.

In the overall picture the four Tigers are the outstanding exception on the positive side, while Sub-Saharan Africa (which is, of course, a much bigger chunk of the Third World) is at the other extreme. Africa, where populations have been growing faster than in other developing regions, and at a rate which rose from about 2.6 per cent a year in the 1960s to 3 per cent in the 80s, experienced slow growth of income per head in the 1960s and 70s, a little over 1 per cent a year on average. And since the late 1970s incomes in Sub-Saharan Africa have been falling. GNP per person declined, on average, by 0.8 per cent a year through the 1980s, with the result that the average income level in the early 1990s was hardly any better, and in a number of cases worse, than when the colonial powers withdrew in the 1950s and 60s. The contrast between the east Asian Tigers and Africa can be illustrated vividly by comparing the cases of Korea and Ghana. In 1960 Ghana's income per head was somewhat higher than Korea's. In 1990 Korea's had risen to $7600, while Ghana's stood at $430.

However, most of the developing world falls somewhere between these two extremes. India is such a case, an example of limited success. India's population has grown over the past 30 years at an average rate of 2.2 per cent a year, not a particularly rapid rate by Third World standards, but enough to have swollen the population from about 350 million at the time of independence in 1947 to over 900 million today. India's record during the 1960s and 1970s was one of GNP growth sufficient to raise income per head very gradually, at an average rate of 1.3 per cent a year. This was an achievement of sorts and to those who remember the Indian countryside, as I do, in the 1940s and 1950s, the improvement in the standard of living since that time is palpable. But such modest percentage increases have only a small effect when the starting base is very low. In the last decade, since the early 1980s, with reformed policies which allow more play for market forces, India has doubled its rate of growth of income per head to over 3 per cent a year; and there are lessons there that I shall come to. But after four decades of development effort it remains a very poor country, with an average GNP per head of about $300 a year.

A number of other Asian countries present a somewhat similar picture: Pakistan very slightly better than India in terms of the growth of GNP per capita, Bangladesh somewhat worse. Indonesia, with the advantage for a while of being a major oil producer, did better from the 1970s onward. Income per head grew at only one per cent a year in the 1960s, but the growth rate improved to 4.6 per cent in the 70s. In the 80s Indonesia began to benefit from improved economic policies and a rapid growth of exports of manufactures, but even this growth leaves it, in the early 1990s, with an income per head of only $670 a year. Malaysia, on the other hand (a country which declined to join the Non-Aligned Movement on the grounds that it was, in fact, aligned with the West) has benefited from market-based policies and attained a GNP per head of about $3160 by 1993.

China is a rather different case. As a highly controlled economy until the end of the 1970s and one which went through the self-destructive effects of the Cultural Revolution in the 1960s, China nevertheless achieved an overall GNP growth of nearly 7 per cent between 1960 and 1980 and improved on that in the 1980s. With population growth also firmly controlled, income per person grew by about 4.5 per cent a year in 1960–80 and, in terms of local currency, the yuan, by an extraordinary 8 per cent per annum in real terms through the following decade.[2]

The Latin American story is a very mixed one. At the end of World War II a number of countries in this area, especially Argentina, were regarded as being on the verge of achieving standards of living comparable with the western democracies. Some, particularly Brazil, achieved rapid rates of growth in the 1960s and 70s, despite social and political instability and high rates of inflation. Brazil's GDP growth rate was 9 per cent in 1965–80 and per capita income grew by a respectable 3.3 per cent a year. Mexico was also a fairly strong performer. In Latin America as a whole average income per head grew in the 1960s and 70s by about 2.9 per cent a year, which was by no means derisory – it was progress at a rate which would take about 25 years to double living standards. But the decade of the 1980s, dominated by the debt crisis which struck in 1982, was a disaster for Latin America and in the region as a whole GNP per head fell slightly. The figures for average income per person in Latin America cover such wide variations, not only between countries but within countries, that they are not very meaningful, but on average they are still substantially higher than in the large Asian economies, at about $2180 in 1990. However, at the beginning of the 1990s the whole area had not escaped from being regarded, not unreasonably, as a "developing" region, part of the Third World.

Another significant indication that the development effort has been less than fully successful is the inability of many countries to repay debt. How much debt a country can carry is a function of its productiveness. Large debts are not in themselves a sign of economic failure – a country may borrow heavily and invest in ways that increase its capacity to service debt. But when the burden of long-term debt is clearly beyond a country's capacity to service, this is an indication that the resources available to the country, including presumably the money that it borrowed, were not used productively. This is particularly clear in the case of Sub-Saharan Africa. The average debt burden now amounts to about 70 per cent of the GNP of African countries and most of these countries are unable to meet their debt obligations. The great bulk of this debt is owed to governments, reflecting aid provided in the past. It is common to treat the debt problem in Africa as indicating that the region needs still more aid – debt forgiveness in the first instance and further assistance in grant form. But the first point to note is that the large quantity of debt which cannot be serviced creates a presumption that aid was not used effectively in the past.

The case of Latin American debt is slightly different. The debt which precipitated the crisis of 1982 consisted of loans, not from official lenders, but from international commercial banks, which were flush with money as a result of the "petro-dollars" accumulated by the oil-exporting countries after the two big oil price increases in 1973 and 1979. The crisis was aggravated by the sharp rise in dollar interest rates in the early 1980s, which the borrowers had not expected, and by recession in the industrial countries and falls in commodity prices. Who was to blame for this debacle is arguable. The commercial banks, which pressed loans on Latin American governments and were ready to make loans for unspecified purposes, must bear a part of the responsibility; but in the last resort it is the borrowers, who borrowed too much, and often to finance consumption and current government expenditures rather than investment, who must accept the largest share.

Again, the contrast with Korea is interesting. Korea was for a time regarded as part of the debt crisis. In 1983 its foreign debt amounted to 63 per cent of its GNP, compared with 51 per cent in Latin America as a whole. But with its strongly growing, export-oriented economy, Korea was able to handle its problem and meet its obligations – a clear indication that it had used resources more productively.

*   *   *

In assessing the success of the international development effort, as I argued earlier, it is right to take account also of important social indicators, such as life expectancy, child mortality and literacy rates. Generally speaking, these indicators make the record look better. In each of these three areas, there has been remarkable progress in all developing regions over the past 20 to 30 years, as Figure 5 and Table 6 show.

These indicators show better levels of performance in East Asian countries and Latin America and weaker performance in Africa and in very poor countries like India and Pakistan. Clearly, levels of attainment in these fields are related to the overall income of the country. But the remarkable fact is that, even while GNP per head was falling in Sub-Saharan Africa, and for a few years in the 1980s in some Latin American countries, there was significant progress in these social fields.

One other area where there has been significant progress is in the efficiency of agricultural production. The so-called Green Revolution transformed the production of food-grains, especially in Asia, in the 1960s and 70s. The original impetus for the change came from research in institutes financed by western governments and foundations, especially the International Rice Research Institute (IRRI) in the Philippines and the Centro Internacional de Majoramiento de Maiz y Trigo (CIMMYT) in Mexico which

Table 6   Literacy, Life Expectancy and Infant Mortality

	Literacy (per cent)		Life expectancy (years)		Infant mortality (deaths before 1 year/ 1000 live births)	
	1970	1990	1960	1990	1960	1990
All developing countries	46	64	46.2	62.8	149	74
Latin America	71	84	56.0	67.5	104	49
Middle East & North Africa	29	54	47.0	61.0	167	60
Sub-Saharan Africa	27	51	39.9	51.8	165	106
South Asia	32	46	43.5	58.0	164	98
East Asia*	64	84	46.9	68.0	124	37

*does not include China and 4 Tigers

Source: UNDP Human Development Report, 1992, 1993 and World Development Report, 1992.

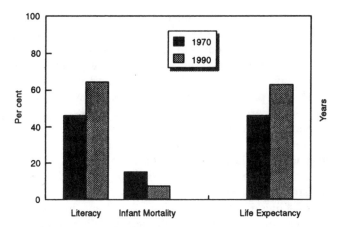

Figure 5   Social Progress (All Developing Countries)

developed new, high-yielding and disease-resistant strains of rice and wheat, capable of increasing the productivity of farming in some countries enormously.

The successful cultivation of these new varieties required plentiful rainwater or irrigation and also substantial amounts of fertiliser, which led to changes in the social organisation of farming, in which aid agencies played a significant part. But not all farmers benefited equally, and in recent times the social and ecological effects of the Green Revolution have been the subject of some controversy. However, we should not fail to recognise the extraordinary advance which it represented. It largely destroyed the spectre of famine, a scourge from which millions died in bad years in the past in some Asian countries. It enabled all the larger countries to produce enough food grains not only to feed their people regularly but to provide reserves against disaster. It was in fact one of the outstanding achievements of the international development movement.

The main achievements of the Green Revolution were in the cultivation of wheat and rice, and prolonged efforts to produce similar advances in crops grown in arid or semi-arid areas were much less successful. One result was that Africa has so far gained very little from the Green Revolution.

*   *   *

How are we to assess this overall record? Would the original participants in the international development movement regard it as showing that their hopes had been satisfied? Some of those original participants may have had naive expectations and it would not have been reasonable to expect the poor countries to be projected into prosperity in a few years or even a couple of decades. But we are talking about an effort by developing country governments and international aid agencies which has now lasted over 40 years.

The general conclusion must be that, apart from a few countries in the far east, the overall record has been, at best, disappointing. World Bank spokesmen are wont to say, with satisfaction, that standards of living in the developing world have doubled over the past half-century, but this has limited meaning if the starting point is woefully low. In most of Asia, the middle east and Latin America the progress which has been achieved has left oppressive problems of poverty unresolved after four decades. And in Sub-Saharan Africa we must frankly recognise failure (and the most acute questions about development methods and policies and about the impact of aid arise here). The majority of Third World countries remain poor, and many people in those countries very poor indeed.

The incidence of poverty is an apt measure of development progress in itself. Poverty is, not surprisingly, a field where statistics are particularly imprecise, but the reality of abject poverty is still all too apparent in much of the Third World today. It is not difficult, on the basis of common observation, to believe that, as World Bank figures show, in the early 1990s there were over a billion people, between a fifth and a quarter of the world's population, living in what the Bank graphically calls "absolute poverty".[3] The great majority of the people of Africa are very poor. Each of the large Asian countries, despite the progress they have made, contains tens or hundreds of millions of people living in squalor with no more than the barest necessities of life. Although India now has a substantial middle class, the number of "absolute poor" was recently estimated at about 36 per cent of the population, or 325 million people. And, of course, statistics of this kind are by no means the full measure of poverty – those living just above the "absolute poverty" line are still, by any standard, poor.

This has been so for such a long time that we have come to take it for granted; but should we do so after over 40 years of effort to achieve economic development and eradicate poverty? During that time a number of countries in east Asia, which started out in the 1950s as poor as the rest, have shown that it is possible to attain rates of growth which have raised the standard of living of their peoples to a different level and eliminated serious poverty. This is the east Asian achievement. Could other countries have achieved the east Asian rate of growth if they had done the right things? Probably not, but there is every reason to believe that they could have done better than they did. I return to the point in Chapter Four.

If there has been failure or partial failure, who is to blame? As a general rule the main determinant of success or failure in promoting economic growth is the policies which governments in developing countries follow and the quality of those governments. Of course there are historical and sociological factors which largely determine what kind of government countries have and limit their effective choices; but the final responsibility for success or failure in development must rest with those countries themselves. Nevertheless, aid donors and international agencies have their influence. What responsibility should be assigned to them?

An aid donor will usually have an influence of some kind on what happens in the recipient country, but it may be a narrow and limited one. Since aid began many years ago, it has mostly focussed on particular "projects", because the donor countries and agencies have sought to direct their contributions to something which they can influence, if not control. The effect that these projects have on the long term development of the country depends on a variety of factors – how well the projects are administered, how relevant they are to the real needs of the country, how they fit into the development programme of the country and whether they are supported by the government or undermined by bad economic policies.

There have been a number of studies of the effectiveness of aid, and these too have focussed on the impact of various kinds of projects. A lot of wisdom has been accumulated about what works and what does not work on a micro scale. A good example is a study, entitled "Does Aid Work?", by a group led by Robert Cassen, in 1986.[4] Not surprisingly, it came to mixed conclusions about the relative successes and failures of various kinds of projects. The Operations Evaluation Department of the World Bank has also produced a wide variety of studies, sometimes quite self-critical, of Bank projects.

However, such studies, valuable as they are, do not enable us to make a judgment about the *overall* impact of external aid on development. A number of studies have failed to discover any clear relationship, positive or negative, between economic growth and amounts of aid received. Regression analyses leading to the conclusion that virtually all aid goes to consumption rather than investment are controversial in the profession.[5] To arrive at a judgment about the impact of aid, there is little alternative to examining the growth record of each country, which depends to a large extent on government policies, and combining this with a view of the influence of aid donors and agencies on those policies and their implementation. The fact is that it is only the major international agencies that are able effectively to impose conditions related to overall government policies. Bilateral donors are usually concerned mainly with the implementation of individual projects and are reluctant to complicate their wider relations with the recipient country by getting involved in their macro-economic policies, even if the amount of aid in question is enough to give them that kind of influence.

The main international organisations which have influenced overall economic policies seriously are the Bretton Woods institutions. The IMF does so when member countries come to it for help. It is not mainly a development agency, and the conditions relating to macro-economic policies which it imposes are, in the main, short-term When it comes to influencing long-term policies for development, there is no other institution with clout comparable with the World Bank. Since the late 1970s or early 80s, the Bank, besides concerning itself with sectoral policies, such as energy, transport or agriculture, has sought to influence macro-economic policies when unsound policies threaten to undermine the effectiveness of development generally – for example by creating inflation. The various regional development banks – in Asia, Africa and Latin America – have largely left this role to the World Bank and confined themselves to projects. Another international agency which could make an impact on macro-policies is the European Commission, but it does not usually seek to do so.

But "conditionality" has its problems. Policies imposed on reluctant governments by outsiders often fail to achieve their objectives – governments which, in the current phrase, feel no "ownership" of reform programmes, implement them without conviction and abandon them as soon as difficulties arise. In the words of Tony Killick of the Overseas Development Institute in London: "Unfortunately, conditionality, being essentially coercive, undermines ownership".[6] According to Killick, three-quarters of World Bank adjustment loans in the years 1980–88 had disbursements delayed because conditions had not been complied with. Clearly, much more is achieved when governments look for outside help to carry out reforms in which they believe.

The influence which donors exert varies widely, depending partly on the amounts of aid being provided in relation to the size of the country, and on how far the country needs those resources. Table 7 tells us something about the amounts of aid received by various countries in relation to their own GNP. In the case of the large countries, such as India and Indonesia (both long-standing

Table 7   Aid as a Percentage of Recipients' GNP* (selected countries)

	1980–81	*1986–87*	*1991–92*
Sub-Saharan Africa	4.2	6.6	13.4
Kenya	6.3	7.1	9.7
Tanzania	12.6	14.3	39.4
Zambia	7.5	25.2	14.0†
Nigeria	–	0.1	0.9
Côte d'Ivoire	2.0	2.8	8.0
Sahel Region	14.8	20.5	16.5
India	1.3	0.8	0.9
Indonesia	1.1	1.1	1.7
Bangladesh	8.8	8.9	6.5
Philippines	0.9	2.6	2.9
Egypt	5.7	5.1	11.2
Turkey	1.5	0.6	0.6

*Note: The figures are for net concessional aid. If non-concessional aid is also included the figures are slightly higher in some cases (e.g. India, 1991–92, 1.2%), but not significantly different.

† 1990–91 figure

Source: OECD/World Bank.

aid recipients), China (a very recent one), and the larger Latin American countries, aid amounts to a tiny proportion of GNP. On the other hand, a number of poor countries, mostly in Africa but including Bangladesh and some in Latin America, have been receiving aid on a scale which amounts to 10 to 15 per cent of their GNP, and in a few cases even more.

Large countries where aid is small in relation to GNP are generally less susceptible to pressures from donors, especially if they have high savings rates and can generate substantial resources themselves, as most of the main recipients in Asia can. But even in a large economy, the marginal need for external finance when the balance of payments is weak and the country does not have access to foreign private capital, can be critical. The amenability of a country to the Bank's conditions also depends on what other pressures the borrower is under. The debt crisis in Latin America in the 1980s drove a number of countries to adopt policies recommended by the Bank which were very different from those they had followed for many years before. The voice of the Bank may have had some influence, but the grim economic realities probably spoke more eloquently.

However, other factors may come into play. The donor may be very anxious to lend and therefore reluctant to impose severe conditions. The World Bank's concern to meet its own lending targets has undoubtedly reduced its willingness to insist on conditions in many cases (I shall quote some examples of this in the next chapter). In the Indian case, an almost intimate relationship developed in which the Indians often influenced the thinking of Bank staff as much as the reverse.

Overall, the international agencies do not appear to have had a strong positive impact on the policies followed in the large Asian and Latin American economies. Even in large countries, however, by providing aid, especially in times of economic difficulty, external donors such as the World Bank frequently encouraged and supported governments in following policies of their own which were harmful from the point of view of economic growth. In the case of smaller countries, on the other hand, especially the poor and backward states of Sub-Saharan Africa, the direct impact of external aid donors and aid agencies was and is greater, and the international development community cannot avoid a large share of the responsibility for what has happened.

Sub-Saharan Africa has not suffered from lack of attention from donors. As we saw, both the share of global aid and the absolute amounts going to Africa have been rising strongly since the early 1960s. But during much of the period since the late 1970s, performance, as measured by GNP per head, has been deteriorating. In the decade of the 80s, a total of $142 billion, at 1990 prices, was poured into Sub-Saharan Africa in the form of grants and soft loans, a rate of flow which rose by the end of the decade to no less than $33 a year for every man, woman and child in the region. This is a rate of aid flow, amounting to about 10 per cent of average income per person in the region, which exceeds anything in the history of aid. Yet during that ten-year period, GNP per head *declined* continuously in most of Sub-Saharan Africa, on average by nearly 1 per cent a year.

It is true that a number of countries such as Uganda, Zaire, Angola, Ethiopia, Sudan, Somalia and Mozambique, have had periods of civil disorder which have made economic progress impossible. No external agency can be blamed for that; but very little of the external aid flow has gone to countries where there has been war and even those which have not experienced civil war have shown a record of falling GNP per head. We have also to acknowledge that weak or falling commodity prices during much of the 1980s made things more difficult for many African countries; and that, in African conditions, very rapid population growth probably makes progress in raising income per head more difficult (and paradoxically, rising populations reflect progress of a sort, as seen in longer life expectancy rates and lower child mortality rates). But the overall picture is one of large and rising volumes of aid combined with falling standards of living, failure by the basic test of development.

However, the impact of aid in Africa is not just a reflection of the amount. Africans are as sensitive as anyone to interference by outsiders in their affairs, but their need for external help, the enormous number of aid missions calling on governments of small countries, and the relative lack of sophistication and self-confidence of their ministers and officials has meant that the influence of the aid professionals of the world has been substantial. Most significant of all, perhaps, is the fact that many years of high and rising levels of aid create a condition in which African governments cannot conceive of doing without it. The corrosive effects of aid dependence and the mentality of dependence are evident in Africa today. Among the difficult questions which have to be asked is whether there is, in fact, some correlation between the amount of aid poured into Africa and the development failure. Is it possible (shocking as it may seem to the good people involved in this business) that excessive aid has actually retarded development progress in Africa? I return to this question later.

✻   ✻   ✻

This brings us to the question of the policies and methods which produced these disappointing results. Could more have been achieved by different policies and methods? The following two chapters review how governments in the developing countries and the international providers of aid have gone about the task of promoting economic development over the past four decades, and what lessons this record offers us for the future.

But there are two basic points to be emphasised. The first is that the only way in which countries with large numbers of people living in poverty can make a real impact on that problem is by achieving *a period of rapid economic growth sustained over a substantial number of years*. The length of time required to achieve a real impact depends, naturally, on the level of GNP per head at the starting point and the speed of growth; but for very poor countries we have to think in terms of GNP growth at rates of 8 to 10 per cent or more sustained over two or three decades.

This is what has not been achieved in most of the developing world, with the obvious exception of the "Tigers" of east Asia; and this is what development policy should be aimed at achieving. It now appears to be within the grasp of a number of Third World countries, especially in south and east Asia and in Latin America, to achieve this kind of growth in the years ahead, and this prospect holds out new hope for the poor in these countries.

The second point is that rapid growth will bring its problems, social and environmental, and one very regrettable consequence of the relative failure of the development effort so far is that most countries now face the challenge of growth with much larger populations, and especially urban concentrations of people, than they had three decades ago. The tragedy of lost time means that the environmental and social problems associated with rapid growth will be more difficult to manage than they would have been if rapid growth had taken place, say, in the 1960s and 70s, as it did in the four east-Asian Tigers. These problems will have to be faced and dealt with because there is no way other than rapid growth by which the Third World can escape from the poverty which has oppressed it for so long.

The Third World is still the Third World because most of it has not yet achieved this transforming growth. It is a reflection of this relative failure that, since the phrase was invented 45 years ago, the boundaries of the area which we think of as the Third World have not significantly changed. A few countries in the far east and some on the southern fringe of Europe (which were dubiously included in the first place) have dropped out, but otherwise the area is substantially as it was 40 years ago. So we tend to think of the Third World as part of the God-given order of things and the poor as always with us. The development task, according to this view, is never-ending and international aid is to be accepted as a permanent fact of life. Both First-World and Third-World people are trapped in this pessimistic mentality. Is this unavoidable, or can the Third World, after half a century, break out of the cage?

3 The Heavy State

In the four decades of effort to promote economic development in the Third World, one striking fact stands out. Over most of that time, developing countries leaned heavily towards state intervention, ownership and control as the means of achieving the objective. Generally speaking, the Third World differed from the Second in that the state did not exercise the total control and ownership seen in communist countries. Third World economies were characteristically mixed economies, but with substantially more state control and ownership than in the First World.

From the 1950s through to the early 1980s the prevailing view in most of the developing world was one which favoured

- state ownership of substantial parts of the means of production, especially industrial establishments of all kinds;
- government planning of the economy and therefore controls, in varying degrees, of investment, employment and production decisions by enterprises, including private companies;
- in many cases, price controls, partly for the purpose of subsidising basic necessities for the population;
- state control of the financial system, often achieved through government ownership of banks, for the purpose of directing credit towards investment in the areas regarded by the planners as deserving priority;
- protection of domestic markets from external competition by barriers against imports combined with policies designed to substitute domestic production for imports; and
- restrictions and controls over foreign investment.

Naturally, the extent and nature of these controls varied considerably from one country to another, but the remarkable thing is how widely prevalent this approach was in the developing world for three decades or more. It was to be found in all major regions, with the very significant exception of a few countries in the far east. In many countries the private sector was not regarded as having a significant role to play in development.

India is a good example. Until the early 1980s India had many of the characteristics of a command economy. A substantial part of the nation's industrial capacity was owned by the state, and virtually the whole of the financial system. There was always a private sector in India, consisting partly of companies going back to the early years of the century, long before independence. But in the 1960s and 1970s it was subject to tight control. Except for very small firms, all important business decisions – decisions about investment, production and employment – required approval by one ministry or another. The government effectively eliminated competition, which was regarded as wasteful, by deciding who should produce what, in what quantity and at what price. Indian entrepreneurs and company managers spent a large amount of their time negotiating with government officials over the permissions they needed to conduct their business.

The Indian market was surrounded by a wall of protection erected to prevent foreign competition and bar imports of products which the government believed Indian firms could make. One effect was that the quality of the products available to Indian consumers and companies was well below world standards. The importation of passenger cars, for example, was not merely restricted by tariffs or quotas, but banned – with the effect that Indians in the 1980s could buy only cars made in India based on European technology of twenty years earlier. In contrast to east Asian countries, India did very little to encourage its companies to export, and world markets for a wide range of consumer goods, where India could have performed well, were lost to other Asian countries.

India was in some ways an extreme case, but the pattern was replicated in varying degrees in many other countries. Egypt, after the fall of King Farouk and the accession to power of Nasser in 1954, moved to a socialist system. A large measure of state ownership and control was to be seen in countries as diverse as Turkey, Indonesia, Ghana, Morocco, Brazil, Argentina, Mexico, Tanzania and of course China where the Communists took over in 1949. And certain countries moved farther in this direction in the 1970s and 1980s – Chile moved abruptly (though temporarily) to a socialist system under Allende in the early 1970s, Jamaica moved to socialism in the 1970s, and Mexico nationalised all its banks as late as 1982.

How did it come about that the Third World was so socialist? A variety of historical and political factors played a part, varying from one country and region to another. In some former colonial countries, particularly British ones, a political alliance between independence movements and parties of the Left in the metropolitan country left a continuing influence. Jawaharlal Nehru, India's first Prime Minister, and his party, the Indian National Congress, had close links with the British Labour Party. The same can be said of a number of African leaders, such as Julius Nyerere of Tanzania, who was at Edinburgh University in the 1940s. India, as a founder and early leader of the Non-Aligned Movement, established a certain moral authority amongst developing countries and influenced the thinking of others.

It was natural for the leaders of the colonial independence movements, many of them educated at universities in Europe and the United States, and some in the USSR, to identify colonialism with the existing political and economic systems in the western world and be sympathetic to those who advocated radical change in those systems. Marxist thinking had its influence on the generation of leaders in the post-colonial countries, reinforced in cases such as India by close diplomatic links with the USSR. In the rhetoric of these leaders, "socialism" went along with democracy as a non-controversial objective.

In other cases, traditions of state management of the economy had quite different origins. In France and Spain the state had always played a more active role in economic affairs, and in the countries of the former French empire this tradition lingered after independence, strengthened by the fact that many French ex-colonies maintained close collaboration with the former colonial power. In the former Spanish empire, the tradition of a dominant state directing the economy was deeply ingrained, and remains part of the political background in much of Latin America, even though these countries gained their independence from Spain very much earlier, in the 1820s.

In a number of Third World countries the state became heavily involved in economic matters more for reasons of nationalism than socialist belief. In Mexico in the 1930s the whole oil and petrochemical sector was taken into state ownership and the constitution was amended to forbid private ownership in this field.

This was done less because of dislike of capitalism than because of a desire to ensure that these assets would not be owned and controlled by foreigners (that is by Americans). This desire to keep important national assets, especially mineral resources, out of foreign hands, combined with the fact that there were few private citizens in the country capable of owning and operating them, was a reason for state ownership in other Latin American countries, such as Brazil. In the Middle East, too, nationalist sentiment was the driving force of Iraqi and Egyptian socialism in the 1950s. And in a number of African countries foreign-owned companies were nationalised, not chiefly because they were privately owned but because they were foreign-owned. The anti-capitalist dependency theory, mentioned in Chapter 1, offered a theoretical justification not only for state ownership as a means of preventing foreign domination, but also for the protectionist, import-substitution policies which were the norm for many years in most of Latin America.

There were other reasons why much of the Third World leaned towards state management of the economy. An apparently good reason was that, especially in very poor countries, even those who believed in the private sector were often at a loss about where to start because there was no private capital to speak of and virtually no private sector, except for tiny, informal businesses and small-scale agriculture. This was particularly true in Africa. Leaders who were impatient to see economic growth and progress get going felt there was no alternative to doing it through the state itself, using the mechanisms of the state to mobilise the savings required and to make the investments. One weakness of this line of reasoning is that, in a good many countries in Africa, foreign private investment could have provided at least part of the answer and was doing so to some extent in the 1960s; but nationalisations and expropriations shut off the inflow of foreign investment. Having started this way, it was difficult for African governments to change.

A less good reason for state management of the economy (but a real one) was that government controls enormously increased the opportunities for ministers and officials to enrich themselves by corrupt means. The more private economic activities are controlled by the state, with agents of the state having discretionary powers of approval or refusal, the more corruption is likely to flourish. This is undoubtedly one reason why governments in some developing countries, especially in Africa, still resist pressures to privatise state-owned companies and to reduce government control of the private sector. Recently the question of corruption has come to be discussed more openly than in the past, and this is a sign of progress. But it remains a question to be addressed in considering the role of the state and the private sector in economic development.

If there is a common thread running through these varying motivations for state ownership and control of the economy in the Third World, it would appear to be a political/psychological one, related to Third World countries' feelings and fears about the First World. The association of colonialism with capitalism, the desire to avoid foreign ownership of national economic assets, the fear of competition from powerful capitalist economies, generally the fear of domination by the (capitalist) First World – in every region, these factors, in varying forms, were part of the explanation for the Third World's preference for state management of the economy. Nationalist sentiments combined with a fear of capitalist exploitation by foreign investors and competitors. The most obvious method of dealing with this perceived external threat seemed to be the state as owner of national assets and controller of the economy. As time went on, however, this would change, as we shall see.

Meanwhile, the First and Third Worlds had another relationship – through a rising volume of aid and strident demands for more. As providers of aid, how did the capitalist democracies, and their instruments like the World Bank, respond to the state-centred policies prevailing in most of the Third World?

It is important to understand that the whole international aid movement arose out of a period when interventionist thinking was much more prevalent in the industrial democracies than it is today. It was widely assumed that governments could organise economic growth. No one questioned that the international effort would take the form of transferring resources to governments. Even the United States accepted this and went along with development planning as part of the process. It is true that the US was the only country that seemed to have some qualms, which led it, in 1956, under a Republican administration, to promote the formation of an affiliate of the World Bank to support private-sector development – the International Finance Corporation. But the IFC was regarded as an irrelevant oddity by most of the development community and remained small and marginal for many years.

Ideas about how aid providers could best achieve their aims went through several phases. As the development movement progressed, the World Bank gradually emerged as the leading organisation in the field and the leader in thinking on the subject. At the same time the Bank was answerable to its main shareholders, and the evolution of its policies largely reflected the evolution of attitudes in the donor community generally. If we look back over the Bank's activities in the past four decades, we can, I believe, identify four main phases.

The first phase covered the 1950s and 1960s. The Bank was led by two very able Presidents with a business-like approach, Eugene Black (1949 to 1962) and George Woods (1963 to 1968) There was not a great deal of economic theory about their approach. It consisted of making loans (and, in the case of very poor countries after 1960, IDA credits on very soft terms) for the purpose of financing capital expenditure. Bank activity focussed chiefly on infrastructure investments – dams, power stations, irrigation systems, roads and railways – involving large capital expenditures. Other providers of aid, mainly bilateral donors at that stage, followed the same approach. It was taken for granted that external resources should finance capital investment rather than current expenditures, which should be financed internally. Sound capital investment was expected to benefit the economy and to help create the resources which would enable borrowing countries to repay the loans. Conditions attached to such loans were mainly to do with the implementation of the projects themselves; and although Gene Black was quite capable of refusing a loan to a country whose fiscal policies were lax, this had more to do with credit-worthiness and the security of the Bank's money than with promoting sound macro-economic policies for development reasons.

This approach also had the advantage, from the point of view of the Bank and other aid providers, that it involved financing discrete projects in which costs and benefits could be calculated relatively easily and expenditure controlled. And since the Bank and other aid providers naturally dealt with governments, the capital investments so financed were those of the state. The second phase began in the early 1970s, when thinking moved on under the influence of the World Bank's most innovative and dynamic President, Robert McNamara, who led the institution from 1968 to 1981. He took the Bank into the financing of new programmes designed to make a more direct attack on poverty, hunger and human misery – rural and urban development programmes, education and population control. McNamara, through a number of powerful speeches at the Annual Meetings of the World Bank in the early 1970s, made the world much more aware of the fact that these ills were not only continuing, but evidently increasing in many countries. The Bank became much more involved, in a "hands on" way, in efforts to improve social conditions and alleviate poverty in Third World countries. These new programmes involved expenditures which would earlier have been regarded as unsuitable for Bank financing because they included current expenditures as well as capital. Other donors and development organisations followed the Bank's lead and the influence of this phase of thinking on aid has persisted. I shall discuss the issues involved further in Chapter 6.

Robert McNamara had another major impact on the development scene. He enormously increased the scale of the Bank's activities, raising its annual lending more than ten-fold from less than $1 billion in 1968 to nearly $12.5 billion in 1981. As I vividly recall from my days as a member of the World Bank board, he simply refused to believe anyone who tried to argue that his aims could not be achieved. By 1981 the Bank's cumulative lending commitments had grown to $92 billion, of which all but $13 billion had been undertaken in the McNamara years. The successful drive to increase the World Bank's lending also changed the mentality of the institution. A rising volume of lending and the attainment of targets for lending became a key objective in itself and this had a continuing influence on the Bank's activities.

The third phase in the history of development policies, overlapping the second, began in the later part of McNamara's period at the Bank. In the late 1970s and early 1980s many developing countries were suffering from losses of export earnings through falls, temporary or more lasting, in commodity prices; and meanwhile the oil shocks of 1973 and 1979 caused serious problems for countries which depended on imported oil. Demands grew for assistance in the form of balance-of-payments financing. The richer countries reacted cautiously – this would be another step away from financing capital investment and would raise further doubts about the ability of borrowing countries to repay. In the late 1970s this reluctance was reflected in a policy guideline that no more than 10% of the Bank's lending should take the form of balance-of-payments support. Later this limit was relaxed as major shareholders and the Bank itself became increasingly aware that balance-of-payments lending could be used as a means of inducing borrowing countries to make policy changes which could be expected to improve their economic performance.

This brought "conditionality" to the centre of the development stage. In the 1980s a high proportion of World Bank aid came with policy strings attached. The conviction grew, supported by much evidence, that the policies followed by developing country governments themselves were of greater importance than any- thing which external agencies such as the Bank or other donors could do to help. Structural adjustment loans and sector loans became part of the scene. Bad economic policies, bad government generally and misuse of resources by developing country governments could make even the best-designed aid projects ineffective. In a positive sense the policies which developing country governments themselves followed would make the difference between success and failure in overall development. Inducing governments to follow the right policies was ultimately more important than providing money.

But what policies should the World Bank and other donors recommend to developing countries? What policies had they in fact been recommending until then?

*   *   *

The truth is that from the 1950s to the early or mid 1980s, the main donor countries and international development agencies more or less accepted and to a considerable extent supported the state ownership and state management of the economy which were the norm in much of the developing world. The question was not one which aroused much controversy.

This was not mainly a matter of policy, but the consequence of a simple, practical fact. Because aid activity consisted of transferring resources to governments for use by governments, it tended to strengthen the role of the state in the economies of developing countries. Donors and development institutions felt they had no alternative to dealing with governments – the private sector simply did not come into the process. But the flow of large amounts of aid money to governments, at a time when there was little private investment or funding from private financial markets flowing into most countries, had far-reaching effects on the shape of developing economies. The fact that money came to governments meant that many investments were undertaken in the public sector which might have been in the private sector. Admittedly, it is hard to quote many cases where a specific private sector alternative was available and was turned down in favour of a public sector solution because aid money was available to the government. But the point is that in countries where government investments were financed by aid, private sector alternatives were usually not considered at all, and private investors did not bring forward proposals, knowing they would be rejected.

Again, India is a case in point. Between 1965 and 1980 the World Bank made loans to state-owned Indian industry, including companies in sectors such as food and beverages, chemicals, oil and gas and power generation, totalling $2.3 billion. These were investments which could have been undertaken by private investors, domestic or foreign. Fertiliser production was another area where India had a substantial private sector, including major companies and groups which could certainly have undertaken many of the investments which the government made itself, with World Bank help. For its own ideological reasons, the government wanted these investments made in the public sector and the Bank facilitated that. Very recently, there has been a more egregious case. As late as 1995, although India had liberalised significantly, the country's banks were still overwhelmingly owned by the state, and hopes were rising that privatisation might be coming. However, the World Bank intervened with a very large loan ($700 million) to enable the Indian government to recapitalise these banks without resort to the markets – which would certainly have been able to provide the capital – thus positively impeding privatisation and market reform.

Between 1977 and the mid 1990s the Bank made six major loans to Egypt for power generation, for a total of $690 million This investment could certainly have been financed at least partly from private sources, domestic or foreign. But it was not the policy of the Bank to refuse its financing until private alternatives had been investigated, although that is exactly what its own Articles of Agreement would require it to do.

In Africa it might at first sight seem less obvious that private alternatives were available. But the fact is that in the later 1960s Africa received significant amounts of foreign private investment: over half a billion dollars a year in 1968 and 1969 (equivalent to about $1.8 billion a year in 1994 dollars). This inflow dried up when a number of countries nationalised foreign companies, sometimes with inadequate compensation to the owners. The aim was partly "indigenisation" and partly to gain control of profitable businesses. In the "Nigerianisation" programme in the 1970s, the government acquired 60 per cent ownership in all companies in designated areas, including banking of all kinds, insurance, energy and iron and steel. In Tanzania, by the early 70s, one third of manufacturing output was in state-owned firms; and in Zambia it rose to 56 per cent, in addition to the state-owned copper mines.

But if private investment inflows stopped, this did not cut off aid. Investments which might have been made by foreign private investors were made by the government instead, and in Sub-Saharan Africa, over the past two decades, public investment has typically been financed wholly by external aid. These public investment programmes have involved most African governments in a variety of sectors of the economy – not only in utilities such as power and telecommunications, but in manufacturing, mining, hotels, cement, banks, insurance and the like. These investments could not have been undertaken without external aid. Not surprisingly, most of them have performed badly and the governments concerned were disappointed in their hope of gaining access to large profits.

Thus, in much of the developing world, the availability of official aid was one explanation of the fact that state ownership was so prevalent. And there is no doubt that many of the providers of aid, bilateral and multilateral, encouraged this approach in the developing countries, or at least did not discourage it. The World Bank, even under the leadership of American Presidents from the private sector, such as Robert McNamara, positively promoted state ownership of industry in the 1960s and 1970s, and did not discourage central planning of the economy in countries like India. Many of the staff of the Bank were believers in planning and state ownership. It is fair to acknowledge, however, that the failures of this approach were not so apparent in the 1960s and 70s as they became later; and that those who did believe in the importance of the private sector were often at a loss as to how to go about promoting a private sector in poor countries. The instruments in their hand, mainly the instrument of loans to governments or guaranteed by governments, led them to a state-centred approach. Planners themselves, intelligent and capable planners, they worked naturally with those who played that role in the governments of borrowing countries.

There was one other critical way in which the supply of official funding retarded the process of development, and that is through its effect on the financial sector. During the period when state-led development was the accepted philosophy, the creation of modern financial systems and capital markets in developing countries was not in the book. It was part of the state-management approach that credit was directed through government-controlled (very often government-owned) banks. There is a long record of development banks in the developing countries and it is generally not one of success. Many of these institutions, operating under political direction and without proper financial discipline, got into financial difficulties and were baled out by governments, sometimes with the help of donors.

These development banks were in many cases created specifically to serve as conduits for aid funds coming from abroad, particularly from the World Bank. They were thus, in market terms, artificial institutions which did not have to meet the market test of mobilising savings domestically. Their dependence on foreign official finance was one reason why most of them were not able to evolve into market-based institutions, as had been intended. They also mostly failed in another objective – that they should assist in the development of securities markets through underwriting activities. Since they relied principally on long-term funding from aid sources abroad, they showed little interest in securities markets.

Thus, in many countries, government control of the financial system, supported by donors and strengthened by flows of aid money into it, meant that there was very little possibility of a market-based financial system emerging. Modern banking systems were not encouraged to develop – very few developing countries, even as late as the 1980s, had commercial banks which could provide private companies with term loans of more than two years' maturity. In the 1960s and 70s, securities markets were not encouraged either – they were not seen as part of the development process. Even in countries which had them, like India, they were regarded as irrelevant to economic development.

*   *   *

The adherence of most developing countries to non-market financial systems for many years meant that the processes by which savings were mobilised in the economy and decisions made about investments were inefficient. It has to be assumed that this inefficiency was one factor in the disappointing economic performance of many countries.

Although the failure to recognise the importance of financial markets continued into the 1980s, there were signs of change in the World Bank even in the 1970s. A Capital Markets Department was set up in the IFC as early as 1971, intended to serve the Bank Group as a whole in this field. But the IFC was then a small organisation with no influence on policy and the form of this initiative only confirms that the Bank regarded the subject as marginal. It was not until the next decade that it began to be understood that an efficient private sector – and that itself was at last being recognised as fundamental to development – required an efficient, market-based financial system. This has since become a commonplace of development thinking, but it is fairly recent. And even now, as we shall see later, there is often a failure to recognise that pouring large amounts of official money into an economy through the government can seriously retard the development of market-based financial systems.

A less fundamental but interesting example is electricity. This is admittedly an area which much of the developed world, as well as developing countries, regarded as appropriate to the public sector. But if in the 1960s private investors had been encouraged to establish power plants in many developing countries, as is happening now, large numbers of people who in the 1990s are still without electricity could have had it. The World Bank estimates that about two billion people in the world are still without electricity. Private investment in power generation will probably reduce that number significantly in the coming decade. Opportunities to get private capital invested in power certainly existed – for example the Calcutta Electric Supply Company, a privately owned utility, was forbidden for years to make any investments, although now in the 1990s it is again being encouraged to do so.

I fully acknowledge that there is more than an element of hindsight about these observations. When governments and aid agencies set out on the task of development soon after World War II, there was very little experience to learn from. In the 1950s, 60s and 70s, the consensus view not only in developing countries, but in most western countries was much more interventionist than now. It was taken for granted that Third World development had to be an activity of the state, and the private sector was regarded with suspicion, except for small businessmen and farmers, about whom aid agencies always tended to have warm feelings. "Development economics" was a mode of thinking which assumed that normal economic principles did not apply in poor countries.

All this was done with the best of intentions. But it often produced the paradox that donors supported economic policies and systems in the Third World which would certainly not have been accepted in their own countries. Some donor countries, whose own economic success – and indeed their ability to offer aid – had come from capitalism in one form or another, somehow felt that when it came to promoting economic growth in poor countries, this was not relevant. The Netherlands is a case in point – a country which undoubtedly owes its wealth, and its ability to provide aid, to capitalism, but where the practitioners of aid have often been from the political left. For them "development" does not consist of trying to replicate the success of the capitalist west, but of building a new kind of economy and society for which there is no example of success in the world – a utopian approach in which rich westerners indulge their taste for experimentation at the expense of poor Third World countries.

The classic case is Tanzania, a country which by the early 1980s had been driven to economic ruin by Julius Nyerere's own brand of "African socialism", expounded in the Arusha Declaration of 1967. This involved total state control of the economy combined with the compulsory movement of large numbers of the population into planned villages. Nyerere, a genuine idealist and perhaps the only one of the first generation of African leaders who was personally incorruptible, was idolised and supported with large amounts of aid, especially from the Netherlands and the Scandinavian countries, but also from the World Bank, which has recently acknowledged its error. The Bank's own report on its relationship with Tanzania is remarkably frank in acknowledging both the disastrous effects of Nyerere's policies and the fact that the Bank supported them strongly for a number of years. External aid enabled Nyerere's misguided policies to be continued, even after the economic chaos and poverty they had caused had become all too evident. Over the twenty years from 1965, income per head fell on average by 0.3 per cent a year to reach $240 in 1986. Eventually, in the 1980s, in the midst of economic collapse, they were abandoned.

The alliance between aid administrators of this mentality in the west and developing country leaders meant that, in some countries, years of opportunity were lost, and the cause of development was retarded. Ghana and Jamaica were two other cases where disastrous policies, rather than war or civil disorder, drove the country to economic breakdown. By the early 1980s normal public services had ceased to function in Ghana and per capita income was a third lower than a decade before. It could not be argued that the aid donors were mainly responsible for this state of affairs, but some continued to support the Ghanaian government during the worst period of its damaging policies. Similarly, during the first administration of Michael Manley in Jamaica, which led to economic chaos, the Bank and other donors provided large amounts of aid. The economic situation began to improve soon after the aid was cut back.

The case of Egypt is also interesting. After the Camp David accords of 1978 Egypt began to receive large amounts of aid from the US. In 1990-91 aid receipts amounted to 12.6 per cent of the country's GNP and no less than 32 per cent of total American aid. But Egypt's economic performance has been poor because of misguided policies, including price controls, subsidies, and a large government deficit. The government has repeatedly failed to come to terms with the IMF and, when it has done so, has failed carry out its agreements. Its ability to resist IMF pressure was partly due to the inflow of American aid, and the disservice this has done to the long term interests of the people of Egypt is substantial.

*   *   *

A large part of the failure of most of the developing world to achieve rates of growth high enough to raise standards of living significantly must be attributed to the fact that, for many years, they followed policies which were not based on sound economic principles. The population problem certainly compounded the difficulties, but faster economic growth, as all experience shows, would have reduced population growth rates sooner and eased the pressures. The ultimate responsibility for all this must rest with Third World governments, but we in the First World have to acknowledge that donors and official development institutions to a large extent supported and facilitated these policies.

Obviously it is easier to perceive mistakes with the benefit of hindsight than it was at the time; but we must learn the lessons of history and not repeat them. Good intentions are not enough. Aid providers should be alert to the fact that aid can have unintended effects, and make every effort to see all the possible effects, not just the wished-for ones. They must put the real interests of recipients before the gratification which aid-giving may give to donors.

In the last few years things have begun to change. The fourth phase of thinking in the history of development is the phase in which we find ourselves now. In the 1980s there was a world-wide change in thinking, including the thinking of the World Bank. It has come to be widely accepted that market-based systems, when combined with sound macro-economic policies, offer the best prospect of rapid economic advance. But the development agencies have found themselves in a paradoxical situation, because their methods of operation and the instruments they are accustomed to using are still to a large extent geared to the old ways of thinking. Their role has to be reconsidered.

But before coming to that, we should look at the momentous changes of the 1980s and early 1990s, amounting to a revolution, and why they occurred.

4   The Market Revolution

The shift towards market-based policies in the late 1980s and early 1990s, remarkable for being virtually world-wide, was a turning point in economic history. It was evident in the industrial democracies about the beginning of the decade and there were some signs of it earlier still. German Socialists moved away from traditional socialism in the 1970s and the French Socialist party did so rapidly while in power in the early 1980s. In Britain, while the Thatcher government was making radical changes, including privatisation, the Labour Party in opposition broke away from its socialist roots, and accepted much of the Thatcherite revolution (as the Conservatives 40 years before had largely accepted the Attlee revolution). In other European countries, such as Spain, there was a similar trend, and even before the collapse of communism in the East, the Communist Parties of Italy and France had moved far from their traditional positions. And in the United States the 1980s were the decade of two Republican Presidents, Reagan and Bush.

Much more dramatic change followed in the Second World at the end of the decade. The collapse of communism in eastern Europe led to rapid moves towards a market economy in Poland, the Czech Republic and Hungary. It is legitimate to regard this as part of the same world-wide phenomenon, but the situation following the break-down of communism in the Soviet Union in 1992 is, at this time of writing, difficult to interpret. It did represent, especially in Russia itself, the collapse of the most formidable anti-market system in the world; but whether it will be possible to describe what replaces it as a market economy is still unclear.

The move to market systems has been very much a phenomenon of the Third World too. Some time before the collapse of communism, many countries had embarked on a process of reform, and by the early 90s the movement had become remarkably widespread. These reforms were of two kinds: first, liberalisation measures to remove barriers to the operation of market forces; and secondly, macro-economic stabilisation

measures to create the kind of environment in which those forces
could work effectively.

Third World economies, as we have seen, were characteristically mixed in ownership and heavily controlled. The first group
of reforms involved removal of many controls over private
business decisions, allowing markets to decide matters which
had required government approval; removal of price controls;
liberalisation of financial systems so as to allow market forces to
determine the allocation of capital; privatisation of state-owned
enterprises; and opening up domestic markets to competition from
imports, combined with removal of barriers to foreign investment.

The second group of reforms was equally important. In the
mid-1980s, a significant group of developing countries came to
recognise clearly the importance of sound fiscal and monetary
policies, above all the reduction or elimination of government
deficits, policies which would reduce inflation and create a climate
of confidence for private investment. By the end of the decade,
many countries, especially in south-east Asia and in Latin
America, had made changes of this kind and were already
benefiting from the shift.

*   *   *

One country which led the way in this change in the developing
world was Chile, where market-based policies were introduced
under a brutal dictatorship. The government of General
Pinochet, who overthrew the socialist Allende in 1973, combined
a bad record on human rights with a highly successful economic
policy. The reforms were in large measure a reaction to the
policies of the Allende regime, whose economic management had
been a disaster. A public sector deficit in 1973 of 30 per cent of
GDP, much of it due to the losses of state-owned companies,
became a surplus by the end of the decade. In the 1970s Chile
went through a deep recession, but the reform programme
continued in the 1980s with further privatisations, liberalisation of
the financial sector, encouragement of foreign investment and
reductions in external tariffs.

The implementation of these policies produced painful effects
for a time, with many company failures and unemployment. But,
having started on market reforms before the debt crisis broke in

1982, Chile was able, despite a heavy burden of external debt, to cope with the crisis better than most of its neighbours, partly by extensive use of debt-to-equity swaps which played an important part in bringing the debt down to manageable levels. Whether these policies could have been implemented effectively under a democratic system of government is a moot point. But as the success of the policies became more and more obvious, and the unattractive aspects of the regime also grew less, Chile achieved a GNP growth of 7.4 per cent a year between 1985 and 1990. When democracy was eventually restored in 1990 the elected government continued with virtually the same market-based policies.

The Chilean experience had a considerable impact in the rest of Latin America. The unpleasant character of the Chilean regime probably discouraged others from following the model for a time, but the economic success became too clear to be ignored. For most Latin American countries, however, the strongest pressure to reform emerged out of the struggle to deal with the debt crisis which broke in Mexico in August 1982 and deeply affected the whole region. It was the need to face hard facts in the midst of the debt crisis that led many of them to policies of stability and private-sector-led growth.

In the later 1980s a remarkable number of changes in trade polices were made. Mexico and Brazil began a process of liberalisation of their import regimes. Mexico broke with its past by joining the GATT in 1986, reducing its external tariffs from an average of 50 per cent to under 20 per cent by 1988, and went on to negotiate the North American Free Trade Agreement with the United States and Canada, which came into effect in 1994. Recently there has been talk of extending NAFTA to include other countries such as Chile. Brazil put in hand a series of tariff reductions in 1987 which continued into the 1990s, reversing a long-standing policy of heavy protection for its domestic industry. The change of attitude in the region is reflected also in other free trade arrangements, such as the grouping known as MERCOSUR, involving Argentina, Brazil, Paraguay and Uruguay, established in 1991. Trade among these countries more than doubled between 1990 and 1993. And older arrangements amongst the Andean group of countries (Bolivia, Peru, Ecuador, Colombia and Venezuela) and the Central American group were revitalised in the early 1990s.

Other reforms designed to encourage market-based activity also swept Latin America. Most countries moved towards liberalisation of financial markets, for example in allowing interest rates to be determined by the markets instead of by the authorities. Exchange-rate regimes also became more market-based – Argentina, Venezuela and Peru abolished dual or multiple exchange rate systems, which had been used to discourage unwanted imports of goods and capital.

In most of Latin America, macro-economic policies aimed at stability have been adopted. One of the most remarkable cases is Argentina, a country whose experience over four decades was mostly of hyper-inflation, but where inflation was reduced to less than 10 per cent a year in 1993 and 1994. Another striking and early case was Bolivia, which in the mid-1980s was setting records for hyper-inflation but reduced inflation to 8.5 per cent in 1993. Brazil in the late 1980s and early 1990s was behind the game through a failure of political leadership. But in 1994 Fernando Henrique Cardoso, who a quarter-century earlier had been one of the leading proponents of the dependency theory[1] but had abandoned his earlier views, was elected President. This was after a period as Finance Minister when he was outstandingly successful in curbing hyper-inflation. As I write, Cardoso is just assuming office and there is now reason to hope that Brazil will join the new Latin American consensus.

Barriers to foreign investment came down all over Latin America in the late 1980s and early 1990s. Mexico, Argentina and Venezuela all introduced major changes in their foreign investment codes. There was a general easing of restrictions on the percentage of foreign ownership allowed – up to 100 per cent in Argentina, Chile and some smaller countries. Brazil, Colombia and Peru also liberalised. Foreign direct investment in Latin America, which averaged $3.7 billion a year in the mid-1980s, rose to nearly $10 billion a year in the years 1988–92.

A wave of privatisation swept Latin America in the late 1980s and early 1990s. Chile was well ahead of the rest and had sold off well over 400 companies by the end of the 1980s. Since 1988 over 300 companies have been privatised in Mexico, Argentina and Brazil. Recently, Peru has joined the reformers and plans to privatise all state-owned companies.

Meanwhile elsewhere in the world also, major changes were taking place. In South-East Asia, Indonesia, Malaysia and Thailand were the leaders, although they in their turn were influenced by the example of the four far eastern "Tigers", whose outstanding success began to make its impact on thinking in the rest of Asia as early as the 1970s.

Indonesia began gradually in the mid-1980s. Protection against imports was reduced sharply; barriers to foreign investment were eased; financial market controls reduced. At the same time, public expenditure and monetary growth were restrained and a competitive exchange rate was maintained. Although Indonesia remains a country where political interference in investment decisions is considerable, the benefits of these reforms have been clear. GDP growth averaged between 6 and 7 per cent in the early 1990s. Foreign direct investment 1993 was nearly ten times what it had been in the mid-1980s; and exports of manufactures, as opposed to oil, on which Indonesia relied heavily for many years, began to grow very fast – they doubled in the five years to 1992.

Sound macro-economic management and market-supporting reforms introduced in the first half of the 1980s gave Thailand one of the fastest rates of growth in the world, around 12 per cent, in the late years of the decade, based on a very strong growth of exports of manufactures (1992 exports were over four times the late 1980s rate). This led to an inflow of foreign investment even larger than in Indonesia.

Malaysia was even more successful. Its policies were always more market-based than those of most other countries in the region, and over 25 years the annual rate of growth of GDP was 6.5 per cent. Recently, good economic management has raised this rate to about 9 per cent, with the result that GNP per head rose to $3160 in 1993, making Malaysia very much a middle-income country, although still behind Hong Kong, Singapore, Korea and Taiwan. As with all the east Asian successes, the strong growth was closely related to a vigorous export performance, and the inflow of foreign investment has been the largest in the region.

India moved more slowly. The first, tentative liberalising reforms were introduced in 1982, when a number of industries were removed from the list of those which required government approval for investment and other plans. Further cautious reform of this kind followed during Rajiv Gandhi's tenure as Prime Minister, but it was not until Narasimha Rao took over in 1991 that the process gathered momentum, the pace of change quickened by the pressures of the balance-of-payments crisis which confronted the new government as it took office. Many of the strangling controls over business decisions, especially investment decisions, were removed. But in many areas where reform has been undertaken, it remains incomplete. Protection has been reduced, but remains relatively high. Controls over foreign investment have been eased, but not removed. Financial markets have been substantially de-regulated – for example, controls over the pricing of new issues on the Indian stock exchanges have been removed – and Indian companies are now allowed to raise capital on international markets, but subject to various conditions. Privately owned banks are now permitted, but the banking sector remains overwhelmingly in government ownership. Politics in India still stand in the way of a vigorous privatisation programme – the most the government will do is to sell minority stakes in some state-owned companies to private investors.

However the atmosphere in India has changed dramatically. The private sector has gained confidence and is facing up to the necessity to compete both at home and in export markets. The Indian government has come to realise that it must look to the private sector, domestic and foreign, for important investments which would previously have been undertaken in the public sector, including investments in infrastructure – power generation, telecommunications and transport. India in the mid-1990s seems to be heading for growth rates of perhaps 7 to 8 per cent, substantially better than in the past.

One of the most interesting examples of movement towards the market economy is the paradoxical case of China – paradoxical because China remains, even now in the mid-1990s, a communist country in which the power of the Communist Party is very strong. Yet there is no more remarkable case now of the vigorous growth which a market system can produce than what is happening in south and east China. The leadership in Beijing, especially Deng Xiao Ping himself, have publicly blessed the market economy, and in the coastal regions around Hong Kong and Shanghai extremely vigorous growth is taking place (accompanied by some inflation which is worrying the authorities). Some estimates are that GDP growth in Guangdong province has been as high as 26 per cent. Figures of this kind are difficult to verify, but for a periodic visitor they seem consistent with the evidence of the senses. Official figures for the Chinese economy as a whole show an annual growth rate of 12 per cent over the years 1988–92.

The example of China, and the competitive threat it seems to pose, is proving a powerful influence on thinking in neighbouring countries. But it is hard to describe China as a market economy – it has rather the aspect of an outburst of laissez-faire capitalism within a communist state, which makes it difficult to interpret the Chinese phenomenon or to predict where it may be going. I revert to this subject in the next chapter.

Others countries have been following down the market road at differing speeds. In the Islamic countries of the middle east, progress has generally been slow and the potential of the market economy has not been realised. The Islamic movement in the late twentieth century has tended to be associated with socialist ideas, as in Iraq and Syria. In Iran, too, the fundamentalist revolution of 1979 led to strongly state-centred policies for a time, associated with hostility to the west and to western companies. However, Iranians are natural businessmen and there is reason to hope that a more realistic approach to economic policy will gradually emerge.

On the other hand, Pakistan has made some gains and has raised its rate of growth in the late 1980s and early 1990s. After a long period when business was heavily controlled by the bureaucracy, the government has abolished many controls. Quite a vigorous privatisation programme has been put in place, and foreign private capital is being attracted particularly for investment in power generation. Pakistan suffers from a heavy burden of military expenditure and expenditure on education is amongst the lowest in the developing world – the literacy rate at 35 per cent (and 21 per cent for women) is also at the bottom of the scale.

Egypt was a leader of the anti-capitalist trend in the developing world in the 1950s and 1960s and has been slow to turn its back on the socialist philosophy it espoused under Nasser. As I pointed out in the last chapter, the pressures on Egypt to undertake effective reform have been reduced by the availability of large amounts of American aid. There were few signs of change in the 1980s. In 1991 a reform programme was begun – stabilisation measures, including a reduction of the fiscal deficit and a unified exchange rate; decontrol of interest rates and financial liberalisation; removal of price controls; and a reduction of trade barriers – but there remains a gap between stated policies and implementation. Morocco, on the other hand, has made impressive progress towards the market economy. In the later 1980s macro-economic stability was firmly established, with government expenditure down from 32 to 26 per cent of GDP. Trade liberalisation was accompanied by a strong growth of exports, and controls over foreign investment were substantially eliminated. A major privatisation programme was begun.

In Sub-Saharan Africa the story has been more mixed, although there have been some moves in the same direction. One striking case is Ghana, a country which got itself into a mess comparable to Tanzania in the early 1980s. The economy in effect sank to subsistence levels, and even the most elementary requirements of modern consumers could not be obtained. It was a leader of leftist inclinations, Flight Lieutenant Rawlings, who began the process of facing up to the facts when he introduced, with World Bank help, the New Economic Programme in 1983. (Was there an echo of Lenin in 1921?) Over the rest of the decade Ghana made steady progress and achieved a rate of growth of 4.7 per cent between 1985 and 1990. Zimbabwe has also moved towards stabilisation and market-based policies in recent years. Zambia, under Kenneth Kaunda, one of the original generation of independence leaders who was removed from office in elections in 1991, was an avowedly socialist country; but it has recently been making moves towards a market economy. The Côte d'Ivoire, which ran into serious economic difficulties in the 1980s because of over-dependence on exports of commodities whose prices had fallen, combined with excessive government expenditure, embarked on reform at the end of the decade. As with other countries in west and central Africa with close links to France, Côte d'Ivoire's problems were compounded through the 1980s and early 1990s by a much overvalued exchange rate, because their currency was linked to the French franc at a rate which remained unchanged from 1950 until the problem was eventually dealt with early in 1994.

Generally, Sub-Saharan Africa remains farther away than the rest of the developing world from an effective market economy. In a number of countries in the region, war and disorder made rational discussion of economic questions irrelevant. Nigeria, which contains nearly a quarter of the population of the whole region, has repeatedly flirted with reform policies but then turned away. In most of the region, the private corporate sector is severely under-developed. There is plenty of evidence that Africa does not lack entrepreneurs, but they operate in a difficult environment. Even in countries which have been peaceful, the quality of government has often been poor and the level of corruption high. Relatively small populations have meant only small local markets for African manufacturers. Total figures for investment in the African economies are not low compared to other developing regions such as the Indian sub-continent; but the return which is earned by investment in Africa, public and private, is poor and has deteriorated in the past 10 to 15 years. Total exports from a region which contains 9.5 per cent of the world's people amount to no more than 1.5 per cent of world trade (it was 2.4 per cent in 1960).

Finally, the most dramatic episode in the market revolution was, of course, the collapse of communism in Eastern Europe and the former Soviet Union, a series of events which cannot be denied the title of revolution. I shall have something to say in Chapter 10 about its relevance to development in the Third World; but, dramatic and important as these changes were, they came after a large part of the Third World had already made the decisive shift towards market-based policies. The collapse of communism may have confirmed Third World leaders in their views, but it was not a factor in forming those views.

Why then, did these remarkable changes occur, after so many years when state-management and socialism were the accepted approach? The first point to note is that the change was generally not an ideological one. The Third World is not peopled with Margaret Thatchers: one would have to search the developing countries very hard to find any important leader who displays convictions and emotions about socialism and the role of the state in the Thatcher style. (Lee Kuan Yew of Singapore may be an exception, but his country has not really been part of the Third World for some time.)

The leaders of this Third World revolution have been of a different character. In Latin America, many of the reforming leaders belonged to traditionally socialist parties but abandoned their former views for practical reasons – President Salinas of Mexico, leader of the Institutional Revolutionary Party; President Menem of the Peronist Party which, more than any other group, had been responsible for state-managed disaster in the Argentine economy from the 1940s onward; Carlos Andres Perez who had been President of Venezuela before, pursuing quite different policies; and Manley, the leader of the Labour Party in Jamaica who was also re-elected to undo his own previous policies. In Indonesia the Economic Team which led the way consisted of dedicated technocrats, such as Ali Wardhana, Radius Prawiro, and J. B. Sumarlin, mostly educated at the University of California at Berkeley. In India change began with a gradual recognition amongst the more intelligent members of the Civil Service that the old system was not working well and was carried forward by the policies adopted by Narasimha Rao, an old socialist, and Manmohan Singh, a technocrat and former head of the Planning Commission. Pragmatism is to be seen in even more remarkable form in China, where the Party still rules and the system requires leaders to use meaningless phrases such as the "socialist market economy", while Deng Xiao Ping confers his blessing on the booming capitalism of the south and east.

In Africa poor political leadership has been an obstacle to reform; but where it has occurred, it has the same pragmatic look – reforming leaders such as Chidzero of Zimbabwe and Botchway of Ghana were certainly not ideologues. In Eastern Europe (which is not to be regarded as part of the Third World), the situation is a little more confused. Vaclav Klaus of the Czech Republic could be called a right-wing ideologue but he is something of an exception even in his own country. And Leszek Balcerovicz of Poland, the man who set the trend towards the market economy in the area with his decisive reforms of January 1990, is a professional economist and a dedicated believer in the market system, but not a right-wing ideologue.

Third World leaders who turned to the new way of thinking were influenced mainly by practical experience of the failures of the previous systems – one key example of this being the poor performance of state-owned "enterprises". Evidence accumulated from many countries that state-owned firms performed much less well than private firms, and the cost of this appeared in the form of losses which had to be financed by the state and which could not be ignored by Ministers of Finance. The pattern was remarkably consistent. In Argentina the losses of state-owned companies averaged 5.4 per cent of GDP for five years in the mid-1980s, and in Brazil 3.3 per cent. The economic crisis in Latin America affected this performance, but the same kind of phenomenon was to be found elsewhere. In Indonesia during the same years state-owned firms lost amounts corresponding to 3 per cent of the country's GDP, and in the Philippines 5 per cent. In India at the end of the 1980s the losses of state-owned companies amounted to 10 per cent of total government revenues. Public disenchantment with the inefficiencies of state-managed enterprises also played a part in Latin America where opinion polls have shown strong popular support for privatisation. In Argentina and Peru polls showed 80 per cent in favour and in Chile 58 per cent.

The problems created by the performance of state-owned enterprises also opened up wider issues. If the response was to be that the private sector should replace the public in these fields, then conditions had to be right for the private to succeed. State ownership of large parts of the productive system was something which fitted into the logic of a closed, protected economy but was demonstrably unsuited to the internationally competitive economy to which they were now aspiring. The failure of state-owned companies in areas such as the export market demonstrated that they were particularly unsuited to activities requiring adaptability, innovation and competitiveness. Many Third World leaders were becoming aware that economic success would not be achieved without moving to a more open economy in which competitiveness would be at a premium. This was how leaders in Latin America, such as Pedro Aspe of Mexico and Domingo Cavallo of Argentina, were thinking in the late 1980s.

The need to deal with the failures of the old system was combined, in a number of cases, with the pressures of economic crisis, which also had an important influence on reform. Latin America is perhaps the most obvious case where the pressure for economic reform was intensified by crisis – the debt crisis of the 1980s, the budgetary problems associated with it and the attendant recession. With budgets under severe pressure there was the problem of financing new investment in important sectors of the economy which were dominated by state-owned companies. Governments everywhere began to turn to the private sector both because the state could no longer assume the burden and because the private sector had shown that it could do it more efficiently. The same logic led directly to privatisation.[2]

In Asia, the pressures of crisis played a much smaller part in bringing governments to reform. It was not a key factor in the south-east Asian countries, although it played some part in India in 1990–91. In Africa crisis was the driving force of reform in Ghana and the Côte d'Ivoire; and elsewhere in Africa those governments which have embarked on reform have usually done so under the pressure of severe economic problems, whether identified as "crisis" or not.

Another factor in the shift of thinking towards market-based policies was the power of example. In Latin America, Chile was an example of the success of market policies. In Asia, and to some extent in the Third World as a whole, a much more powerful example of success was to be seen in a few countries in the far east. Japan itself was an early and important demonstration that an Asian country could attain First World standards of living, but in the post-war period Japanese industrial success was no longer a great novelty and it was the performance of the four Tigers, Korea, Taiwan, Hong Kong and Singapore, which commanded attention.

Two questions arise, which have been much discussed. Do the east Asian Tigers present a model which others can imitate, demonstrating what developing countries in general could achieve? And are they examples of the market economy, or of something else?

Few would argue that the Tigers offer a readily exportable model. These are unusual countries, two of them densely populated city-states, three of them having been on the cold-war front line for many years, all lacking natural resources. Korea and Taiwan received large amounts of American aid in the 1960s, for cold-war reasons. The four have in common that, through their years of very rapid growth, they all maintained sound macro-economic conditions, and competitive exchange rates, unlike many Third World countries. They all relied heavily on export growth and so benefited from international competition. In all of them the private sector, operating in conditions of competition, was the driving force of growth, particularly in the export sector – government ownership of industry was not a significant part of the scene in any of them. It is also significant that they all devoted substantial resources to education – for both sexes – with the emphasis on primary and secondary schooling. As early as 1965 Korea, Hong Kong and Singapore all had universal primary education.[3]

In Korea and Taiwan, and sometimes in Singapore, governments did engage in "industrial policy", playing a role in the investment decisions of larger firms by establishing priorities, especially for exports, and did exercise considerable influence over the allocation of credit to private companies. The evidence is inconclusive as to whether this contributed positively to growth or not. The relationship between government and industry, as in any country, reflects national traditions and culture which cannot readily be replicated elsewhere.

The conclusion is that, although the east Asian Tigers do not offer a simple, comprehensive formula for success which other countries can adopt in its entirety, there are clearly a number of factors in their success which could be imitated, and might help them achieve faster growth. Above all, the four Tigers show us an example of a framework of national institutions (or rather four different ones) within which market forces have been able to operate successfully – an example, not of socialist economies, but of a form of market economy.

It is sometimes argued that the example of the small far eastern countries is not very relevant to a very large country with a huge rural population, such as India. But the example of China cannot be ignored, both as an illustration of what can be achieved in a country which is in many ways similar, and as a warning that India may find itself left behind its neighbours to the east. In fact Indian policy-makers sometimes seem almost obsessed with the example of China. This competitive attitude may produce benefits. In fact an influence supporting change in India at present is a new self-confidence in the business community. For most of the post-war period Indians have assumed that their firms could not be expected to compete in international markets. This misplaced humility lay behind the heavy protection of the home market from imports for four decades and the small attention paid to exports. And indeed the quality of Indian products was not generally competitive by international standards, not because Indian firms were inherently inferior, but because they had not been exposed to competition. India has at last begun to emerge from this cocoon.

*   *   *

Finally, one more factor in the shift towards market policies in the developing world was the influence of the IMF and the World Bank. These institutions certainly played a part in the process, but in my view their impact is often over-stated. John Williamson of the Institute for International Economics in Washington DC coined the phrase "the Washington consensus" to describe the policy reforms that were urged on developing countries by the IMF and World Bank, but he himself describes this list of proposals as "embodying the common core of wisdom embraced by all serious economists".[4] How much part the two Washington institutions played in moving Third World governments towards these precepts is a moot point.

The roles of the two institutions differ considerably. The IMF's basic concerns – with balance-of-payments problems, currency and exchange rate questions and macro-economic stability – and its own intellectual rigour have always driven it towards market economics and kept it away from the illusions of "development economics". In fact it has been criticised frequently for being unconcerned with development and for adopting a harsh and doctrinaire approach. There have been cases where the Fund's prescriptions have taken too little account of political realities. This, combined with the fact that the Fund frequently has to deal with acute problems within a short time-horizon, means that although it has been effective in imposing its requirements, it has been less effective as a persuader. The IMF has obliged many developing countries to adopt at least short-term policies based on sound analysis and market economics, but its unpopularity has limited its influence on the thinking of Third World leaders. In the years 1980 to 1993, according to Killick, over half of the medium-term adjustment programmes "imposed" by the Fund in developing countries broke down before the end of their intended life.[5]

The World Bank, on the other hand, has been more ambivalent about market economics. As we have seen, in the 1960s and 1970s the Bank had no serious doubts about going along with development policies involving a large measure of state owner-ship, controls, planning and protection. In the 1980s the failures of these policies were increasingly recognised in the Bank and market economics became the generally accepted doctrine in the institution, which began to use its influence to persuade governments to accept this approach. "Policy-based" lending was used to promote reforms such as trade liberalisation, privatisation and liberalisation of financial systems.

But the Bank was not a very effective persuader either. Its known previous attitudes sometimes made its advocacy of the market approach unconvincing, and in any case, not all of the Bank's staff shared the new convictions. One example of the persisting ambivalence of Bank attitudes, of which I had personal experience, concerned a discussion with the Indian government in the late 1980s about a proposed financial sector loan designed to help India improve its capital markets and banking system. At the time there were differences of opinion on these matters in India and an intense debate between reformers and conservatives. A prestigious committee appointed by the government had recom-mended reforms, but there was opposition. In this situation World Bank staff supported the conservatives rather than the reformers, with the result that opportunities for progress were lost. Some of this ambivalence was probably due simply to a lack of familiarity with market systems and the private sector on the part of World Bank staff who were long accustomed to dealing only with governments and socialist systems.

I return to the question of the role of the Bank later. The point here is simply that the influence of the IMF and the World Bank on the historic shift towards market-based policies in the Third World was limited. That shift got going in earnest whenever leaders in the countries concerned became convinced that it was necessary. In any case, forcing change down the throats of reluctant governments by attaching conditions for loans was never likely to be really effective. For the policies to succeed, governments had to believe in them – if they did not, they would be likely to renege as soon as difficulties arose.

*   *   *

In short, the last 10 years have seen a general, although not universal, shift in the Third World towards policies which encourage markets to work and also an increased readiness to follow policies aimed at macro-economic stability. This trend in thinking seems to be continuing and indeed strengthening. There is great hope for the people of the Third World in this fact, a prospect of faster growth and rising living standards. Underlying this change is the recognition by a majority of Third World economic leaders that the interests of their people lie in their own hands. An era of illusions seems to have passed.

Rapid economic growth in any country is not caused by a single factor, but many. Natural resources must have their impact, although some countries which lack them, such as Japan and Korea, have done spectacularly well, whereas some well-endowed countries, such as Nigeria and Venezuela, have not. Access to technology and export markets can be important. Levels of saving and investment are critical (although the efficiency of the use of investments is more important still), including investment in education and in adequate infrastructure and in the handling of environmental questions. And there are factors affecting social cohesion and indefinable cultural influences on economic behaviour.

Many of these factors are beyond the power of governments to change, but probably the most important factors are within their power. The evidence of the past 30 years shows that the framework of government policy is fundamental – policies which provide stability and at the same time allow and encourage market forces to work offer the best prospect of rapid growth. The absence of such a policy environment will deny a country rapid growth. The private sector has to be the driving force if rapid growth is to be achieved.

It is probably right to assume that the rates of growth achieved by the Asian Tigers, and those being achieved by China now, will not be exceeded by many other developing countries. No one can be sure that there are no other "miracles" in the making, but rates of growth of real incomes in most other developing countries seem likely to be lower. However, this still leaves room for a substantial improvement on the record of the past three decades, and the most important single factor which will determine whether this is achieved or not will be government policies.

However, we cannot take it for granted that improved policies will be sustained everywhere, especially macro-economic policies. Populist pressures can undermine sound economic policies anywhere, and more easily in democracies. Turkey is a country which accepted fiscal discipline in the early 1980s and achieved low inflation and a few years of growth averaging 5 per cent, only to slip into huge deficits and high inflation again in the 1990s. After a period of reform, Venezuela, a country whose oil revenues were used for many years as the basis for a subsidised economy, elected a new populist leader in 1994 – the budget deficit has soared again, inflation has risen and growth has come to a halt. The danger is not confined to developing countries: Britain in the early 1990s, with the departure of Margaret Thatcher, quickly slipped into fiscal laxity, from which it is now struggling to recover. The United States in the 1980s developed huge budget deficits. It is very much on the cards that some countries which have introduced market reforms will nevertheless fail to achieve their potential growth because of weak macro-economic policies. Few countries are likely to have governments which will show the same skills in helping the economy to work effectively as the Asian Tigers. However we can probably expect that Asia, especially undemocratic Asia, will do better than Latin America or Africa in this respect.

The world-wide shift towards the market economy is not, I believe, a change in the wind of fashion, but a response to the lessons of experience everywhere. The century which is now in its closing years has been a period of extraordinary experimentation and we have learned something from the process. A hundred years ago, as the nineteenth century was coming to an end, socialism and communism were emerging as new, challenging ideas. As the twentieth century progressed, and especially in the 1930s, capitalism seemed on the defensive, and many well-thinking, sensitive people turned their backs on it. In all parts of the world different forms of socialism were tried, from full-blown communism in the Soviet Union and its satellites; to varying forms of state-management and ownership in much of the Third World, as we have seen; to milder forms of "mixed economy" socialism combined with a welfare state in a number of western countries. For a time some of these systems seemed to achieve some success: even Soviet communism appeared from the outside to be moderately successful for a short time. But longer experience, in the second half of the century, taught us more. If socialism has been abandoned by the industrial democracies; if Soviet communism has collapsed dramatically and China has opted for the market economy; and if most of the Third World has turned in the same direction – all this is surely not an accident.

We now know, although many will regard it as regrettable, that the socialist method of running an economy does not work well. Experience has shown that state-owned enterprises do not function efficiently, and that competition is crucial to economic efficiency. There is not a single case in the world where the pattern of state ownership of the means of production and state control and management of the economy has produced high rates of growth for any extended period. The only arguable exception would be the USSR in the period just after World War II when Nikita Khrushchev made his hollow threat to bury the West. Growth was achieved through totalitarian state pressures, in conditions which were appalling from the point of view of human liberty, and, probably for that reason, proved unsustainable.

What is the lesson for the Third World and for the donors and international agencies whose concern is economic development? The primary objective of development policy must be to achieve rates of growth high enough to raise living standards generally and to produce the resources needed to deal with poverty, social problems and environmental problems. There are now enough examples to convince us that the combination of market systems with sound macro-economic management offers the best prospect of achieving this. The world-wide consensus in favour of the market economy is just as relevant for the Third World as it is for the advanced industrial countries.

I conclude that *the basic development task now consists of creating a successful market economy* and that *the main challenge to aid donors is to help poor countries achieve this.*

But this raises some further questions. What exactly do we mean by the market economy? Capitalism has emerged the victor in the twentieth century duel and socialism the loser, but that cannot mean that we should now cease to be concerned with the moral and social issues about capitalism which have pre-occupied so many people for so much of this century. The honourable opponents of capitalism, repelled by its unattractive aspects, were not simply wrong-headed to look for an alternative. That search has failed. No doubt from time to time we shall see the search for alternatives to capitalism renewed, but these will be a diversion from the main road ahead. What we cannot escape is the need to shape forms of capitalism which are acceptable in terms both of economic efficiency and of social cohesion and justice. These questions are especially difficult to deal with in Third World conditions. Unrestrained capitalism, and nothing more, can hardly be an adequate answer to the continuing challenge of development.

The next chapter discusses what is meant by a "market economy" and following chapters consider what Third World governments and international aid agencies can do to promote it. This will take us to the heart of the development question today.

5 Is Capitalism Right for the Third World?

The very word "capitalism" offends many people to whom it suggests a jungle-world of unfettered market forces, driven by greed, in which the rich become richer and the poor are neglected or exploited. Can this be the "development" we want for poor countries?

If we reject "socialist" methods of economic management as inefficient – as we must – it is necessary to define the alternative. Alongside the long battle between capitalism and socialism in the twentieth century there have also been a number of efforts to redefine capitalism, mostly in the First World. In the 1930s President Franklin Roosevelt, leading one of the century's great efforts of this kind, spoke of capitalism as a tiger which must be tamed. In the 1970s it was a British Conservative Prime Minister, Edward Heath, who spoke of the "unacceptable face of capitalism". We need to consider these issues in the context of the Third World.

First, a word on terminology. The "market economy" is a less provocative phrase than capitalism, and the concept of an economic system based on market forces has been endorsed by no less a person than Pope John Paul II in his encyclical *Centesimus Annus* of 1991. But the encyclical also emphasises the need to restrain and regulate markets in the interest of the larger freedom of society as a whole. Perhaps the market economy is best defined as properly regulated capitalism, a system which seeks to maximise economic efficiency, while minimising the social ills and injustices which unfettered capitalism can throw up.

By this I do not mean some kind of half-way house between socialism and capitalism, in which some degree of state ownership, economic planning and control is retained. We have to accept without reservation the lesson that the market is the most promising road to economic success; and at the same time we have to learn how to civilise capitalism in ways that will not deprive it

89

of its dynamism. For dynamism is exactly the characteristic of capitalism that the Third World needs most.

Beneath these issues lie important questions about human motivation. The market philosophy reflects a realistic view of human nature: it harnesses some less-attractive human motivations for the common good. This is not to say that greed is the only or even the main driving force of a successful market economy. Much nonsense is talked about the profit motive in capitalist societies, both by those who find it distasteful and by others who naively believe it to be the only means of achieving efficiency.

In reality, a more important characteristic of the successful market economy is freedom; and in conditions of freedom, motivations can be very mixed and complex. It is a matter of common experience that motives of public service can and do operate powerfully in capitalist societies. No good doctor, judge, professor or policeman is driven chiefly by profit, but highly competent and dedicated people are to be found in these professions (and many more) in capitalist societies. Even amongst those involved in more commercial activities, motivations are complex and mixed and the drive for profit is often more institutional than personal. A society in which monetary gain was the only driving force – if such a thing can be imagined – would be an extremely unattractive one.

It is this freedom and the complexity of motivations it encourages and tolerates which are the ultimate strength of the market economy. Even amongst entrepreneurs, who play a vitally important, creative role in capitalist societies, profit is by no means the only driving force. But clearly the profit motive is an important source of the vigour of market economies; and a key characteristic of those economies is that they recognise and accept this fact. At the same time civilised capitalist societies also recognise the need to place restraints on the profit motive and subject economic behaviour to some public accountability.

The failure of socialism, on the other hand, stems ultimately from the fact that, as a philosophy, it rests on a naive view about human nature (although of course the rulers of socialist countries have often been anything but naive). Some definition of terms is needed here too. "Socialism" is often used in the sense of an ideal – a type of society in which co-operation and caring prevail over greed and profit-seeking, a state of affairs which must always be preferred to capitalism as experienced in practice. However, I use the word here to refer to socialism as it too has been experienced in practice. Socialist systems, as actually experienced in the history of this century, have resulted in a concentration of power in agents of the state, through the collective ownership and control of substantial parts of the economy. Such systems failed partly because it is simply impossible for those who govern large countries to have enough information to decide everything; but, more fundamentally, because of the human tendency to be corrupted by power. In the rush of idealism which follows a socialist revolution, this power may, for a while, be used benevolently, but as time goes on human nature prevails, power is used selfishly, the creativity which is needed to drive a modern economy forward is suppressed and concern for the collective good becomes no longer dominant.

No more striking example can be found of the consequences of this naivety about human nature than the handling, or rather mis-handling, of environmental issues in the Soviet Union and Eastern Europe under communism. The collapse of communism revealed a disastrous situation, in which pollution resulting from industrial operations had reached a scale never seen in the capitalist west – although the record of western countries was far from perfect. Now, preventing ecological damage is a communal need and a system which purported to place the communal good above the interests of individuals might, therefore, have been expected to perform better in this respect. The opposite was the case, because authority acted in secret, without accountability to the public. The more realistic view of human nature which underlies capitalism would not have naively assumed that public officials would act in the communal interest without the sanction of public accountability. And just as the absence of public accountability was one of the deepest flaws of communism, it is also the most critical requirement for taming the tiger of capitalism – I revert to this point at the end of this chapter.

* * *

When we consider how, in the Third World, or anywhere else, an acceptable form of capitalism is to be created, we cannot avoid the central issue of the role of the state. Any model for a market economy can be defined mainly in terms of the role of the state.

For a market system to function successfully, the state must withdraw and be excluded from activities which should be left to private market participants. But a successful market system also demands that the state should perform other critically important functions. If it fails to do so, the system will not succeed, either in the sense of economic efficiency, or of social fairness and acceptability. In the Third World, in particular, where state control has been so prevalent, there is an urgent need not only to re-define the role of the state in the economy, but to equip it to play its proper role. The success of the market revolution in these countries will be closely linked to the competence of the state in performing its essential functions. Moises Naim of Venezuela, a former Executive Director of the World Bank, has written interestingly about this subject, expressing concern that many governments, especially in Latin America, are not well equipped to do what is needed.[1]

Naturally the role of the state will be influenced by the culture, traditions and history of each individual country. But certain principles should be recognised as of general application if an efficient and fair market economy is to evolve. I claim no originality for the list which follows, but it seems salutary to try to lay them out, as a basis for discussing the development task in a world of market economics. The principles are concerned with two things: ensuring that the economy itself works efficiently; and ensuring that the needs of the community are adequately met in cases where market forces alone will not supply them. The list does not cover non-economic roles of the state, such as civil order and defence, with which we are not directly concerned here.

First, the state must ensure that the *systems and services* needed for a market economy to work efficiently exist. The legal system is the most fundamental of these. No market economy can work well without a satisfactory system of commercial and corporate law and a system of courts which provide a reliable means of settling disputes; requirements for proper disclosure of company activities; and a common and adequate accounting system. An efficient market economy also depends crucially on the existence of a financial system in which capital can be raised and allocated to productive use by transparent market means. The state need not create each of these systems itself – in some cases it may be better to rely on other, semi-private or private agencies to do so – but ultimately it must ensure that they exist in acceptable form.

Secondly, the efficiency of the market economy requires *an environment of competition*. A point on which Adam Smith, the apostle of capitalism (although he never used the word), and Karl Marx, its most radical critic and opponent, were agreed was that capitalists do not naturally seek competition, but try to avoid it. Success in business consists in defeating "the competition", and no businessman can be criticised for pursuing that aim. It is not his responsibility to ensure that there is a competitive market place, but the government's. The early history of capitalism in Europe is full of examples of entrepreneurs and companies seeking, and often getting, monopoly rights from kings and governments. Only in the nineteenth century were the benefits to the community of competitive markets clearly recognised in the capitalist world. The United States, in the twentieth century, took the lead, through its anti-trust laws, in introducing legal systems designed to prevent markets being overwhelmed by monopolists. In Europe the enforcement of competition is still less far advanced, although the European Union has taken strides forward in the past decade.

It is naive to assume that competition will occur naturally if the state just leaves well alone: the state must be active in this field if the market economy is to work well. An effective competition policy calls for legislation, backed by independent means of enforcement, to prevent or break up monopolies. It calls for laws requiring proper disclosure by companies of their activities and the use of regulatory and tax powers to ensure, as the saying goes, a level playing field. Competition is also encouraged by maintaining open borders for trade and commerce so far as possible: in smaller economies, this may be the most effective means.

Thirdly, there is the need for *basic infrastructure* – power supplies, transport, telecommunications and the like – and *basic social services* such as education and health. Whether these requirements are provided by the state itself or by private entities operating under state supervision, or by some combination of the two, is a matter of national choice. There can be considerable advantages in engaging the private sector to provide many of these things; but the state must ultimately be responsible for ensuring that, by one means or another, the needs of the community and of the economy in these matters are adequately met.

Fourth, the market system in itself will not prevent, and may actually encourage, economic activities which damage the *environment* or that are dangerous or injurious to the *health or safety* of employees or the public. Only the state can establish and enforce regulations in this field to protect the interests of the community as a whole and of future generations. The role of the state will be increasingly important in this field in the future and special problems already present themselves in developing countries.

Fifth, a free market system will not, of itself, protect the *unemployed and the weak and disadvantaged* in society, those who for reasons of age or disability cannot provide for themselves. The case for the state to assume some responsibility is particularly cogent in the case of the unemployed, because unemployment can be the consequence of the functioning of the market economy. A flexible market system involves labour moving from one employment to another, implying at least transitional unemployment. Considerations of economic efficiency and social justice alike call for this process to be eased by unemployment pay and re-training, but the state's ability to provide such a safety-net naturally depends on the wealth of the country and the resources it can spare for this purpose.

As for others in society who are unable to fend for themselves, any civilised society, whether capitalist or not, will ensure that, within reason and subject to the resources available, such needs are met. Whether this is necessarily a role of the state is more arguable – it is possible for them to be met in other ways – but in the modern nation-state, it is probably right to regard the state as having ultimate responsibility of ensuring that they are met. And most advanced industrial countries now regard this as including an obligation to ensure, by one means or another, that there is adequate health care for the whole population.

These principles describe, in broad outline, a kind of model for a market economy. It is a model which exists in all its aspects hardly anywhere, although closer approximations to it are to be found in the western industrial democracies than elsewhere. Capitalism comes in many forms: American capitalism is very different from the French version or the German and the versions found in the far east are very different again. It has also gone through other forms in the past. The market economy, as we see it in the more advanced countries now, has taken a long time to develop, and has often looked very unlike the model suggested in the principles I have listed.

Clearly there can be no single model of the market economy which should be recommended to all developing countries. There is room for difference of opinion about many aspects, such as priorities in government expenditure, approaches to inequality and poverty and to remuneration in the public and private sectors. A tolerant and flexible approach, recognising differences of culture, moral codes and history is essential. At the same time we should recognise that the problems involved in civilising capitalism and building a successful market economy – which is the essential development challenge now – are both different and more difficult in poor countries.

The following pages consider these issues in more detail. They discuss the role the state should play in Third World countries in creating successful market economies. They also touch on the question of inequality in developing countries and its relevance to the development challenge. Finally, there is the basic issue of accountability in a market economy and therefore of the relationship of the market economy to democracy.

* * *

It is sometimes argued that no western model of a market economy can be suitable for the Third World because it reflects a western culture which countries elsewhere do not share. But if this is true, can alternative forms be developed which are more compatible with the culture of countries in Asia, the middle east, Africa or Latin America? Or indeed to the confused cultural heritage of Russia?

Oddly enough, the region where there is the most talk about a conflict between local cultures and western capitalism is Asia, and especially east Asia – which is precisely the part of the Third World where capitalism is advancing most rapidly and successfully. There is much talk, for example by former Prime Minister Lee Kuan Yew of Singapore, about western ideas and methods being unsuited to Asia, where other traditions, such as Confucianism, prevail. And what is meant by Confucianism today, beyond respect for elders and family, is not always clear.

But the reality is that, in an important sense, the market economy is a culture in itself and does not merely reflect a more general western culture. The earlier culture of Europe in which capitalism developed, and the culture of pre-industrial America were very different from what prevails in these regions in the twentieth century. It is probably true that Europe and North America were particularly fertile soil for the growth of a market economy, with an individualism, not found in other parts of the world, embedded in its history, and legal systems which were adaptable to the needs of the new economic environment. But Japan has developed a highly successful capitalist system, despite the fact that its own culture is profoundly different, and collectivist rather than individualist. Decision-making processes in the Japanese corporate world will never be the same as in the west, but the growth of capitalism in Japan has meant the emergence, in effect, of a new Japanese culture, containing much that has been imported from the west – that is, from the modern capitalist west, and especially the United States.

Other Asian societies too are loosening their roots in their pre-existing cultures as the market economy advances, just as Europe did a century or two ago. This is not to say, of course, that the market economy, as it evolves in Asian countries, will or should be exactly the same as the western version. The Japanese case strongly suggests otherwise. But "cultural" issues are not always what they seem. Objections to what are criticised as western ways of doing things are often, in fact, objections to the logic of the market economy.

An important part of that logic is openness to international market forces. A lot of the benefit which countries that have moved to the market economy are already gaining comes from opening their economies to international trade and investment. This is happening at a time when industrial countries too are much more open and integrated – in the catch phrase, "globalised". The players in this increasingly integrated and open world economy will inevitably tend to become more alike in their economic behaviour. The "culture" of the market economy will be a common, global culture, with local variations.

The role of the law is important here. I have suggested that amongst the *systems and services* essential for an efficient and fair market economy is a predictable, above-board system of settling disputes. It is certainly a western tendency to assume that the market economy requires a legal underpinning. Is this a western cultural prejudice or is such a legal system an essential part of a market economy?

Japan shares with China and other east Asian countries a tendency to believe that business matters – amongst other things – can best be dealt with by consultation and agreement under the guidance, very often, of those in authority. But there is a big difference between Japan and China. Although Japan is still very different from the United States or Europe, it has developed a system of corporate law, and litigation does occur between Japanese companies (less commonly than in the US, it is true, but that is not the ideal standard to conform to). China, on the other hand, lacks both a coherent system of corporate law and a judicial system to enforce it. Foreign investors in China, including Japanese investors, have found that, if obligations between corporate entities are to have the force of law, contracts have to be extremely detailed and there is always much uncertainty about what will happen in the event of a dispute. "Overseas Chinese" – businessmen from Singapore, Malaysia or Hong Kong, for example – making investments in the home country, accept that everything depends on trust. They accept that going to court to settle a dispute in connection with one of their investments would be futile.

China is a country where, as any visitor quickly realises, market forces are being allowed a great deal of freedom, but within a strongly authoritarian system, managed by the Party. The Chinese way of handling contractual obligations and other business obligations reflects not only ancient Chinese tradition, but the lack of public accountability of power within the Communist state. Business dealings rely to a disturbing extent on informal relationships in which power and privilege can all too easily be misused. The lack of a modern legal system seems certain, as time goes on, to cause growing problems not only in China's international business dealings, but in the internal working of the market economy. As business relationships become more sophisticated, including the operations of the banks and the nascent stock markets which the authorities are encouraging, the need for greater transparency and predictability will become clearer. Pressure for a more modern legal system will probably grow. Hong Kong, which will be part of China after 1997, although under a special regime for 50 years, may play a part in this. As a mixture of the western and the oriental – Chinese entrepreneurship and British commercial and company law, enforced in British-style courts – it may, as a model, exert a considerable influence on the way the market economy develops in other parts of east Asia.

China and India present an interesting contrast in the matter of law. India's British-style legal system is by no means perfect, but it is one factor which attracts foreign investors to India and offers great advantages as the country moves into the market economy. Elsewhere in the Third World the picture is very varied. In the better-governed states of Africa and in most of Latin America, legal systems for the settlement of disputes, more or less modelled on the west, exist and operate with varying degrees of efficiency. Building legal systems to underpin a market economy is a major challenge in the former USSR. The First World is by no means perfect in all this, but it is fair to say that in the Third World it is more common for courts to be susceptible to pressure and influence, especially if the government is involved. This is a deterrent to foreign investment in many cases and a source of inefficiency in the operation of domestic companies. Building successful market economies requires more attention to be paid to enacting modern corporate and commercial laws and developing transparent and reliable courts. Equally, there is a need in many countries to ensure modern, transparent accounting systems if business is to be conducted efficiently.

Under the general heading of systems and services for the market economy, we should also recognise the fundamental importance of financial markets. Market forces should govern both the mobilisation of savings in a market economy and the allocation of resources for investment. Efficient financial markets can have far-reaching effects on the efficiency of the economy as a whole. Legislation which encourages the growth of healthy capital markets is important. Financial markets require more regulation and supervision than markets in physical goods, simply because it is a world in which, without regulation, it is relatively easy for people handling large amounts of other people's money to cheat.

In recent years there has been progress in many developing countries in these matters, as the importance of the subject has come to be better understood. But many countries still lack an efficient banking system, which has often been held back by heavy state ownership in the sector, and although stock and bond markets have been developing very fast in some countries, regulation in these "emerging markets" is still very variable. There is still a large uncompleted agenda here.

Then there is the question of *competition*. Few developing countries yet have formal systems for enforcing conditions of competition. In many of them, especially smaller countries, competition can be better ensured by maintaining reasonably open borders for trade and investment. During the last ten years, many countries in Latin America and Asia have moved forward in this respect, and the creation of free trade areas in Latin America is a very positive development. But large countries should also make it part of their development policy to establish mechanisms to prevent monopoly, or at any rate the abuse of monopoly. There is room for argument about whether areas of "natural monopoly", or areas where competition is difficult to organise, should be in public or private hands; but in either case regulation to protect the consumer and the public interest is important. The leading industrial democracies have made some progress in organising this type of regulation over the past two decades, but the First World generally has some way to go in this matter. And in Third World countries the subject needs much more attention than it has had so far.

When we turn to *basic infrastructure and basic social services*, there is no need to emphasise that Third World countries have a long way to go. In the coming decades the requirement for investment in electricity generation, telecommunications, roads, ports and the like will be enormous. All the indications are that private capital, domestic and foreign, will play a much larger part in meeting these needs than in the past, and if the external aid agencies have a role to play, it is likely to take the form of mobilising private capital.

It is worth stressing the importance of education here. A number of World Bank studies have demonstrated that investment in education, particularly primary education and the education of girls, provides very high returns to the economies of developing countries.[2] This is a service to the community which, in most developing countries, the state must provide because for the most part no one else will. With all the budgetary pressures that developing countries have to cope with, there is long term wisdom in giving priority, so far as possible, to expenditures that will foster growth, and this is one.

The fourth principle concerns the *environment, including health and safety.* There can be no doubt that environmental and related social issues will present Third World countries with enormous and growing problems in the coming years, and the state has a crucial role to play.

In the 1990s there is reason to hope that many Third World countries will be able, after decades of slow progress, to embark on a period of rapid growth. I believe this is essential if standards of living are to be raised and poverty reduced. But one hard reality to be faced is that many countries are embarking on this process after decades during which their populations have grown enormously. Many of the poorest countries are now densely populated and, as I pointed out in Chapter 2, this means that the environmental and social problems associated with rapid growth are going to be more difficult to cope with than they would have been two or three decades ago. A characteristic of the Third World in the past two decades has been the emergence and growth of mega-cities – Mexico City, São Paulo, Bombay, Calcutta, Cairo, Lagos, Jakarta, Bangkok, Guangdong, Beijing and many, many more, all far larger in population than any city of Europe or North America. All these cities face environmental problems including pollution, poor sanitation and congestion which are certain to be aggravated by rapid economic growth. China, which at the beginning of the 1990s appeared to be the fastest growing economy in the world, is beginning to worry seriously about these urban problems and the social unrest that they may engender. If one walks through a city like Bombay or Calcutta now, not much imagination is needed to envisage the challenges which fast growth will present. India embarks on high growth with a population of 900 million (still growing at about two per cent a year), of whom 70 per cent still live in rural villages. Rapid growth will change this too and no doubt new mega-cities will emerge. Without growth, the problems would be worse still, but that challenge to the state in dealing with urban problems during the period of high growth will be formidable. Industrial pollution will be the easier part of the problem. Government controls have been greatly intensified in the advanced industrial countries over the past decade or more and although the developing world generally lags behind in this matter, there is progress. Awareness of the dangers they face if they fail to develop proper environmental control systems is growing.

The role which external aid agencies can usefully play in this field is a difficult question. Ensuring that proper environmental standards are adhered to in projects financed by aid agencies is clearly essential. Providing technical assistance and advice can be valuable where it is wanted and not resisted. Some of the slowness of developing country governments in facing these issues stems from resentment of what they regard as unjustified interference in their affairs. The self-righteous attitudes of many non-governmental organisations coming from rich industrial countries – countries whose record on the pollution of the global atmosphere, the use of energy per person and the destruction of forests in the past should in fact induce some humility in their citizens – have done much harm to their own cause in developing countries. The harm is intensified when such people, who often know little about the developing world, seem to show no concern for economic development and raising standards of living.

Environmental problems which are essentially local must be distinguished from those which have a genuine global dimension. Shrill self-righteousness from American and European organisations about how many people will be displaced by a hydro scheme in India is out of place: that is a matter for the Indians. On the other hand, there can be a legitimate concern about the large-scale destruction of tropical forests because it can affect global warming. But if the concern is a genuinely global one, it is logical that the global community should bear the cost to the developing country of saving the forest.

Finally, protecting the *unemployed and disadvantaged* in a market economy is another area where poor countries obviously face more difficult problems than advanced countries. So long as they remain poor and the market economy has not yet raised the general standard of living significantly, it is very hard to find the means of paying for a safety net – unemployment pay, social security benefits for the old and sick and the like. Extended families can play a part in meeting these needs, but amongst the poorer sections of the population this is, to say the least, an imperfect solution, and is reported to be breaking down in many developing countries. Charity and religion play a part too.

Some developing country governments have tried to prevent unemployment by simply forbidding it. In India the law has for many years prohibited companies from going into liquidation without approval from the authorities, which was normally withheld. This often meant in practice either that the law was flouted and companies remained in existence legally but did in fact close down and lay off their work-force, or alternatively, a bank or a state-owned company would be brought in to run the bankrupt company so as to avoid layoffs. This could be seen as a form of unemployment pay, keeping the work-force occupied, but it is costly for the community. It perpetuates the production of uncompetitive goods or services and tends to undermine the financial health of the company which takes over and creates a vicious circle of inefficiency.

Until a country can afford a system of unemployment pay, this is a difficult problem, to which there is realistically only one answer and that is to achieve a momentum of growth in the economy sufficient to create new jobs faster than old jobs are lost. The successful far eastern countries, including Japan itself, did achieve this in the 1960s and 1970s. During those two decades Japan, Korea, Taiwan and Hong Kong all grew at average rates in the region of 10 per cent a year. In the far eastern countries, unemployment was not a significant problem in their transition to a successful market economy.

This momentum of growth is just what India has not achieved. Through the 1960s and 1970s India's average GNP growth was about 3.5 per cent a year, although over the past twelve years this has improved to 5.3 per cent. This has been sufficient to bring about a very gradual rise in living standards over the past three decades, but not enough to create a "virtuous circle" in which rapid re-deployment of labour minimises social problems and also contributes to the rising efficiency and growth of the economy. Fortunately, there are now signs that India may be entering a new period.

China in the past decade has achieved overall growth at an average rate of over 9 per cent a year and there has apparently been still faster growth in the southern and eastern coastal regions of the country. If India and other large Asian countries, through market-based policies, can achieve and maintain for two or three decades the kind of growth rates we are now seeing in China, they will be able to cope with the problem of unemployment through the rapid creation of new jobs. And as the nation's wealth increases, provision for unemployment pay and some kind of public support for other disadvantaged groups will be possible.

*   *   *

When thinking of capitalism in the Third World, the question of inequality of income immediately comes to many people's minds. In the midst of poverty, often abject and degrading poverty, it seems scandalous that some should be very rich, and both the riches and the poverty are commonly associated with capitalism. In fact, the proposition that wide inequality of incomes is an essential characteristic of capitalism can be disputed. Amongst capitalist countries there is considerable variation in degrees of inequality. Some Third World countries have achieved high growth rates and rising standards of living through market policies without extremes of wealth and poverty. But because it is often argued that creating greater income equality should in itself be an aim of "development", it is appropriate to consider the question here.

The available data on this subject[3] present a varied and somewhat confusing picture. A reasonable measure of inequality is the percentage of total household income received by the richest 10 per cent of the population together with the percentage received by the poorest 20 per cent. In the richer industrial countries, including the United States, Germany, Britain, France and Japan, the share received by the top 10 per cent is in the range 22 to 28 per cent, while the share of the lowest 20 per cent is in the range of 4.5 to 9 per cent. The United Kingdom, according to the most recent data, shows a relatively high degree of inequality by both measures – higher now than ten years ago – while Japan is the most egalitarian of this group.

Developing countries, on the other hand, vary very widely. Most Latin American countries display high degrees of inequality by both measures. Brazil is the country where extremes are greatest, the champion of inequality, with over 51 per cent of total household income going to the top 10 per cent and just over 2 per cent going to the bottom 20 per cent. There are a few examples of extreme inequality in Africa too. Asia, on the other hand, is generally much more egalitarian, although less so than the advanced industrial countries. India, Pakistan, Bangladesh and Indonesia are typical: they report figures in the range of 25 to 31 per cent at the top end and 8 to 9 per cent at the lower end. Korea, which can hardly be classified as a developing country any longer, also seems to have relative equality of incomes – 27.6 at the top end and 7.4 at the bottom.

In 1955 the American economist Simon Kuznets put forward a theory which has dominated discussion of this subject ever since.[4] He argued that in the period of rapid growth which usually occurs in the early stages of industrialisation, inequality increases, but then declines again later to produce a more equal distribution of income in mature industrial societies. This, Kuznets argued, applied not only to capitalist countries, but to all countries making the transition to an industrial society. Recent work, especially by Nancy Birdsall and Richard Sabot of the World Bank, has shown that there is nothing inevitable about the Kuznets pattern.[5] There are cases where high growth has been accompanied by a relatively high degree of equality, especially in east Asian countries such as Japan, Korea and Taiwan. It has even been argued that equality contributes to high growth. This is difficult to demonstrate, but it does seem clear that high inequality is not a necessary concomitant of high growth. However, the Kuznets tendency for inequality to increase in the early stages of industrialisation and then diminish probably still rules in many cases.

There are, I believe, four important points to be made about inequality in the context of Third World development.

First, the scandal of riches is not nearly as important as the scandal of poverty. The most important problem, whether the country is poor or rich or in between, is not inequality but poverty. If, in the course of a process of growth which enriches the country as a whole, some people make a lot of money, this need not be a cause for concern; but if many are very poor while the economy is growing, there should be concern.

Secondly, however, extremes of wealth and poverty are socially divisive and seen as unjust in most societies. Where there are extremes, there is always degrading poverty. One does not need to be a doctrinaire egalitarian to believe that the degrees of maldistribution to be found in Brazil and some other Latin American countries should not be acceptable. However, what degree of inequality is tolerable, and when it becomes unacceptably divisive, are questions on which societies will inevitably differ.

Thirdly, where there is serious poverty, it is right that governments should accept some responsibility for trying to alleviate it. In the last twenty or so years, much has been learned about how to reduce poverty – and not by means of charity. Some countries, such as Indonesia and Malaysia, have made considerable progress with market-based policies which raise the productivity of the poor. This can be achieved by encouraging labour-intensive forms of production in suitable cases, by training, by land reform where necessary and by providing the kind of social services which also raise their productivity. The evidence shows that a strong emphasis on universal education, especially primary education in the early stages of economic development, contributes to both equality and growth. On the other hand, state-imposed egalitarianism is likely to be economically damaging, retarding the creation of resources which could be used to alleviate poverty, amongst other things. Heavy-handed government intervention in the distribution of income, through heavy redistributive taxation or regulation of salaries by law, will have negative effects on growth, and measures of this kind should be employed with care and restraint. But when a reasonable distribution of incomes, without divisive extremes, can be achieved by consensus rather than government regulation, the benefits can be great. This is one of the main lessons to be learned from Japanese and Korean capitalism, where the divergences of income between the rich and the poor were less than in the older industrial countries of the west even during their period of very rapid growth.

But fourthly, there is no escaping the obvious and basic point, confirmed by all experience, that if poverty is to be attacked successfully, the economy as a whole must grow and so produce the expanding resources needed for this task. There has been no example of success in attacking poverty without substantial overall growth. And the market economy, some version of capitalism, is the only effective way to achieve that.

In most countries and cultures, the flexibility and freedom required for a market economy to function efficiently and achieve high rates of growth are bound to be accompanied by some degree of inequality, at least in the sense that some people will make a lot of money. But that does not mean that there is bound to be abject poverty – that is not a necessary adjunct of the market economy. But it behoves those who believe in the market economy as the answer to the problems of less-developed countries to pay careful attention to the question of poverty. The avoidance or reduction of poverty, rather than equality of income, is an appropriate aim of development.

*   *   *

Finally, there is the question of the links between the market economy and democracy. Can democracy be in any sense a legitimate aim of development? If international development agencies are right to urge Third World governments in the direction of the market economy, are they entitled also to persuade them towards democratic systems of government?

As a matter of observation, democracy (I use the word in its western sense, or in Peter Berger's words as meaning "a political system in which governments are constituted by majority votes cast in regular and uncoerced elections")[6] has always gone with capitalist economic systems; but the reverse is not the case. There have been plenty of Third World examples in the past half century of reasonably successful capitalist economies existing under authoritarian regimes – Chile, Korea, Taiwan. The historical record also seems to show that full-blown socialism in the sense of a "command economy" where all economic activity is controlled by the state has never been combined with democracy, and probably cannot be. But the Third World record is more of mixed systems: heavily *dirigiste* systems which fall short of full-blown socialism. But even these systems, in the Third World, have mostly been combined with authoritarian governments. The exception, and it is an interesting one, is India, which for at least a couple of decades, bore some resemblance to a command economy but which was also, in a real sense, a democracy – an imperfect one no doubt, but a democracy nonetheless, in which the incumbent government could be, and sometimes was, turned out of office. Berger's summary ignores these nuances, but is substantially right as a comment on the historical record: "all democracies are capitalist; no democracy is socialist; many capitalist societies are not democracies".[7]

This would lead us to the conclusion that democracy is not necessary for a market economy. The market economy, no doubt in imperfect form, has existed under authoritarian governments and can no doubt do so again. But to stop there would be to miss some important points.

First, it can surely be said that there is an *affinity* between democracy and the market system. In both, power is diffused – economic power to the consumer who by his or her choices in the market ultimately decides what will be produced in the economy; and political power to the same people as voters.

Secondly, the market economy in its fairest and most efficient forms requires an environment which is most naturally produced in a democracy – a system of law which operates transparently, systems of supervision of commercial activity which are subject to public scrutiny, and similarly transparent systems of environmental control. Capitalism under authoritarian regimes tends to be accompanied by secret and corrupt relationships between the powerful and the rich. As I argued earlier, public accountability in various areas is needed for a market economy functioning with optimal efficiency and fairness and that is not to be achieved without democracy.

Thirdly, there is some reason to believe that successful market economies, which raise the standard of living of the people as a whole and result in improved levels of education and public communications, will in the course of time lead to pressures for democracy. We see this happening in some Asian countries such as Korea and Taiwan. The influence of example from the western democracies, especially the United States, through modern media, is no doubt a factor here too, but it has much greater impact in countries which have themselves achieved significant progress through the market economy.

This presents a difficult question as regards the role of aid donors and agencies. For very understandable reasons, they usually avoid getting involved in political matters. Some would have the World Bank and similar institutions impose conditions requiring progress towards democracy on countries which receive its loans; and a case can be made, on the basis of the points above, for regarding this as a legitimate adjunct to the role of promoting economic growth through market systems. The formal objection to this is approach is that it involves an intrusion into the sovereignty of Third World countries. This objection may not be entirely compelling, but some caution is in order here, if only because democracy, if it is to succeed, has to be home-grown, and probably the best way to assist its growth is to promote successful market economies.

Heavy conditionality in this area would certainly be ill-advised, and persuasion will always be preferable to pressure. But an important part of the process of developing a successful market economy, as we have seen, lies in ensuring the competence of the state to perform its functions well; and ideally this involves public accountability in various ways. There is a fine line to be trodden here, but some external pressure in matters such as establishing a system of corporate law administered by competent and open courts, or transparent systems for stock-market supervision or for environmental control may be appropriate; whereas pressure from aid agencies for a multi-party election system would not.

So is capitalism in some form the answer to the development needs of the Third World? There are those who argue that "development" should not consist of exporting the ugliness of industrialism to poor countries. Some of that ugliness can be avoided by learning from the experience of the existing industrial countries, using the latest technologies so as to leap-frog phases of technological development through which the older industrial economies have had to pass; and handling environmental and social issues related to industrialisation and urbanisation better on the basis of their experience. Development does not consist solely of GNP growth, but without economic growth there will be no development and no successful assault on poverty, hunger and misery. But the question is not only whether the Third World can achieve high rates of growth through the market economy – the evidence strongly suggests that if governments do the right things, it can be done – but whether socially acceptable forms of capitalism can be developed in Third World countries, forms that are sufficiently rooted in the local culture to be stable.

It is obvious that the difficult task of building market economies that are both efficient and socially acceptable is one which falls squarely on the shoulders of the leaders of each developing country. What then is the message for aid donors and the international development agencies? Are they any longer relevant? The next chapter addresses the question of their future role.

6 Re-inventing Aid

If the international development task must now consist primarily of helping developing countries to run successful market economies, the question is how this is to be done. International aid has mostly taken the form of financing governments and the change in the role of governments which the move to the market economy requires must also mean a change in the activities which aid finances. At the same time, if the private sector is to play the leading role in economic growth, much more attention needs to be focussed on aid to the private sector – a task which also needs careful definition. Aid needs to be re-invented.

Some conservative economists have argued that any development aid is inconsistent with the market philosophy. On this view, any development activities undertaken by governments or international organisations are *ipso facto* an interference in the market economy and therefore damaging to economic efficiency and growth. The interests of Third World countries, and of the donor countries themselves, would be served best if the whole aid and development effort were abandoned. The foremost proponent of this view has been the British economist Peter Bauer.[1]

This extreme and rather simplistic position, apparently based more on *a priori* arguments than on an examination of the evidence, unfortunately diverts attention from some real issues. It is true that international aid grew out of a period when there was a prevailing belief in the ability of the state to promote economic growth, through public investment, ownership of enterprises and planning. As I have argued, aid to governments encouraged many of them in such policies in the past. These beliefs are shared by few serious people now and the acceptance of market principles must raise questions about the impact of much traditional aid activity.

But the view that market economics completely invalidate the case for any kind of aid is altogether too sweeping. The question is: what kinds of aid can be consistent with a belief in market economics and what kinds are not? Bauer does us a service when he asks why the case for aid "has come to be taken as practically

111

self-evident"; but he himself is open to the charge that he treats the case *against* aid as self-evident and does not distinguish between one kind of aid and another.[2] The case for aid does indeed need to be argued and justified, both on the basis of principle and case by case.

I believe we need a new intellectual basis for the whole aid activity. This new basis must be fully consistent with, indeed built on, the market philosophy, so we might well start from the challenge of those who believe that the market philosophy invalidates aid in its entirety. The extreme proposition that *any* form of development aid is inconsistent with the market philosophy fails on two counts.

First, it ignores the important positive role the state must play in an efficient market economy – a role which I discussed in the previous chapter and which normally includes some public investment. This role of governments is a non-market activity – governments cannot be market operators because they do not operate in an environment of market risk – but necessary to create the conditions in which the markets can function well. In the Third World many governments are not able to perform this role satisfactorily and can benefit from external assistance. Economic progress can be accelerated by selective and targeted assistance to help governments perform these functions. But it is of crucial importance that any aid activities carried out under this rubric must assist the development of a healthy market economy and not hinder it.

Secondly, so far as the private sector is concerned, the extreme view fails to distinguish between a fantasy world in which market forces function perfectly and the world as it actually is. In the market economy the private sector will be the driving force of growth, operating in an environment of market forces and subject to market risks and incentives. But the truth is that in most Third World countries this environment is highly imperfect and market forces work less efficiently than in more developed countries. This retards the processes of investment and growth. In fact under-development could almost be defined as a set of conditions in which markets can only work badly. So certain aid activities which enable private companies and investors to cope with these conditions and facilitate markets in making sound investments can be beneficial. But, as in the case of aid to governments, the intervention of aid agencies must be very carefully designed to ensure that they do not hamper or undermine the working of markets, but help them to work more efficiently.

In fact these two propositions form a good basis for a redefinition of the aid task now. It falls into two parts. First, helping the state to play its proper role in the market economy; and secondly, helping the private sector to overcome market imperfections and so make sound investments in difficult environments. As part of the process of re-inventing aid, we should try to define the main disciplines to which aid of both kinds should be subjected.

But before we do so, there are two general and fundamental points which are relevant to all aid activity. To some, they will seem obvious, but if they were taken seriously they would imply far-reaching changes in the business of aid as it is practised at present. They are all too often ignored.

First, it is important for aid practitioners to recognise that *aid can be harmful*. The point is not just that it is sometimes ineffective (which is also true), but that the wrong kind of aid can be positively injurious to the basic objective of economic growth. There is a naive tendency to assume that good intentions validate aid. Aid programmes are usually managed by people who are trying to do good, but they are not prone to ruthless self-criticism, rather more to a kind of moral satisfaction which can blind them to the effects of their actions. The unwillingness of some of them to recognise the importance of sound economics brings no benefit to the people of Third World countries.

The wrong kind of aid can retard the development of a sound market economy, and quite frequently has done so, as I argued in Chapter 4. It can damage the ability of poor people to be productive and support themselves – a blatant example being some past food aid programmes which undermined the productivity of Third World farmers. The wrong kind of aid can inhibit the evolution of efficient, market-based financial systems and capital markets, as I argued in Chapter 3, with harmful effects on the economy as a whole. The development banks promoted by international agencies have not only misused donors' money, but the savings of poor countries too, and have thus done positive harm. And aid can do damage by supporting mistaken policies. The people of Tanzania suffered grievously in the late 1970s and early 1980s when external aid supported and encouraged policies that drove that country to economic disaster.

One factor which can increase the danger of aid being provided in harmful ways is the pressure in some aid organisations to achieve targets for lending. This has the effect of making quantity more important than quality and can easily result in poor judgment. The World Bank since the days of Robert McNamara as President has, as I pointed out in Chapter 3, been more prone to this than most aid agencies. Once again, Tanzania illustrates the point. The Bank's own report on its dealings with that country over 25 years said: "The Bank sometimes lent for the wrong projects . . . This may have been due to the need to meet Bank lending targets. In retrospect, Tanzania could have been better off with less Bank lending." This was probably true of World Bank lending in other countries, which was equally driven by volume targets, in Africa and elsewhere.

And perhaps the least recognised form of harm done by aid is pauperisation. Bauer quotes the example of the Navajo Indians in the western United States, overwhelmed with well-intentioned subsidies, destroyed as a society. We are not enough aware of the danger of creating a mentality of dependency. Just as individuals can be corrupted by charity which makes it unnecessary to earn their own living, whole societies can be corrupted or pauperised. This danger is seldom discussed by aid organisations and professionals, although in fact there are signs that this is exactly what is happening now in a number of countries, especially in Africa. Pauperisation is an addiction to charity, undermining the ability of the addict to be productive (and aid in the form of grants, involving no obligation to repay, creates the greatest risk of addiction). Donors who fail to recognise the danger react by providing the addict with more of the drug. This too is what appears to be happening in Africa now.

The second general point, in effect the positive side of the first, is that, as a general rule, *aid, whether to the government or the private sector, should take the form of investment designed to promote economic growth, not of subsidy.* Aid should not finance recurrent expenditures. (I am not speaking here of disaster relief which is obviously a special case.) Aid should finance expenditures which can seriously be expected to raise the productivity of the recipient country and contribute to faster economic growth. The principle of aid-as-investment is an elementary one which used to be adhered to much more rigorously in the early days of the aid business. Many development agencies and donors would not dispute it today and would claim that their activities are guided by it. But investments should earn a proper return and the record of international aid, especially in Africa, does not suggest that this is how aid has been managed.

The principle of aid-as-investment does not mean that it must necessarily be spent on plant and machinery or the means of producing goods and services for the market place. Expenditure on basic infrastructure – roads, railways, ports, telecommunications services, electricity supply, water supplies – can be essential investment which increases a country's productive capacity. Education is a long term investment in a nation's productive capacity. The question is how to ensure that aid is used for investments that will secure a proper return to the economy of the country concerned.

When aid takes the form of investment in private companies which operate in genuine markets, the test is clear – the enterprise will succeed or fail in the market place. In case of public sector investments which face no market test, including investments made by governments but financed by aid, one has to rely on techniques, which are now very sophisticated, for estimating the potential "economic" return to the recipient country. But these calculations are notoriously vulnerable to optimism and wishful thinking before decisions are taken and to poor record-keeping afterwards. Providers of aid, if they are to ensure that their resources are efficiently used, have to adopt an extremely rigorous approach in such cases.

Where aid takes the form of loans at market-related rates, another quasi-market test is available: the ability of the recipient country to service and repay debt over a reasonable period of time is a rough indication whether resources provided through loans (though not necessarily by any particular loan) have been used effectively. As I have argued, the fact that many African countries have for many years been unable to service huge amounts of debt to foreign official lenders – debt originating from development aid – raises serious doubts about how that money was used. This burden of debt is often quoted as evidence of those countries' need for more aid, but the situation is primarily testimony to the misuse of past aid.

The problem of the debt burden is avoided if aid takes the form of grants or of credits, like those provided by the IDA, on such soft terms as to be little different from grants. But this only makes it more difficult to answer the question whether the aid is being used in a manner that enhances productive capacity commensurately with the quantity of aid. It would be surprising if the use of grants did not tend to reduce the rigour with which the impact of intended aid projects is estimated. In countries where loans seem to have been misused, what reason is there to believe that grants will be more efficiently used? In fact the overall record of growth in African countries which have been receiving large amounts of aid, mostly in the form of grants, strongly suggests that aid projects and the economic returns to be expected of them have been assessed with insufficient rigour in many cases.

And no one should suppose that if grant-financed projects fail no harm is done. There may be no debt to repay, but failure is always damaging, especially if programmes are abandoned, and if not, they are likely to require either continuing subsidy from the donor or continuing recurrent expenditure by the recipient country.

*   *   *

In the last chapter I discussed how the role of the state might be redefined, recognising that there will be differences of opinion about exactly where the boundaries of state activity should be set. Co-operation between external aid agencies and recipient countries will be effective only if there is agreement on this point: forcing change of this kind down unwilling throats will not achieve results. But the reality is that if developing countries are to get the benefit of a healthy market economy, the state will have to withdraw from many activities in most countries, and reduce the share of the national resources which it pre-empts. At the same time, the state will have to be better equipped to perform certain positive functions.

Against the background of the market economy, the scale and nature of aid to governments must change. Its basic purpose should be much more carefully defined in terms of helping governments (those which really do need help) to do the things that will promote the development of a healthy market economy, and to perform these tasks efficiently. In many developing countries expertise in the creation of legal, regulatory, accounting and other systems for the market economy is badly needed. There is an important, positive role to be played by aid agencies here. Technical assistance, as opposed to capital financing, becomes increasingly important as we move toward a modern market economy. The international agencies have moved with the times and are now providing more of this kind of aid, but the point needs more emphasis.

There is also a role to be performed in the financing of public investments in infrastructure, education, health and the like which are needed to promote economic growth. This has of course been one of the main activites of external development agencies since the beginning of international aid. It is here that the redefinition of the role of aid to governments has to include restraints. This re-definition needs to be based on a much greater awareness that injecting official finance into a country can harm and retard the development of a market economy. Development institutions should adopt new guidelines for aid to governments which, I believe, should require all such aid to meet two basic criteria.

First, aid to governments should be used only for investments which the private sector (domestic or foreign) cannot or will not undertake, either alone or in association with the state, or where there are compelling reasons of public interest why they should be undertaken by the state and not the private sector. Aid must not be used to draw into the public sector activities which can be undertaken in the private. This is a principle which has not always been observed in the past but which the World Bank has recently espoused officially. However, it is not clear that all other donors have accepted it. As we have recognised, the boundary between public and private will vary to some extent from one country to another, and external development agencies should not seek to impose rigid views about this on developing countries. But they can and should decline to provide finance for purposes which seem inconsistent with the development of a healthy market economy.

Second, as I have already suggested, aid should finance only priority investments (and not recurrent expenditures) which are likely to earn a high rate of return for the country. In view of the record in this respect, the minimum projected rate, or "hurdle rate", should be set high and every proposal should be subjected to rigorous scrutiny, making due allowance for the danger of over-optimism, before any decision is taken.

Over many years, development agencies have helped govern-ments undertake public investment programmes without con-sidering sufficiently the impact on the private sector and the efficiency of the economy. It is essential that this should change, but unfortunately the tendency to ignore or make light of these issues is still there. Old habits die hard and institutional behaviour changes reluctantly. An obvious case is when loans are made for the purpose of rehabilitation of inefficient state-owned companies which ought either to be privatised or closed down. The World Bank approved such a loan as recently as 1993 for China. The risk that such resources will be used inefficiently is very high. In 1990 the Bank made a substantial loan to India to rehabilitate six inefficient state-owned cement plants when more efficient private sector alternatives were available. Enabling inefficient state-owned companies to continue in business by providing capital which they could not get on the market must retard the development of a healthy private sector in the country.

Channelling money through the system on non-market terms – for example in the form of loans for on-lending to the private sector at below-market rates – was a significant part of World Bank activity in the early 1980s, but has been reduced in recent years. This type of lending can only retard the emergence of an efficient financial system. Loans for the purpose of recapitalising inefficient state-owned banks can be even more damaging. These have become less common recently but there have been recent cases such as a $350 million World Bank loan for this purpose to Indonesia in 1993, and the even larger loan to India in 1995 which I mentioned in Chapter 3 (p. 61). Chapter 7 will discuss in more detail what can be done positively to help developing countries to create healthy financial systems.

The use of guarantees to support private sector lending is another area where institutions financing governments need to proceed with care. It is easy to see how problems arise. For example, a big infrastructure project calls for substantial amounts of loan finance. The private commercial banks are interested but, seeing a chance to reduce their risk, ask the World Bank or some such institution, to guarantee their loans. The Bank finds this appealing because it enables them to say that they have mobilised a large amount of private finance for the project. But comprehensive guarantees for commercial bank lending defeat the purpose of involving the private sector, which is to achieve efficiency by ensuring that capital comes on the basis of market risk, which gives lenders the incentive to make sure that the project is well planned and managed. If the lenders rely for their security solely on the guarantee of an international institution, they will have no such incentive to ensure efficiency.

Comprehensive guarantees which remove commercial risk for private financiers of projects are therefore to be deplored. A case can be made, however, for more limited guarantees covering non-commercial risks – particularly the political risk of damaging interference by the government concerned or failure by official bodies to fulfil their obligations. Facing risks of this kind does nothing to improve the efficiency of investments. At the same time, guarantees by international institutions have to be regarded as a second best solution to this kind of problem, because they alleviate the pressure on the host governments to do what is necessary to remove the risk. Far better that the government of the country concerned should conduct itself in such a manner as to make any guarantees unnecessary. If they are necessary, a reasonable form of guarantee is for the government of the host country to guarantee that an official agency in the country, for example, an electricity board which is contracting to buy power from a private company, will fulfil its contractual obligations. But when a powerful external agency such as the World Bank introduces its own guarantee as well, the situation is significantly changed. The Bank has recently announced a new guarantee policy which shows awareness of the dangers, but the wording is flexible and it remains to be seen what it will mean in practice.[3]

The second basic aid role which we should recognise in the new world of market economics is aid provided directly to the private sector. This is the subject of the next chapter, together with the question of the balance between the two roles.

7 Aid to the Private Sector

The second aid role consists of assisting the private sector, on which successful economic growth will crucially depend. It is no less important to define and limit this aid function carefully.

The leading organisation engaged in this type of work in the Third World is a part of the World Bank group, the International Finance Corporation or IFC, which I headed for over nine years.[1] The IFC deals with private companies direct, providing both finance and advice, in pursuit of the basic aim of economic development. There are also parallel institutions in a number of donor countries, such as Britain, France and Germany.

As in the case of aid to governments, this type of aid activity has also to be justified in the light of market principles. The obvious question is: why not simply leave it to the private sector? Why should any official agency concern itself with what private companies do? The basic case for aid to the private sector rests on the proposition that markets work imperfectly, and that it is, therefore, legitimate to look for ways of facilitating the working of markets and helping private companies and investors to cope with these imperfections. To begin with, however, it is important to understand just how imperfect and flawed the market environment is in much of the Third World.

First, in varying degrees, the legal systems through which business is conducted are deficient. In most countries companies, domestic or foreign, do not have access to an efficient system of courts in which disputes can be settled reliably. For example, enforcing a foreclosure on a mortgage is often either impossible in practice, or at least very difficult, even assuming that all the documentation is in good order. In many cases the law does not impose satisfactory accounting and disclosure requirements and it is often difficult to secure good accountancy services. In a number of countries, even after the general improvement in the past decade, government regulation and interference are burdensome, sometimes including price controls. And in a number of cases, especially in Africa, corruption is a barrier to the efficient conduct of business.

121

Secondly, the backwardness of financial markets continues to be an obstacle to the smooth functioning of the market economy in many countries. This has been changing in the past ten years or so, but there is still a long way to go. In most developing countries, it is still difficult for companies to raise finance from local banks in the form of term loans, except on a short-term basis. This is slowly improving, but conditions are still very different from those in the advanced countries. Equity markets are developing fast in many countries, but markets in debt securities are much less advanced. And in many countries economic conditions are such that real interest rates have to be very high.

Thirdly, there are barriers to investment, especially foreign investment, stemming from lack of information and understanding, and of confidence related to these things. Investors in advanced countries are less familiar with conditions in Third World countries and more cautious about investing there. Political risks, real or perceived, can discourage foreign investment even where the commercial case is strong. Again, things are changing in some parts of the Third World and investment is beginning to flow on a larger scale; but the perception of higher risk is still there.

All this adds up to an environment (and of course the situation varies widely from one country to another) which makes business more difficult than in the advanced countries. This applies to both domestic and foreign companies, but the difficulties are usually greater for foreigners. So to assist the progress of the market economy, there is room for a market-facilitating aid role which consists of helping companies and investors to measure and manage the risks of investing and operating in developing countries.

But we must be aware of the dangers. The IFC, like the World Bank itself, is owned by governments, which provide its capital. (Since Russia and the other members of the former Soviet Union joined, these owners are virtually all the governments of the world.) The danger is that, because it is a powerful government-owned agency, its efforts to help the private sector will in fact undermine the private character of its clients. Official financing of the private sector, like investments undertaken by governments, may displace and crowd out market financing. It may reduce or even remove the discipline of risk from which the efficiency of the market economy derives; it may substitute bureaucratic processes of decision-making for entrepreneurial decision-making; it may introduce political factors into the allocation of resources. If these things happen, the intervention of such an agency will weaken the market economy rather than support it.

The history of development demonstrates that these dangers are real. I have spoken of the development banks that were established in many countries in the 1960s, often with the encouragement and help of the World Bank and the IFC. These were usually government-owned, and created for the purpose of providing investment capital to both public and private enterprises. They were quite often used by governments, which appointed presidents or chairmen who would follow instructions, to make investments for political and sometimes corrupt purposes, and to keep unviable enterprises going. By the early 1980s many of these institutions had investment portfolios which made them unviable themselves (the losses of state-owned enterprises often made a big contribution to this), and they had either to be closed down or rescued by the injections of additional capital by the state.

One reason for the creation of these development banks was the absence of market-based financial systems. But it was not uncommon for their activities to become an obstacle to the emergence of such systems, because private banks and financial institutions could not compete with the easy money they offered. And it was not only the financial system which suffered. Just as an efficient financial system transmits discipline to the companies it finances, a feather-bedded system transmits inefficiency and indiscipline. Many of the clients of the official development banks did not take their financial obligations to those banks at all seriously.

So we do know something about the dangers inherent in using official funds to support the private sector. The IFC itself is a kind of development bank and subject to some of the same dangers. However, as an international organisation supervised by an international Board, it is less at risk of political pressures and is also able to benefit from a wide knowledge of the experience of national development banks in many countries. But it is crucially important that the role and method of operation of institutions like the IFC should be defined carefully and clearly, and the IFC's own experience shows that, if this is done, such institutions can make a significant contribution to economic development.

The role of a private-sector-supporting aid agency is a complex one. It is not so much a matter of following precise rules as of adhering to certain underlying principles. What follows is a discussion of these principles, based very much on my experience at the IFC.

The first is the principle of *additionality*. The agency exists not to substitute for the private sector, but to engage the private sector in sound investments which would not proceed without the agency's participation. In Third World conditions, potential investors, domestic or foreign, may be unwilling, for one reason or another to accept the risks alone. Or the project might be one which would proceed without the agency's participation, but in a less satisfactory form – for example, the agency's participation might make it possible to get local investors to join a venture which would otherwise be wholly foreign-owned; or a company might be persuaded, with the agency's participation, to list the company and invite participation by the public.

The central aim must be to promote profitable, economically sound, private companies which will be successful in their own economies, making a contribution to output and employment and avoiding environmental damage. The investments it supports must be sound financially: they must pass the test of the market and be profitable. But if they are to contribute to development, they must also be sound from an economic point of view, that is, their profitability must not depend on subsidies, protection, price controls or other market distortions.

The second principle is that the agency should act as a *partner of the private sector*. Although its own basic purpose is development rather than profit, it must operate as a business, which is not, in practice, as much of a contradiction as some might think. To be a partner of private companies and investors, the agency must fully understand and to a considerable extent share their objectives. If the companies it supports succeed, the agency will benefit from a flow of interest payments and dividends, and in due course capital gains when investments are sold off. So it is healthy from the point of view of its development role that the agency itself should also have to look after its own bottom line.

Functioning as a business means that the agency should be a genuine risk-taker. This is a fundamental point. The founders of the IFC were wise enough to include in its Articles of Agreement a section which prohibits it from accepting government guarantees of any of its financing. The reasoning behind this is sound. The management of market risk is a source of efficiency in the private sector and the same must apply to the agency itself. If, as an investor or lender, the agency is protected from market risk by government guarantees, it will be likely to take less care in the appraisal and design of its investments, knowing that, if an investment fails, it can fall back on its guarantor. Good investments succeed by creating competent management, technology and marketing systems to cope with market risk. An aid institution which supported the private sector while protecting itself from commercial risk would be in danger of promoting companies which would not have the strength to survive market pressures.

One might also ask whether it is in fact realistic to expect an organisation funded and controlled by governments to operate like a business in the full sense? It is true that such an institution is likely to be better placed than private investors to carry certain risks, especially political ones. Does this invalidate its role? I believe not, because no one would argue that it is the management of political risk which makes for efficiency in the private sector. Participation by the IFC as a minority investor often encourages investors to proceed who would otherwise be deterred by fear of government interference or political instability. The IFC "umbrella" operating in this way allows decisions to be taken on the basis of an assessment of genuine commercial risk.

So far as commercial risk is concerned, however, the private-sector aid agency should not enjoy any privileges. What it should bring to the table is experience and expertise as a specialist in investing in developing countries and in making the difficult judgments which are often involved. This contribution can take a variety of forms. The financial structuring and planning of projects is an obvious one. There may be a technical contribution to be made, especially if the sponsor is a local company without access to such advice. A foreign investor is less likely to need technical help, but may have problems in negotiations with the host government. For example there may be issues about taxation, or, in the case of mineral and mining projects in particular, a government's insistence on some measure of ownership in the venture for itself. In the case of private investments in infrastructure, there are always issues involving the government, and private-sector aid agencies with the appropriate skills can play a useful role.

Should a private-sector aid agency provide subsidised funding or operate on market terms? Some of the existing agencies do offer subsidised finance while others, including the IFC, do not. The argument against subsidy is that it runs the risk of weakening the rigour of the investment appraisal. In principle, if a project requires subsidy to succeed, it does not meet the full test of the market. The principle of partnership with business suggests that subsidy is out of place because it tends to put the agency on a different footing from the others with whom it seeks to co-operate, leading them to expect that it will be a "soft touch" and less than fully business-like. It is therefore preferable, in my view, from the point of view of the long term success of its client companies, that the development agency should lend on market terms and expect a satisfactory return on its equity investments. The concept of "soft equity", of Scandinavian origin, where a normal return is not expected, has led to well-meaning aid agencies supporting unviable ventures – which is no contribution to development at all.

On the other hand, one cannot be too purist about this. It might be argued that there is a kind of subsidy implicit in the fact that private-sector aid agencies are content with a lower rate of return than private investors. Whether lower returns which are the consequence of deliberately operating in difficult and risky places are properly described as subsidies is perhaps a matter of semantics. These lower returns mainly stem from the fact that costs are higher, because of the need to spend more staff time on the design of projects in difficult circumstances. For the client company, the "subsidy" arrives in the form of free advice (although in the IFC's case, it has been the practice for some years to charge fees for such advice where the amount involved is large and the client can pay) and it is true that "subsidies" of this kind are by no means unique to development activities in the Third World – for example, most western countries have programmes to assist small businesses, including free advice and often tax concessions.

The important point, in the end, is to ensure that the ventures which a private-sector development agency supports are fully able, when launched, to stand on their own feet in the market. This strongly suggests that they should pay normal market rates for loans and be judged by normal standards on the performance of their equity.

The third basic principle for a private-sector development agency is that it must operate as a *catalyst* – using its own resources economically to encourage and help private investors and entrepreneurs to commit private capital to sound enterprises. The bulk of the capital and the leadership and management in client companies should come from the private sector. But I believe it is a good principle that the agency itself should provide only a minority of the funding, avoid being the largest shareholder and not get involved in management, which should be undertaken by genuinely private parties. This detachment should not, of course, prevent the agency from taking a close interest, at the planning stage, in the structure of the management and the personnel involved. This is a necessary part of the process of risk-management for investors, which is central to the role. And it may be right for the agency to take a seat on the Board of the company, when it is an equity investor, so as to make sure that it is kept properly in touch with the affairs of the company and to make a contribution to them.

However, practice varies amongst the private-sector agencies. The Commonwealth Development Corporation, an older organisation than the IFC, has always managed a number of its investments itself and does so very competently. This can set a standard of good management in the country and if the aid agency eventually moves out and hands over to local owners and managers, the benefit to the private sector in the country can be real.

The catalytic role means mobilising funding, in whatever form is required, to enable a good project to go ahead. The agency's ability to do this will depend partly on its own record. If it builds up a reputation as a successful investor, its participation in a project will be taken as a "seal of approval" which can make the difference for other investors and lenders. But the key point is that the seal of approval consists not of an opinion which is delivered in return for a fee, but of the fact that the agency, with its record of success, risks its own money in the investment. Besides this, the development agency may be able to mobilise funding because its presence in a venture is seen to reduce the non-commercial risks, such as the risk of unfriendly government intervention.

The catalytic principle would also indicate that the development agency's own input of funds should be tied up in a project only for as long as is needed. Loans should be repaid over a period determined by the need of each individual project and equity investments sold when the agency's presence is no longer necessary for the company to operate successfully. When it comes to selling equity stakes, the agency should look for a fair market price, including a capital gain where the client company has been successful, but with development objectives in mind too. For example, selling the shares to the public on the local stock exchange, if that is possible, can widen share ownership in the country and help to open up the company.

There is also the question of what happens when a company in which the agency has invested runs into trouble. For a risk-taking agency this is bound to happen from time to time – indeed, if it never happened, that would suggest that the agency was not taking enough risk. It is common for the IFC, in such circumstances, to be asked by the other investors and lenders to work out a solution. Its first aim should be to find one which will enable the company to recover and go on to be successful. However, if this is not possible, there may be no alternative but for the agency to extract itself on the best available terms.

* * *

If these principles are observed, they can be a basis for a variety of other activities by a private-sector aid agency, beyond the central role of financing projects. There are specialised areas where such agencies can be of help. The experience of the IFC suggests three in particular: capital market development, small business development, and infrastructure.

We have already noted the importance of *capital market development* and the creation of efficient financial systems in building a successful market economy. The IFC has been particularly active in this sphere. Provided the host government's attitude is positive, it provides expert advice to the authorities –

the government, the Central Bank, the stock exchange – on the development and regulation of securities markets. The 1980s and early 1990s saw an extraordinary development of equity markets in the Third World, the so-called "emerging markets", which are gradually becoming part of the world financial system. The IFC played an important role in forging links between the emerging markets and the major world financial centres, thus promoting flows of portfolio investment to developing countries. This activity was a creative response to a particular situation in the mid and late 1980s, and is now less needed because the private markets are themselves vigorously promoting these flows.

But the more basic task of capital market development consists of initiatives to strengthen domestic markets and equip them with institutions which can provide finance and financial services to the country's private sector. In common with some national private-sector aid agencies, particularly the British CDC, the IFC has invested in a very large number of local, private financial companies, which become operators in the capital market. Private banks, merchant banks, housing finance companies and venture capital companies all help the financial markets to function more effectively. Experience has shown that in countries where the banking system does not readily provide term finance for the purchase of capital equipment by local companies, the establishment of leasing companies can be very valuable.

Then there is *small business development*. Most governments in the world, in advanced as well as developing countries, are interested in encouraging small businesses. If the economy is not to be dominated by an oligopoly of large companies, new ones must grow up alongside them. In developing countries, the interest in small businesses springs partly from an understandable desire to see indigenous businesses grow so that foreign companies do not dominate. In very under-developed areas like most of Africa, the hope of a healthy private sector in the future must rest to a large extent on such new businesses.

Can an external private sector development agency help with this? It is obviously a local task, requiring local knowledge and local decision-making. Many, but by no means all, small businesses in developing countries depend on local markets rather than exports and are therefore not well placed to accept hard-currency loans, which is what international development agencies generally have to offer. So the conclusion is that such an agency can realistically help small business development mainly by working through local intermediaries.

This brings us back to development banks, whose record of success, especially in Africa, is far from encouraging. Most development banks in the past were wholly or partly government-owned and government-controlled. The causes of failure lie largely in this fact. An alternative is for international agencies to use privately-owned banks and other financial companies as intermediaries, institutions which are subject to market discipline so that the risk of failure is much less. The agency may provide loans to local banks for on-lending, or guarantees of local currency lending by the banks. It may prescribe conditions for the use of its funds by intermediaries and provide training for local staff to do the work of appraising and advising small businesses. Or it may provide funds for investment as equity in local companies, through venture capital companies or the like.

However, in the more backward countries, such intermediaries often do not exist and the small business challenge will not be confronted successfully without creating new institutions. So support for small businesses links up very closely, in such countries, with the development of the financial system. The lack of such local institutions is particularly acute in Africa where the development of small businesses is also of particular importance. External agencies may have to consider establishing their own local mechanisms, using local staff as much as possible, for small business development, as the IFC has done in the form of the Africa Enterprise Fund. And besides institutions which provide finance, there can be great value in systems to provide guidance and advice to small and medium-sized enterprises and to entrepreneurs embarking on new ventures, such as the Africa Project Development Facility, to which I return in Chapter 11.

One other area where private-sector aid agencies are likely to play an important role in the future is the financing of *infrastructure*. Private capital for infrastructure in Third World countries is relatively new. Not ten years ago it was taken for granted in most developing countries, and in most of the industrial world except the United States, that investments in telecommunications, electricity generation, roads, ports, water supply and the like would be made by the state. The change towards looking for private capital for these purposes, a world-wide phenomenon, has stemmed from two things: first, the fiscal problems of governments and the consequent difficulty of funding new investments in the public sector; and, second, the growing evidence that private investment in these activities is more efficient.

In the mid-1990s investment in infrastructure in the Third World has been about $200 billion a year and rising, the main demand coming from Asian and Latin American countries. A significant part of this need continues to be met from the public sector, but very large amounts of private investment will also be needed. International agencies can do much to facilitate this.

One might regard this as just one form of project financing, but infrastructure investments involve special problems and require special skills. These investments almost always involve the state in a regulatory role or as a buyer of the product or both. The introduction of private capital is often associated with changes in the regulatory system or the creation of one. The private investor in infrastructure seldom operates in a free market: there may be partial competition or a monopoly supervised by a regulator. Difficult negotiations take place between private investors and the government about many matters, including prices and the level of profit the investor can expect. India, for example, is now seeking large amounts of foreign investment in power generation and, as I write, protracted negotiations between would-be investors and the government have not yet produced a model for investments by foreign companies. In many cases the relationship between the private investor and the state takes the form of a "Build-Own-Transfer" arrangement in which the plant built, owned and operated by the private investor, becomes the property of the state after a fixed period of years.

In all such cases it is important that the interests of the public in the country concerned should be protected, and also that the investor should earn an adequate return in a form which gives him an incentive to be efficient. An international private-sector development agency, understanding both points of view, can be a useful intermediary. It can often play an important part also in raising funding from international markets for infrastructure projects. In the IFC's experience so far, 80 per cent of the financing for infrastructure projects has come from private sources, domestic and foreign, 9 per cent from governments and 11 per cent from the IFC, but the tendency in future will probably be for the the IFC percentage to be smaller still.[2] Very large amounts of loan finance are often needed for such projects and this is another reason why the growth of debt markets in developing countries, so far less advanced than equity markets, is so important especially in Asia.

*   *   *

How should these two roles of development aid – one focussed on the state and the other on the private sector – be related to each other? There are two aspects to the question: first, how to determine the balance of resources to be devoted to each activity; and secondly, how to ensure co-operation and complementarity between the two functions. Change is needed in both cases.

Despite the shift in thinking towards the market economy and the general recognition of the importance of the private sector in development, by far the largest part of the international development effort still takes the form of providing finance to governments. The IFC has grown, but otherwise the shift to the market philosophy has not been reflected in any significant change in the balance between the two types of aid to the Third World. On the other hand, the European Bank for Reconstruction and Development, a creation of the 1990s, has been given a major private-sector role in the ex-communist countries.

A number of leading aid donor countries do have private-sector development agencies,[3] in particular Germany, France, Britain, the Netherlands and the Scandinavian countries. Most of these agencies have been expanding their operations in support of the private sector, although they do not all provide finance solely to private companies. But their activities remain relatively small compared to each of those countries' total aid programmes. Amongst the main European countries, the British CDC's investments have amounted, on average, to about 8 per cent of the British aid programme over the past three years. The commitments of corresponding organisations in Germany, France and the Netherlands, where total aid programmes are somewhat larger, are smaller in relation to national aid programmes, ranging in 1992 from 2.4 to 4.4 per cent. In the case of Japan OECF commitments to the private sector represented only 0.5 per cent of gross aid.

In the World Bank Group in 1993–94 the IFC approved financing for private sector investments of $2.5 billion, while the World Bank itself (IBRD and IDA) approved loans and credits of $20.8 billion. IFC funding was thus 11.8 per cent of the Bank's. This percentage has risen sharply in the last few years, as the IFC's funding has risen and the Bank's has fallen. In 1990–91 it stood at 6.8 per cent.

Within the Third World aid programmes of the European Union, the only private-sector component is a small part of the lending of the European Investment Bank. But it is worth noting that when making a loan to a private company in a developing country, the EIB insists on a guarantee from the host government – the EIB takes no commercial risk and is not, therefore, a private-sector aid agency in the same sense as the rest.

In short, although aid provided directly to the private sector has increased in recent years, it still amounts to a relatively small part of total aid. International aid as a whole is still heavily skewed in favour of funding for governments and the public sector. At a time when almost all donors purport to believe that economic growth must be driven by the private sector, the bulk of aid continues to be directed in ways that must tend to strengthen the role of the state in developing countries. Institutional inertia and habit would seem to be the main reason why the pattern of aid has not been adapted more decisively to the new world environment.

We need to move to a new concept of the development task in which aid to the private sector (of the right kind) plays a much larger part. What would be an appropriate balance between aid to governments and to the private sector? The case of the European Bank for Reconstruction and Development is of interest here, although it exists to provide aid not to the Third World but to the former communist countries. The EBRD is *required* to allocate 60 per cent of its outlays to the private sector.

This approach is questionable. The catalytic function of private-sector aid should mean that a limited amount of official aid is used in such a way as to mobilise a large amount of private funding. A well managed private-sector aid programme should support investments many times the size of the aid contribution.

Aid to governments, on the other hand, typically finances a higher proportion of the costs of the projects concerned. Sixty per cent therefore seems a high proportion of total public- and private-sector aid to dedicate to the private sector. But in any case, a fixed ratio of private- to public-sector aid every year is unduly arbitrary – the balance between the two should be influenced by the circumstances of each country. There may be more scope and need for productive use of private-sector aid in one country than in another. If resources are available for both types of aid, and if the criteria I have suggested in the preceding chapter and this one are conscientiously applied, the result may be a 50/50 ratio in country A and 25/75 in country B.

At the same time, there is every reason to believe that in the world-wide aid effort today, the ratio of private- to public-sector aid is too small. The IFC has been experiencing a strong and rising demand for its assistance for a number of years now, beginning in the late 1980s. Meanwhile demand from governments for IBRD financing has been declining and the World Bank has repeatedly fallen short of its financing targets. None of this should surprise anyone: it is entirely what one would expect to result from the economic changes especially in Asia and Latin America, from where much of the private-sector demand comes. In Africa private-sector demand is also strong but takes a different form – financing for small businesses, which are the growth point of the private sector in that region.

Rather than setting percentages for private- and public-sector aid, the best response to this situation would be to provide the resources needed for private-sector aid agencies as a whole to expand their operations. Where necessary, new agencies of this kind should be created. In Britain, the CDC is also experiencing strong demand, despite the fact that it is required to make 70 per cent of its investments in very poor countries. The CDC is an efficient organisation with long experience in this field, and the British government should be looking for ways of enabling it to expand its operations rapidly. I believe ways could be found of engaging some private capital in this task, as the Dutch have done with their FMO, and the Corporation should be freed from the restrictions which prevent it from borrowing on markets to finance its activities. The CDC should be treated as an important arm of British aid policy and provided with the resources it needs to play this role.

In the case of the IFC and the World Bank Group the adjustment in favour of private-sector aid which has been taking place needs to be carried further. This can be achieved by a rapid expansion of the IFC's activities, combined with the application of tougher criteria to public-sector aid, as I have suggested. Fortunately, the financial basis for fast growth by the IFC is more or less in place. The IFC will need no additional capital for some time and maybe never, assuming that the capital increase which the shareholder governments have approved is duly paid in, as agreed. And there has been a recent change in the Corporation's gearing or leverage policy which will allow it to continue to expand its investments rapidly.

I believe this headroom for growth should be used. The strongest rise in the demand and need for the IFC finance is likely to come in the next ten years – up to, say, 2005. The IFC is the best placed amongst world development agencies to respond to the need during that period. If the Corporation's annual rate of investment grows strongly in the years immediately ahead, it will reach a high level from which further growth will be less necessary, and a period of slow or even zero growth may well be appropriate then. And in due course, there must be a time for contraction. For the IFC, as for all other aid organisations, success must mean moving to a point where its efforts and money are needed less, or not at all. But that is certainly some way off in the case of the private-sector aid agencies: the immediate need is for growth.

The second aspect of the relationship between the public- and private-sector aid functions is equally important: how to ensure proper co-ordination between them. Both forms of aid have the same ultimate objective – to promote economic growth and thus raise standards of living. Each must preserve its distinctive character, but a continuing dialogue between those responsible for each activity should enhance the value of both. This is sometimes difficult to achieve in practice. Methods and mechanisms are bound to vary from one case to another. The next chapter includes some comments on this issue in the context of the World Bank Group.

8 The International Finance Corporation, 1984–93

One evening in July 1984 Tom Clausen, then President of the World Bank, telephoned me in London to ask if I would take over the position of executive head of International Finance Corporation. I had been aware that the offer might be coming, but I was delighted and accepted there and then.

I knew that the IFC was then a relatively minor organisation on the fringe of the World Bank Group, and had been so since it was created in 1956. Its initial capital had been a mere $100 million and it was not until 1977 that this was increased for the first time. In 1984 the IFC's authorised capital stood at $650 million and its new investments in the whole of the developing world that year were only $400 million.

But I sensed that the potential was great. The time was ripe for the institution to grow and assume a bigger role on the development scene. The climate of opinion had been changing, as we have seen. Development thinking was shifting towards market-based policies and governments everywhere were beginning to look to the private sector to play a much larger role in economic development. It was against this background that my predecessor, Hans Wuttke, had succeeded in getting agreement from the shareholders to a substantial capital increase, doubling the authorised capital to a total of $1.3 billion. This increase was linked to plans to raise the Corporation's annual investments from $400 million to $1160 million over five years.

The IFC's constitution has always been different from that of the World Bank and the main regional development banks, because its task is different. These institutions' capital is largely not paid in, but available on call so as to provide a guarantee against which the institutions can borrow on international financial markets. The IFC's capital, although much smaller, has always been fully paid in, as is appropriate for an organisation taking commercial risks and making equity investments. The Corporation uses this capital as a basis for borrowing, up to a limit of about three times its equity capital. Thus, the IFC has three sources of finance – its capital, its borrowings and its accumulated profits (the shareholders have never expected a dividend).

The IFC is an "affiliate" of the World Bank, but not a subsidiary because its capital is owned not by the Bank, but directly by governments which subscribe it. However, these governments are mainly the same as the shareholders of the Bank itself – a few, mostly very small countries are members of the Bank but not of the IFC – and the IFC is very much part of the World Bank family. The President of the Bank is also President of the Corporation and the IFC's Board consists of the same people as the Executive Directors of the Bank. Administratively, too, there are close links. Staff is easily interchangeable and the salary structure is shared. Although the key skills required by the two institutions differ, there is an overlap – for example, the IFC makes much use of the Bank's economic skills and research, which it would be foolish to duplicate.

The task of leading the IFC is a mixture of business and development, politics and finance, but also, most importantly, one of managing a high quality staff of people from all over the world. The core staff of the IFC are the investment officers, who usually have an MBA (Master of Business Administration) and often some previous experience in an investment bank or other private institution. Typically, they are able and creative. They have a good opinion of themselves too. Before I joined, I was told by Hans Pollan, who was then the IFC representative in London, that I was joining "a good regiment" and, years on, as the retired colonel, I can hardly disagree with this view. A few years in the IFC usually make an investment officer a very saleable commodity, but a surprising number prefer to stay in the IFC. This is partly because of the sheer interest and variety of the work, as compared with a New York investment bank or a London merchant bank, where the pay would be higher, but the field of work narrower and more specialised. But besides this, most of the

IFC's staff are motivated by a strong spark of idealism, although they do not display it very publicly. The appeal of being able to use high professional skills not only to make money but to do some good in the world is strong, especially to young people. Project finance work involves a variety of skills, financial, legal and technical, and economic. The Corporation has its in-house lawyers and technical staff, with a considerable knowledge of business in Third World countries, working with the investment staff. The technical staff ("engineers") are experienced industry experts, mostly a good deal older than the investment officers (which could cause problems sometimes) and usually with some experience in managing companies in Third World countries. I realised as time went on how much their advice was appreciated by client companies – although there were some clients who hardly needed technical advice, so that the engineers' role was simply to examine the project to protect the IFC's interest as an investor.

IFC engineers often make a valuable contribution in helping a company to keep costs down. Choice of technology can obviously affect running costs. And in many cases, advice from the IFC engineers, based on much experience, often enables a client company to reduce the initial cost of an investment, which can make a marginal project viable. Formal competitive bidding does not necessarily produce the best results. In the late 1980s, the IFC was involved in a major fertiliser plant in India and was able to keep the cost well below that of an exactly comparable plant being planned at the same time, but in the public sector where the cost was determined by competitive bidding because this was what the World Bank, as the financier, required. In other cases, IFC clients were advised to use something less than the most sophisticated equipment available, or even second-hand equipment, so as to achieve competitive costs and make the business a success.

In staff matters the Washington-based Bretton Woods institutions have an advantage compared with the United Nations, in that there are no national quotas for personnel from each member country. Having to fill particular positions with persons of certain nationalities in order to meet quotas can obviously lead to inefficiency. In the IMF and the World Bank Group the management is expected to maintain a reasonable balance of nationalities, but is seldom under pressure to select someone of a particular nationality for a particular post, except for a small number of high-profile top posts, for which lobbying does take place. In the regional development banks, such as the Inter-American Bank in Washington, it is common for governments, through their representatives on the Executive Boards, to put pressure on the management to get particular individuals appointed or promoted. I did experience occasional efforts of this kind by Board members, but the managements of the Bretton Woods institutions are normally able to resist such demands. Pressure to recruit more people of nationalities which are under-represented on the staff is a different matter – I often sympathised with these concerns and tried to do something to meet them.

The mixture of white, black, and various shades of brown faces, and the differences within these groups, the huge variety of cultural backgrounds and of native languages, create a stimulating atmosphere in which to work. But there can be problems which do not appear in single-country organisations: undercurrents of misunderstanding and suspicion. I sit in a meeting at which we are to decide whether to invest in an Indian company in controversial circumstances, and it dawns on me that, by accident, half those at the table are Indians. The discussion seems to be entirely objective and professional, and certainly no reference is made to anyone's nationality; but is there something more going on? Am I influenced myself when a British company is involved? Probably everyone is aware of this danger and, in the interest of his or her career and reputation, leans over backward to avoid it. After some time at the IFC I realised that the atmosphere of professionalism is such that experienced members of staff have become largely free of any national bias in business matters – in fact, an Indian with a knowledge of business conditions in his own country is more likely to warn the others of risks they may not be aware of.

But problems can arise in other ways. Undercurrents of misunderstanding do cause difficulties in management, especially in relations between staff members and their bosses. Problems of "chemistry" between boss and subordinate can occur anywhere, but in a multi-national staff they are complicated by differences of style and custom amongst people from widely differing backgrounds. One result has been a tendency in the management of the World Bank Group to deal with the problems of this kind by writing more and more detailed management rules, leaving as little as possible to discretion. Management by the rule-book often results in mechanical and inappropriate responses to personnel problems.

On the other hand, for good or ill, a unifying force in the Bretton Woods institutions, and certainly in the IFC, is the dominant and pervasive Anglo-Saxon (or, more accurately, American) business culture and professionalism. The Bretton Woods institutions, although global in their responsibilities and activities, do not operate on the basis of a global cultural mix. The sole working language of the institutions is English (if that is the right name for a medium of communication which begins from the American version of the language and is then modified, in a bureaucratic environment, by people from many other countries, into something known as "Bankese"). But more important is the fact that the sphere of economics and business studies, in which most of the staff are trained, is dominated by American academic institutions. A high proportion of the professional staff of all nationalities have qualifications from American universities or business schools. This is especially true of the Bank and the IFC – the IMF with its European head has always been slightly more international in its ethos.

This Anglo-Saxon dominance is, of course, disagreeable to some people of other cultures. The French, who feel this most strongly, have nevertheless provided three heads of the IMF, more than any other country. They have made somewhat less impact in the Bank, where American domination is at its strongest. Germans seem to find the pervasive culture more tolerable and have been effective in both institutions. The British naturally find little difficulty in adapting to it and provide a more-than-proportionate number of staff in both the Fund and the Bank Group, although for the last two decades British staff have occupied very few senior positions in either. Indians and Pakistanis are easily at home and provide large numbers of able staff. Latin Americans, accustomed to dealing with the United States and often educated at US universities, fit in readily, but have not been present in large numbers in recent years, perhaps because political stability in many Latin American countries and the availability of higher-paying positions make it attractive for them to stay at home.

The Japanese are a special case. Obviously, there is a great reservoir of business ability in Japan which the IFC should be able to tap, especially since Japan is the Corporation's second largest shareholder. But the Japanese seem to find it particularly difficult to adapt to the environment of international institutions, whose mode of operation is very different from Japanese business or government; and the tradition of life-long employment with one employer is an obstacle for most Japanese professionals. The difficulties spring not only from the cultural and social differences between the Japanese and almost everyone else (the American dominance is, if anything, a help since it is the foreign culture with which the Japanese are probably most familiar), but also from the way government works in Tokyo. The Ministry of Finance, with which I had some difficult dealings on staff matters, not only wanted more Japanese staff in the organisation, but wanted to appoint them itself. We obviously had reservations about that approach, although I acceded to it by accepting short-term secondments in a limited number of cases because of the general difficulty of finding acceptable Japanese staff. This problem should ease as time goes on. The tradition of life-long employment is weakening in Japan and we are beginning to see the emergence of a generation of internationally minded young Japanese, who may make a greater impact on international organisations in the future.

The fact that the Bretton Woods institutions are so dominated by one language, culture and professional tradition has good and bad aspects. It is a flaw in the sense that it makes the institutions less than wholly international; but there are practical advantages. It is hard on those from other backgrounds that, if they work in the IFC, they must not only be proficient in English, but familiar with American methods of business analysis. But without this coherent basis of operations, the organisation would be less effective in the world than it has been.

✳   ✳   ✳

The kaleidoscope of cultures in the Bank and the IFC's staff is to be found also in the Board, which consists now of 24 members representing the shareholder governments. It was an important part of my work to keep in touch with the Board and to preside at its meetings in the absence of the President.

The Bank and the IFC have structures which bear a superficial resemblance to a private corporation. There is a Board of Governors, one from each country, typically the Minister of Finance, which meets annually – in effect, the Annual General Meeting of shareholders. And there is an "Executive Board" to supervise the ordinary operations of the institutions, to which the larger countries appoint one member each while smaller countries are represented in groups, normally on a regional basis. But there the resemblance stops. In a private company the Board will typically consist of a mixture of executive directors who work full-time as part of the management, and some non-executive or outside directors, who are not part of the management and work only part-time. But the Board of the World Bank and the IFC, of which I was a member for four years in the 1970s, consists of officials who are not part of the management, but who nevertheless work full-time, have permanent offices on the premises and Alternates and substantial staffs to assist them. Despite the fact that, in the Bank, they are called Executive Directors, they are not executives at all: on the other hand none of the executives, including the President himself, has a vote in the Board. The reason for this curious and cumbersome arrangement is that the Board represents a very unusual group of shareholders, namely the governments of the world. Their job is to keep an eye on what the management of these important organisations is doing, on behalf of the shareholders, and to approve important decisions for recommendation to the Board of Governors.

Over the years there has been an unfortunate tendency for governments to regard their representatives on the Board as mere delegates who carry out instructions. This being so, there is no reason why Board members should not be changed frequently, and in fact, few of them stay long enough to gain any deep knowledge of the institutions or their work. This attitude is probably also responsible for the deterioration in the quality and standing of Board members which has often been noted – most recently by the prestigious Commission appointed by the American organisation known as the Bretton Woods Committee to consider the future of the IMF and the World Bank. Their report, in July 1994,[1] commented that many of the Executive Directors of the IMF and the World Bank did not enjoy direct access to the top level in their own governments. It is true that only a few of the current members of the Boards of the Fund or the Bank are individuals who carry any weight in the outside world.

From the point of view of the management of the IFC, the main problem about the Board, in my experience, was that many of them displayed little understanding of the business problems in which the IFC was involved. The Board consists of civil servants who are more at home with the World Bank and its dealings with governments. What is more important, only a few of them, in my experience, developed a real understanding of the IFC's role as a development organisation. Many did not seem to grasp the significance of the shift to market-based policies and its implications for the development role.

The Board, in my time, focussed a good deal of attention on the question of the "development impact" of the IFC's activities, as is proper and right. Seeking to ensure that the Corporation contributes to development should be the Board's key role. However, these discussions often threw up misunderstandings which seemed to reflect underlying differences of view about what was meant by "development". To my mind, the main (but not the only) test of the Corporation's contribution to development should be one which is consistent with the definition of "development" I offered at the beginning of Chapter 2, as the promotion of economic growth and rising incomes. Seen in this light, the IFC's success or failure might be indicated by the number and size of the successful companies operating in developing countries, contributing output and employment to those economies, which owe their success at least partly to the IFC. How to *measure* "success" in the IFC's client companies is indeed a problem. The data, such as they are, suggest that most the IFC investments earned reasonable economic rates of return, after a period of about five years, and benefit the countries concerned.

The misunderstandings which sometimes arose on this issue seemed to stem from a difference of view about the IFC's role. Some members of the Board found it difficult to see the creation of profitable companies as an objective of "development". Some favoured what I can only describe as the romantic approach to private sector development. This approach gives overriding priority to helping small businesses and is suspicious of any proposal to work with large, well-established companies. The assumption behind this "small-is-beautiful" view is that no large company could need the IFC's help. But even large international companies will not necessarily invest in certain countries and projects without the encouragement of the IFC participation, and even strong sponsors cannot necessarily raise all the finance needed for some investments. In large investments involving international companies, the IFC's participation can often be highly catalytic – a contribution to the financing of no more than 5 per cent may make the difference for other investors and lenders. And of course major investments of this kind can bring large benefits to the economy of a developing country in terms of employment, output, exports and government revenues.

Others found some difficulty in the proposition that the IFC itself should seek to be profitable, although the US representative, in the Bush years, pressed us strongly to aim for higher profits. The level of profitability which is appropriate for an institution like the IFC is indeed an issue and I return to it later. The key point is that the IFC's profitability must be a reflection of the success of the companies it supports, rather than an end in itself. To do its basic job properly, the IFC must seek profit; but beyond a certain point, pursuit of profit would be inconsistent with the development role.

There is also another important development test: the effects of efforts to promote private sector development, for example by assisting in the creation of financial companies to serve the private sector, the development of stock exchanges, or initiatives for the promotion of small businesses. Here measurement of the Corporation's impact is even more difficult. A judgment must be made, but we should beware the beguilements of quantification.

*   *   *

The IFC is part of the World Bank Group, and the question of the Corporation's relations with its big sister was one which arose in many different aspects during my tenure. The IFC's close relationship to the senior institution is an enormously important source of strength, in a variety of ways. As I suggested at the end of the previous chapter, it is important that those engaged in the two complementary types of aid activity should consult and co-operate closely. During my time at the IFC, we did make progress on this point, but problems remained.

The two types of aid activity are complementary but different in character, requiring staff with different skills and backgrounds. The Bank, staffed by economists, and dealing with governments and the public sector, has – or at any rate had in the past – only limited understanding of business or the private sector. Difficulties of understanding and communication between Bank and IFC staff sometimes emerged in institutional rivalry (people in the aid business have the same human failings as others). In the mid 1980s Bank staff regarded the IFC as a fringe activity and took little notice. IFC staff responded by going their own way independently. Many of the IFC's staff could legitimately be criticised for being interested solely in concluding transactions and showing insufficient awareness of the wider development role. On the other hand, as the IFC grew, some in the Bank argued that the answer to the problem of co-ordination was to absorb the private-sector aid function within the Bank's plans for each country, failing to understand that private-sector support cannot be planned in the same way as assistance to governments. The IFC staff naturally reacted defensively to ideas of this kind. The private-sector support function, as I have described it, requires that those responsible should make and be accountable for their own business decisions.

But that function consists of more than doing deals. As part of the relationship between the Bank and the IFC, the Bank should draw on the practical experience of the IFC for advice on how the environment for private-sector growth can be improved in particular countries. It should, I believe, be the Bank's role, and not the IFC's, to handle relations with governments, although the IFC can usefully provide advice on technical subjects such as the organisation of stock exchanges. At the same time, the IFC should consult regularly with the Bank about investment priorities in all the countries and regions where it operates, and take account of Bank policies, although in the end it must make its own investment decisions.

In the early 1990s, in the course of discussions with the United States about a capital increase (on which more below), we set up some new arrangements for co-operation and consultation along these lines, including the preparation by the Bank and the IFC

jointly, of a series of "Private Sector Assessments" which reviewed
the situation of the private sector in most of the more important
member countries. As recognition of the importance of the private
sector grows, a balanced and constructive relationship between
the two institutions should develop, aimed at genuine complementarity.

*   *   *

The core of the IFC's activity is project finance, and it is involved
in a huge variety of projects and companies around the world.
This work is governed generally by the principles I laid out in
Chapter 7. But how does the IFC go about this business in
practice?

When I arrived, I was a little surprised to find that the IFC
initiates very few projects: for the most part, it finances other
people's ideas. This does not mean that it waits passively for
proposals to be brought to it. Looking for good promoters with
good ideas is a vitally important part of the work. The aim is to
give the Corporation a degree of choice between a number of
ideas. But for a financial institution like the IFC, without
experience of managing companies itself, to produce ideas for
business ventures and then try to sell them to investors would be
risky.

In one important area, however, the IFC does initiate proposals
– the financial sector, nearest to the Corporation's own expertise.
The IFC is well placed to judge what kind of new initiatives are
needed in a country's financial sector. Venture capital companies
to make equity investments in small companies, leasing companies
to provide finance for investment when bank loans are not
available on acceptable terms, and on the international side,
funds through which foreign investors can invest in developing
country stock markets, are examples of capital-market investments initiated by the IFC.

In the IFC's project work, there is no standard product. Every
proposal has to pass the basic test of viability – on the basis of
prudent analysis, it must hold out the prospect of being profitable
– and must be judged likely to benefit the economy of the country
concerned. All the obvious questions about costs of production,
markets and margins, which basically determine the profitability

of any company, have to be examined with care. However, some issues typically recur.

The *debt-equity* balance is frequently an issue. Proposals coming to the IFC often over-estimate the ability of a project to carry debt because the shareholders, often a tightly held family company, want to keep the equity base small so as to avoid sharing control and to maximise their returns in the long run. There is no standard formula for determining the appropriate ratio of debt to equity: the cash flow simply has to be forecast carefully and conservatively and in the light of experience with similar projects, to determine how much debt the project will be able to carry. In a few cases, it may be possible to finance as much as 75 or 80 per cent of an investment by borrowing without being irresponsible; but in others 50 per cent may be too much. Quite often the IFC has to insist on more equity.

Management is always an issue. When a company fails, some weakness in the management is usually part of the problem and often the main problem. Is the proposed management strong? Have they a track record and experience in the field and in the country? Does the team depend too much on one person who may leave or die?

Relations with the government are often important, especially in the case of foreign investors: for example there are royalty and taxation questions in oil or gas or mining ventures. The IFC can often be of help as an honest broker. Infrastructure investments, such as electricity generation, usually involve some formal agreement between the investors and the government, for example for the sale of power over a number of years.

The economic situation of the country can be highly relevant to a project's prospects. Is there a risk of a major devaluation and how would that affect the company's operations? Is there high inflation or a situation in which severe corrective measures may become necessary? Each IFC Investment Department has an economist to help with these issues.

Protection, price controls or subsidies are sometimes an issue, although less so than in the past. A company whose profitability depends on subsidies or tariff protection or controls over the prices of its products or inputs takes resources out of the economy rather than adding them. It is no contribution to development for the IFC to support such a company.

Environmental issues are critical in a number of IFC projects. All investments are examined from the point of view of their ecological impact by a special team in the IFC, working in co-operation with the World Bank. Those which raise serious environmental issues ("Category A" projects) are subjected to rigorous scrutiny by the Environmental Unit, and the results are publicised in the country concerned and in Washington. It is a condition of the IFC's participation in any project that it must conform to World Bank ecological standards.

The *sponsors' commitment* can be an issue. Those who sponsor projects may do so for a variety of reasons – for example, for the purpose of selling their product to the project company or purchasing its product. In such cases, a sponsor may propose to run the company but make only a small financial commitment itself, so that it might not have enough at stake to stand behind the venture if it ran into difficulties.

Government ownership is still occasionally an issue, though less often than in the past. The IFC prefers to finance wholly private companies, but in some countries where private capital is scarce, a measure of government ownership in some projects is unavoidable. The general rule is not to finance companies which are more than 50 per cent government owned, but even this is occasionally breached where there is no alternative way of ensuring that a useful investment will proceed, provided that the company is privately managed and the government plans to divest when it can.

Foreign ownership is an issue only where it is complete, without any local participation. In the interests of developing a local private sector, the IFC prefers to see foreign investors joining with local investors in a joint venture, or at least to see some minority local participants. But this is not always possible, in which case the IFC may take a share of the equity itself and "warehouse" it for sale to local investors later.

Public listing of the shares of a company is sometimes an issue. The IFC uses its influence, where possible, to persuade companies, as they grow larger, to open themselves up to wider ownership. Families, who own a large proportion of the medium-sized companies in Asia and Latin America, are sometimes reluctant to share ownership with the public, even though this may increase the value of their assets. Sometimes the IFC

participates in a project on condition that the company will float
some shares on the local stock exchange at an agreed time.

The IFC's finance is offered on market terms – loans in a hard
currency of the client's choosing at a fixed or floating interest rate
which is set for each project by reference to the risk of lending to
the country concerned and of the project itself. This contrasts with
IBRD lending which is at a fixed rate for all borrowers – by
definition a non-market system of lending. Many of the IFC's
clients do not have access to the range of financial services now
available in international financial markets, and the Corporation's Treasury department has been working to bring them the
benefit of some of these services – for example, swap arrangements
designed to protect clients against interest-rate and exchange-rate
risk.

It has been an IFC aim for some time to maximise the catalytic
effect of its own investments by increasing the "mobilisation
ratio" – the ratio of the IFC's own funding to the funding
provided by other investors and lenders. In the mid-1980s, on
average every IFC dollar was associated with four from other
sources. In the early 1990s the ratio was about 1:6.

Besides encouraging other investors and lenders simply by
participating in the project itself, the IFC has a more direct
method of mobilising capital through its loan syndication
programme, in which international banks participate in project
loans made by the IFC. This has served as a useful technique for
raising loan finance for many years. The IFC makes the loan to
the Third World client company and remains the lender of
record. International banks refinance a part of the IFC's loan,
taking the same risk, with no guarantee. The IFC always makes
part of the loan on its own account, so that it fully shares the risk
with the banks. Despite the absence of a guarantee, many banks
regard a loan thus made through the IFC as carrying less risk
than direct lending to a company in a developing country,
because of the Corporation's good record in getting project loans
repaid. Recently the IFC has been raising more funds for projects
in this way than it lends itself. European governments and Japan
have encouraged their banks to participate in these IFC loans by
making them exempt from provisioning requirements; and the
European Bank for Reconstruction and Development has begun a
programme of loan participations similar to the IFC's.

* * *

I argued in Chapter 7 that the development of capital markets should be a key role for a private-sector aid agency, and so it has been in the IFC's case. The Capital Markets Department, first established in the 1970s, was led for 15 years by the highly creative Canadian David Gill. Long before most people, Gill grasped the significance of the growth of stock markets in a number of developing countries – the "emerging markets" as they came to be called, a phrase invented by Antoine Van Agtmael who was, for a while, Gill's deputy at the IFC.

From the 1970s on, the IFC was engaged in advising governments about the encouragement and regulation of stock markets. During the 1980s the Corporation began to forge links between these new markets and the major international financial markets, so as to bring foreign capital into the emerging markets. The IFC sponsored a number of Funds through which international investors, mainly large institutional investors such as pension funds, could invest in the new markets, beginning with the Korea Fund of 1984. Two years later the first Fund for investment in emerging markets generally, the Emerging Markets Growth Fund, was launched. This was an idea of Gill's which took him 18 months' hard work to sell to investors but was a huge success. The fund was launched with a capital of $50 million. Four years later, in 1990, with more capital paid in and market appreciation, this had risen to $650 million and by 1994 to $4.7 billion.

After a few years however, the creation of country funds ceased to be a pioneering activity – the private markets took over and launched a huge number of emerging market funds. By early 1995 the number was 397. The IFC moved on to sponsoring only specialised funds in new areas, such as funds for investment in particular sectors such as telecommunications or (an interesting innovation) gold-mining companies in developing countries. There will probably be less work for development agencies to do in this field in the future, but the episode is a good example of a creative response to a situation of opportunity – in this case, doing something which both encouraged flows of private capital to developing countries and also assisted in the development of their stock markets.

More recently, in the 1990s, a growing part of the flow of portfolio equity capital has taken a different form – issues of shares by individual Third World companies on international markets. This is an interesting new trend, especially in south and east Asia and Latin America. From the point of view of private sector development, it is a healthy trend because a company selling its shares on international markets confronts very discriminating investors and so is under pressure to raise its efficiency. At the IFC we were interested in helping to bring some client companies to the international markets in the late 1980s, and indeed the Corporation did play a part in the first equity issue by a Latin American company in New York for 27 years, the Chilean Telephone Company, in 1990. But in fact this business quickly became highly competitive, with many investment banks active in it. The IFC's activities in this field have always been limited and it should now probably be recognised as something which should be left to the market.

Some have questioned the value of flows of portfolio capital (purchases of company shares and bonds) to developing countries because they do not represent "real" new investment, but changes of share ownership. This cannot be said of new issues, where individual companies raise new capital, typically for new "real" investment. Obviously, purchases of shares from existing holders on secondary markets bring no new capital to the company, but if foreigners buy from local investors new capital does enter the country, freeing locally owned capital for other use. In fact, a large part of the portfolio investment in developing countries has been through closed-end funds, where the money invested cannot be withdrawn from the country for a fixed period, typically five years or more. Just as important, the participation of foreign investors in local markets helps to develop and deepen those markets. The volatility of these capital flows is another question, discussed in Chapter 11.

In the later 1980s and early 90s, with Dan Adams in charge, we shifted the emphasis of IFC capital-markets work back to promoting and investing in local financial companies in domestic markets. Most of these were small companies, many of them sponsored and promoted by the IFC itself. In the field of industrial leasing alone, between 1977 and 1993, the IFC helped to establish 27 such companies in 21 countries. About half of these were the first such companies in the countries concerned, but were quickly imitated, leading to the growth of an industrial leasing industry. Latterly, about one third of all the IFC's new investments were in this sector, a total of over 50 a year, although the dollar amounts involved were much less than a third of total dollars invested. This was creative work and of high developmental value, in my view.

*　*　*

Life at the IFC involves dealing with all kinds of companies and businessmen in Asia, Africa and Latin America, which certainly has its fascinations. Are they different from companies and businessmen in the First World? Fundamentally I think not, but of course they often operate in situations which compel different behaviour. To survive in Argentina or Brazil in the days of hyper-inflation required skills that no businessman from Chicago or Birmingham had to develop. Until five years ago, to run a major company successfully in India required above all an ability to influence ministers and officials and obtain approvals for investment and other decisions. The taxation environment differs from the First World. In most Third World countries personal income tax either does not exist or is insignificant, but governments try to tax companies heavily and companies often respond by keeping dual accounts. In any case, although there is a trend of improvement, accounting standards used by Third World companies are still variable. In these circumstances, assessing the true financial position of potential business partners and negotiating deals with them can sometimes be difficult.

The contrast between the IFC's western way of doing business and the varying traditions and methods to be found in the Third World is heightened by the fact that the IFC, as a public, government-owned body, has to be as transparent as it is possible to be, more so than western private companies. The IFC tries to operate as if it were in a properly regulated market economy, knowing, however, that the systems required by a proper market economy do not yet fully exist. This makes the task of the IFC lawyers important and difficult. The Corporation has to protect itself by carefully drafted legal agreements, even if there is often a degree of doubt about their enforceability in practice in local courts. However, I sometimes wondered if we had allowed our American-style legal documentation to get out of hand.

I am by no means implying that businessmen in Third World countries are generally less scrupulous than those in the west. Of course, crooks do exist in the Third World (although probably not less or more than elsewhere) as the IFC occasionally found to its cost. But in my experience businessmen in these countries include roughly the same mixture of the crooked and the public-spirited as elsewhere. But they often operate in an environment which can be compared to the early days of capitalism in the west – Britain around 1820, say, or the United States towards the end of the nineteenth century. The successful capitalists in these countries are naturally a varied bunch – ranging from the cowboy element to outstanding industrial statesmen such as Syed Babar Ali of Pakistan, Julius Tahija of Indonesia, or Keshub Mahindra of India.

It is characteristic of many Third World countries that the corporate scene is dominated by family companies and groups, some very large – the Tata or Birla groups of India, the Vitro or Apasco groups of Mexico, the Bunge y Born of Argentina, the Sabanci and Koç groups of Turkey or the Astra and Bakrie groups in Indonesia. Many of these companies are headed by very able entrepreneurs, and in the faster growing countries now, especially in Asia, it is fascinating to watch the emergence of entirely new family groups of this kind, industrial empires in the making. In India the big and growing groups often operate successfully in a bewildering diversity of activities, from petro-chemicals and fertiliser production to textiles, cement, power generation and even financial services. As time goes on, market pressures are likely to lead to more specialisation. Market pressures of another kind are already leading family groups in many countries to list their shares on local stock markets, opening themselves up to wider ownership and raising capital from both domestic and foreign investors in the markets. All this is part of the process of the development of a modern market economy.

In this formative stage of the market economy, a private sector aid agency such as the IFC has to be constantly thinking about its role, looking for the opportunity to make a creative contribution. It is important to avoid being too much involved with big companies, although new investments by such groups can bring major benefits to the country and do sometimes need the help of an agency like the IFC. I would acknowledge that, in a number of countries, the IFC has probably been too prone to fall in with strong, established groups just because the task of seeking out partners amongst the smaller, emerging companies is much more difficult. It is important to get this balance right.

*   *   *

The basic challenge for the IFC is to combine successful operation as a business with maximum development impact. It was clear when I took over that the IFC's impact had to be increased by expanding its operations, for which a capital increase had just been approved. At the same time, the financial position of the Corporation was not too strong, mainly because of some weaknesses in the portfolio of investments. This was partly due to the economic difficulties which most developing countries were facing in the mid-1980s. The IFC's net income was running at about $25–30 million a year, a return of only 3.5 per cent on its net worth.

In the next two years we devoted much effort to correcting the portfolio weakness. We were quite properly pressed to do this by a few members of the Board, particularly Frank Potter of Canada, one of the two or three Directors at that time with a business background. In the management, Dan Adams and Will Kaffenberger, as successive Vice-Presidents for portfolio matters (a position created in 1985), carried the burden of this effort. By 1987 we had improved the position of the loan portfolio substantially and, as stock markets in the developing world strengthened, the equity portfolio began to do very well. In 1989 our net income had risen to $196 million.

We were also expanding the business. I put Judhvir Parmar, a very experienced IFC man from India, in charge of all new investments. Business expanded in all the main areas where the IFC was operating, but, in the late 1980s, was particularly strong in Latin America. In this region there was an active private sector in most countries, but in the conditions of the debt crisis, which dragged on through the 1980s, it had very little access to foreign exchange finance other than the IFC. Later in the 1980s, and in the early 90s, other forces drove the IFC's investments in Latin America forward. Reform, liberalisation, privatisation, private-sector growth and private investment in infrastructure created strong demand for the IFC's finance, and another period of rapid growth in investment in that region began.

Over the years from 1984 to 1994 the IFC's new investment approvals rose from a rate of $400 million a year to $2.5 billion. The portfolio of existing investments rose from $1.4 billion to $6.2 billion and the number of companies in that portfolio from 350 to 870. The total volume of the projects supported by the IFC's financing rose from about $2.5 billion to about $16 billion.

In the mid-1980s business was rather sluggish in most of Asia. Although China was a member of the Corporation, doing business there was difficult in the mid-1980s and we progressed only slowly. India for a number of years after I joined the IFC was difficult for a similar reason – the whole financial sector and the whole national investment programme were closely controlled by the government. We were repeatedly disappointed at how little we seemed able to do in India in the mid to late 1980s. In both countries things loosened up in the 1990s. Our shareholders decided that the IFC should stay out of China for four years after the events in Tiananmen Square in 1989, but then strong growth began. In the early 1990s India became the largest country in the IFC's portfolio of investments. IFC investments in Indonesia, Thailand and the Philippines, including infrastructure investments, were expanding strongly.

The Middle East was also sticky in the mid-80s. The region includes a number of countries where the IFC could not operate in practice, such as Syria, Iraq and Iran. But in the 1990s, after creating a special department for the Middle East, we moved ahead in some countries – Egypt, Morocco, Tunisia.

Sub-Saharan Africa was a difficult area for the IFC throughout my time. There was very little in the way of an indigenous private sector. In about a third of the countries in the area – the proportion varied — it was impossible to contemplate investment activity because of war or civil disorder. The opportunities for co-operation with foreign investors were, in practice, confined to a few large oil and gas or mining operations in a small number of countries – Gabon and Nigeria for oil, Ghana and one or two others for gold mining. The over-valuation of the currency of most of French-speaking west and central Africa, the CFA franc, linked to the French franc at a rate which, until early 1994, had not changed since 1950, depressed the economies of that area increasingly in the late 1980s and all but destroyed the banking system.

We did succeed in making some medium-sized investments in Africa every year, but in the early 1990s, just before I left the IFC, the situation seemed, if anything, to get more difficult. Investments in Sub-Saharan Africa, which had been about 12–14 per cent of the IFC's total for some years, fell to below 10 per cent, and also fell in absolute terms to below $200 million.

But this is not to say that there was no demand and need for IFC finance. It took a different form – there was always evidence of a strong demand for both finance and advice from new and small businesses. It became clear to me at an early stage that this was the real development challenge in Africa. The question was how an organisation like the IFC could operate effectively in this field. As an international agency, dispensing hard currency finance, the IFC, although experienced in making investments itself, was not well suited to making and supervising them in small African companies. However, we decided to create an organisation to provide advice to small and new businesses and help them raise funding. The Africa Project Development Facility, modelled on an earlier initiative of the IFC's in the Caribbean, was a big success. I return to this subject in Chapter 11.

And in another part of the world, another type of challenge, and a completely new one, was presented to the IFC by the collapse of communism at the end of the 1980s and in the early 90s. This is the subject of Chapter 10.

*   *   *

Meanwhile, in the management of the IFC's finances also there were many changes. Until 1985, the IFC's borrowed funds came directly and only from the IBRD. I had been at the Corporation only a few weeks when Richard Frank suggested to me that we should experiment with borrowing in the IFC's own name on the markets. (Richard Frank later became Vice-President for Finance and Planning and the Corporation's Chief Financial Officer, and after I left the IFC went on to occupy the position of Managing Director in the World Bank, one of the most senior positions in that institution.) It was a bold idea, bearing in mind that the

IFC's financial position was not strong at the time, and that the paper we would issue would not in any way be backed by the World Bank. It encountered opposition in the Bank, especially from then Treasurer, Eugene Rotberg, but we persevered and later had support from Ernie Stern when he took over the finance side of the Bank under Barber Conable. In fact the experiment, which began with modest private placements, was very successful, and we went on from there to secure a Triple A rating from the New York rating agencies, and to a major annual programme of bond issues on the international markets. IFC bonds with a total face value of $6.6 billion are now held in the markets.

The AAA rating and the borrowing programme have done much to establish the IFC on the world financial scene. They also mean that the Corporation is subject to a strong financial discipline. The rating certainly owes a lot to the fact that the IFC is owned by the world's governments, with the main industrial countries having the largest shareholdings. But the New York agencies are also very conscious of the fact that the IFC is a risk-taking investor, operating in many difficult environments, and the rating depends critically on the Corporation's financial performance and profitability.

This troubles some people who fear that concern for profitability will make the IFC less developmental. What level of profitability is right for the IFC? Too low a level would slacken discipline and endanger the AAA rating with all the advantages it brings. Too high a target would run the risk that the IFC might shy away from risk too much and so achieve less development. Much discussion brought us to the view that a return on the Corporation's equity of roughly 8 per cent on average would enable us to perform our development role with financial integrity. This is, of course, less than most private investors would look for and we were sometimes pressed by some members of the Board, but not the majority, to aim for higher profitability. We felt that might put our development role at risk.

However, we knew that an 8 per cent rate of return could be achieved only with good performance by the IFC's equity investments, which was, in fact, a feature of the late 1980s and early 1990s, when equity markets in developing countries were buoyant. But of course such markets are also volatile and unpredictable. Income from lending operations is more predictable, but in the IFC's case much less profitable. In fact, for most of my time, lending operations only just covered their costs. The cost of staff work on projects, much more complex in the IFC's case than for commercial lenders, and the need to make significant provisions for possible losses on risky projects, use up most of the spread between the Corporation's borrowing costs and the interest rates paid by clients. Towards the end of my tenure, we embarked on a more determined effort to reduce the staff costs associated with lending, which my successor has carried further. But the IFC's lending, for reasons closely associated with its development role, is never likely to be very profitable and equity investments will probably always be critical to the Corporation's financial success.

In the course of a long period as the executive head of the IFC, I was probably too slow in shifting the organisation towards more specialisation in the project-finance business. We had always had a specialised Capital Markets Department. But most of the IFC's business was conducted by regional departments which, within their own areas, managed all types of business. There was resistance to change in the organisation, but the old system could not go on. We had to develop deeper skills in areas such as agribusiness, telecommunications, energy, power generation, mining, chemicals and perhaps others to enable us to deal effectively with companies operating in these areas, which would account for a large proportion of the Corporation's business in the years ahead. At the same time, it grew clearer every year that the nature of the development task varied widely from one region to another and that it was essential to maintain, and in fact improve our country and regional expertise. The capital-markets challenge, in particular, was widely different from one country and region to another, whether it was the far east or Africa or the former communist countries.

So we faced a problem familiar to many organisations which operate in many countries, but overlaid in our case by the combination of objectives entailed by the development role. We dealt with it by means of a major re-organisation of the IFC in 1992, creating a number of new Specialist Departments, including an Infrastructure Department, within a matrix system of management, designed to build up and combine country and regional expertise with much deeper expertise in certain key sectors. That change seemed to release a strong new impulse of energy in the IFC.

* * *

As we reached the end of the 1980s two things were clear. The IFC had demonstrated that it was capable of playing a much more significant role in international development; and the demand and need for the IFC's assistance were growing more strongly than ever, including demand from the liberated countries of Eastern Europe. However, at the beginning of the 1990s the situation was that, without a new injection of capital, the IFC would be compelled to slow its rate of growth of new investments from about 20 per cent a year to 4 or 5 per cent.

Early in 1990 we embarked on consultations with the shareholders about a capital increase, suggesting an increase which would double the authorised capital from $1.3 billion to $2.6 billion. This met a generally favourable response from most of the membership, although not everyone was committed to the figure. Amongst the developed countries, the Germans and the British were particularly positive, and most developing countries were the same.

The surprise was the attitude of the United States. They held back agreement for two years, despite their strong interest in private sector development, which had led them in the mid-1980s to press for a larger capital increase for the IFC than others. In the Bush Administration policy towards the international development institutions was almost solely in the hands of David Mulford, Under Secretary for International Affairs at the US Treasury (the Treasury Secretary, Nick Brady, left these things entirely to Mulford). There was Congressional support, coming from both parties, for an increase in the IFC's capital, but Mulford had his own agenda. Part of this was to give priority to a new plan to get the Congress to create a $1.5 billion fund for private-sector development in Latin America, to be administered partly through the Inter-American Development Bank, an institution in which the Americans have a much stronger influence than in the World Bank Group.

Mulford had developed what appeared to be a personal antagonism towards Barber Conable, the President of the World

Bank, an ex-Congressman who had been nominated to the position by the preceding Reagan Administration. There was a tendency in the US Treasury to assume that the American President of the Bank would toe the US line obediently. In fact, no person of the quality to be chosen as President of the World Bank was likely to do this, and Conable, a friend of George Bush and with a considerable reputation on Capitol Hill, certainly did not.

Mulford used the IFC's need for more capital as a bargaining counter, trying to force changes on the World Bank and the IFC, designed to make the whole Group more private-sector oriented. This general aim was welcome to us in the IFC, but for many months the US Treasury held up the proceedings without putting forward any precise proposals, apparently because Mulford found no time to deal with the matter. When they did make proposals, they were a curious mixture, some well conceived, others verging on the absurd. In fact, I was surprised, and not only on this occasion, by the poor quality of staff work in the US Treasury. An unsatisfactory proposal was that the IFC should make its investments conditional on governments adopting sound policies towards the private sector, which would have resulted in governments bargaining with the IFC about its investments. No other country supported this idea. A long debate ensued, in which the World Bank management adopted a generally constructive and helpful attitude: in fact, from this dialogue some new arrangements for co-operation between the Bank and the IFC emerged which produced good results. After 18 months of discussion, pressure from the Congress and finally the intervention of the White House, at Conable's request, a compromise was reached on the Treasury proposals and a capital increase of $1.0 billion was agreed in the IFC Board in May 1992.

This increase, combined with the additions to the Corporation's capital which had resulted from a number of years of substantial profits, put the IFC in a position to continue to expand its operations strongly through the 1990s. As I said at the end of the previous chapter, I believe that the IFC should aim to meet the strong and growing need for its finance and services by vigorous expansion for some years to come.

9 What Future for the World Bank and IMF?

The importance of the Bretton Woods Institutions (so-called because they were designed in the New Hampshire town of that name in 1944) in the whole story of development and aid, and in the relationship between the First and Third Worlds over the period since the war, cannot be doubted. Together the International Monetary Fund and the World Bank have had an extraordinary impact on the shape of the post-war world, and particularly on the developing countries.

In the immediate post-war years this pair of institutions was a new phenomenon on the world scene. International economic co-operation through multilateral organisations set up for the purpose was new – it became significant for the first time in the second half of the twentieth century. The International Labour Organisation, set up under the aegis of the League of Nations, was the most important previous example and it was limited in scope. At this point we cannot be sure whether this pattern of international economic co-operation will continue in the next century and whether, in a world of markets, there will be a role for international agencies like the Bank and the Fund, and if so, what it will consist of.

The effectiveness of these two institutions over the last 50 years is to be attributed partly to the fact that, unlike the New-York-based organisations of the United Nations and its other specialised agencies, they were founded on financial realism. As in the UN, financial contributions were based on economic and financial strength, but unlike the UN, voting power was related to these contributions. Because the stronger countries were able to influence decision-making in these organisations, they were prepared to endow them with substantial resources and use them as mechanisms for international co-operation.[1] Much that has affected the shape of the post-war world flows from this fact.

However, a long stretch of time has passed since the creation of the Fund and Bank. The world has changed out of recognition over the past half-century and the purposes for which they were created are no longer fully relevant. If these institutions are to go on serving the world well, they will have to adapt and change. So they have done to a fair extent; but as time has passed, they have acquired a lot of institutional baggage and developed ways of life of their own. Just as their creation after the war was pure innovation, the challenge of the renewal of such critically important organisations is an entirely new one.

What follows in this chapter is a somewhat personal view of the evolution of the IMF and the World Bank, their impact on the Third World and the role they may play in the future. It is based partly on my involvement with both institutions in various capacities. If the emphasis is rather more on the Bank than on the Fund, that is, of course, because it is the institution concerned mainly with Third World development, indeed the world's leading development institution.

In both cases there are two aspects to be considered: the question of *role*, both in the past and in the future; and a number of *institutional* questions which affect their ability to perform their roles. However, I have already discussed the evolution of the role of the Bank over 50 years in Chapter 3, and its future role in Chapter 6. What remains to be said about the Bank, therefore, mainly concerns institutional questions. In the case of the Fund the institutional questions are less pressing, but there are major questions about its role in relation to developing countries.

* * *

The role of the IMF has changed significantly over the past half-century. The Fund we see today is an institution largely occupied with the problems of Third World countries, and lately of the former Communist countries too, and exercising an important influence in the affairs of some of them. But originally it was created primarily as an instrument for managing the world monetary system established at the end of World War II, the system of fixed-but-adjustable parities. Its ability to provide credit to its members, subject to increasingly stringent performance criteria for larger amounts, was intended to give member states in balance-of-payments difficulties time to adjust, and thus avoid the protectionist reactions to such problems which plagued world trade in the 1930s. And in fact the system of fixed-but-adjustable exchange rates, which survived for a quarter of a century, was accompanied by a rapid growth of world output and trade which looks, in retrospect, like a golden age.

The watershed which split the history of the IMF into two distinct phases was the breakdown of this system in 1971–72. When the United States was compelled in 1971 to abandon the gold convertibility of the dollar, the anchor of the system was lost and the major currencies began to float against each other, as they have done ever since, despite unsuccessful efforts in the early 1970s to revive the old system in some form. Whether we may now be at the beginning of a third phase is an interesting question to which I return later.

This fundamental change in the exchange system meant that the role of the Fund also changed. In the 1970s the last two drawings on the Fund by major industrial countries took place – Britain and Italy, both in 1976 – and from then on the Fund became in practice an institution whose main activity was to assist developing countries. In the developed world it became an agency for consultation, research and advice. It was given an advisory role in connection with the attempts in the early 1980s to co-ordinate economic policies through the Group of Seven leading industrialised countries, but so far, it has never fully recovered the position it once occupied in the affairs of the developed world.

Soon after the Fund had crossed this watershed, however, it faced a challenge which presented an opportunity to develop a new role, namely the developing-country debt crisis which broke in 1982, when Jacques de Larosière was Managing Director of the IMF. Most experts would agree that the response of Larosière at the IMF and of Paul Volcker, then Chairman of the US Federal Reserve Board, almost certainly saved the international banking system from a much more serious crisis, which would have had world-wide economic effects. The Fund developed the instruments to provide resources to the countries in difficulty, subject to requirements for corrective action, and involved the commercial banks in the discussions, in a way that had not happened before. The debt crisis continued throughout much of the 1980s, but the threat to international financial stability was contained.

One lesson we may draw from this episode is that although the Fund appeared to some to be marginalised by being confined, in practice, to assisting developing countries, in fact the affairs of some of those countries were no longer marginal. At the end of 1994 Mexico, the country that had precipitated the debt crisis by defaulting on its debts in 1982, ran into serious financial problems again. This time the crisis was more a specifically Mexican affair, although it had repercussions around the "emerging markets" generally, especially in Latin America. It was precipitated by economic mismanagement, including a rash attempt by the incoming government of President Zedillo to devalue the currency, but it highlighted the fact that Mexico had become vulnerable to the withdrawal of large amounts of liquid or short term capital, held partly in Mexican government bonds and partly in equity investments on the stock exchange.

The outflow of funds was eventually stemmed, partly by a massive rescue package financed by the United States, the IMF and others. But it left the financial markets very uncertain about two points: whether the Mexican crisis was a phenomenon likely to be repeated in other developing countries; and whether any further episodes of this kind would or should be dealt with by massive official intervention. In the Mexican case, although the IMF played a significant part and provided a larger credit to Mexico than any other country had ever received from the Fund, it did not command resources on the scale needed to do the whole job.

In short, new questions about the Fund's future role are thrown up by the Mexican crisis. One possible reaction might be called the interventionist approach: the view that when markets behave wildly, and seem to pose a threat to the stability of the "system", this calls for official intervention, if necessary on a large scale. This approach has been characteristic of much of the last half-century. In the early 1960s the ten leading industrial countries set up the General Arrangements to Borrow, which provided for the resources of the IMF to be supplemented by loans from the ten countries if the Fund had to deal with a serious crisis in a major currency. Some argue that similar arrangements are now needed to enable the Fund – or the international community generally – to come to the aid of countries like Mexico in future. On this view the 1994 Mexican crisis point to an enhanced role for the IMF in relation to developing countries in the future, that of protecting them from irrational markets and thus enabling them to get on with the essential task of economic development.

On the other hand Mexico, bordering on the United States and a member of NAFTA, is clearly an untypical case, and even in that case, a method had to be contrived of providing help without seeking approval from the US Congress. Although the G7 summit in June 1995 recommended an enlargement of the General Arrangements to Borrow, it is doubtful whether in practice any new system could provide resources on the scale of the Mexican package ($50 billion) to other countries in similar difficulties – and still more unlikely that resources could be mobilised for more than one such crisis at a time.

In the case of the developed countries, the interventionist approach through the IMF was, in practice, abandoned nearly twenty years ago. The drawings by Britain and Italy in the 1970s are to be seen as a hangover from the previous period, and the GAB is likewise a relic of the past. (Interventionism continues within the European Union, but the context of a regional arrangement in which economies are closely linked together in many ways does make this case different; and recent experience raises some doubts about whether interventionism without full unification of currencies can be effective even in these circumstances.) In the last few years we have seen a number of developing countries becoming integrated into the world monetary and financial system, with access to international capital markets and large inflows of volatile capital. With this goes the vulnerability to market sentiment which the developed countries have lived with for a number of years now, and the consequent pressures from the markets on economic policy making.

I discuss these new capital flows and their implications for the countries concerned in Chapter 11. The point here is that the recent episode seems unlikely to lead to an enhanced role for the IMF in a financing sense. The Fund cannot effectively protect these countries from the markets. Its role in relation to Third World countries and their development seems more likely to decline than to grow in the years ahead, although it will no doubt continue for some time to assist the more backward countries, which are not linked to the world financial system. So far as the developed countries are concerned, there is no likelihood of the Fund reverting to an active financing role. It has been suggested (for example by the Commission appointed by the American

Bretton Woods Committee in 1994 to examine the future of the two institutions)[2] that the Fund should be used by the Group of Seven as an instrument for the co-ordination of their economic policies; but there has been no sign of any serious interest in this idea so far. However, the long term role of the IMF seems likely to be in the field of information-gathering, monitoring and analysis in international monetary matters.

*   *   *

It is entirely to be expected that institutions which have been in existence for half a century should have developed a marked institutional character, but the strength of these institutional traditions after so much time has passed can be an obstacle to necessary change. The professional staff of both institutions consists largely of people who have spent and intend to spend all their working lives in them. Anyone who has dealt with the staff of the Bank and the IMF over a period of time would confirm that they are generally people of very high professional quality and integrity. The institutions are fortunate that their reputation enables them to recruit and retain first-class people. It is not uncommon for people to move from senior positions in national governments to relatively junior positions in the Fund or Bank. The appeal of life in Washington and the pay levels in the Fund and Bank no doubt play a part in attracting staff from some Third World countries, although much nonsense is talked about these salaries which, especially at the middle and higher levels, are less than competitive in many member countries in continental Europe and Latin America. But the key factor is the high reputation of the institutions.

Given the quality of the staff, it is not surprising that the studies produced by both institutions are generally of a high standard. They are world leaders in their fields. Where then is the problem?

The World Bank has been subjected to a barrage of criticism in recent years, much of it ill-informed and unfair. Criticism comes partly from people who are disillusioned with Third World development generally. A lot comes from unrepresentative groups, people who in a previous generation might have supported development causes, but who today are typically concerned with the protection of the environment. We must all be very much concerned with the environment, but there are groups, including some of the Bank's harshest critics, who pursue this cause to the total exclusion of all else, and even if the costs effectively fall on very poor people in developing countries. The World Bank is in fact dealing with a social phenomenon which does not stem from concern with Third World problems but is internal to the western democracies – the hostility of the natural dissenters within the rich societies, motivated by antagonism to established authority and what they see as concentrations of power. For people with an inclination to believe in international conspiracy, the size and financial power of the World Bank is a natural object of hostility. And of course, the Bank has sometimes played into their hands by errors of judgment, such as the Narmada Dam in India, which provoked a major dispute with environmental organisations, leading to the Bank's withdrawal from the project in 1993.

Besides all this, the Bank has not been good at public relations. It was slow to appreciate the image problem which was developing during the 1980s. For many years the Bank behaved as if it was unnecessary to respond to criticism, assuming that because it was engaged in good work, for the benefit of poor countries, there must be basic public support. This cannot now be taken for granted at all.

Although many of the attacks on the World Bank in the past decade or so have been unjustified – and sometimes quite irrational – the ineffectiveness of the Bank's response to these attacks may be a symptom of problems of another kind. They lie in a number of institutional characteristics of the Bank which are difficult to change.

One such characteristic is that the World Bank is a surprisingly academic institution. In an organisation dedicated to a practical purpose, it is remarkable how intellectual performance seems to be valued almost above all else. A young professional member of staff gains reputation by producing a good report or paper or speaking brilliantly at a meeting, rather as if he were at a university. All this would be fine, if it did not have the effect that lower importance is attached to practical achievements on the ground – the real work of development. Lewis Preston, who became President of the Bank in 1991 and died tragically in 1995, made a start with tackling this problem by commissioning a report on it by Willi Wapenhans, a former Vice-President of the Bank. But there is still a long way to go.

The World Bank is excessively bureaucratic. Procedures for processing projects are cumbersome and over-complicated. There is an almost complete lack of cost-consciousness. The Bank's income comes easily – its borrowing on the markets is guaranteed by its powerful owners and the loans it makes are guaranteed by the recipient governments. A net income of about $1.5 billion a year is earned effortlessly. The Bank is overstaffed, but this is not apparent to many people in the organisation because most people in the Bank work conscientiously, usually producing high quality papers and reports. If a proposal is made for an interesting study, it is unlikely to be opposed on grounds of cost. Much work is done on voluminous studies, sometimes of dubious practical value, where shorter, simpler studies would do. Missions to borrowing countries tend to be large – sometimes twenty people or more. The budgeting system puts little pressure on managers to make economical use of staff.

In this comfortable atmosphere it is perhaps not surprising that for years hardly anything was done about overstaffing. One effort was a reorganisation undertaken by Barber Conable as President in 1987. But it was badly mishandled, causing an unnecessary degree of upheaval and the expenditure of huge amounts to compensate staff members for leaving, many of whom came back to work for the Bank as consultants. Within three years the size of the Bank staff was back to what it had been. In 1994 Preston embarked on an effort to reduce the budget by 6 per cent a year in real terms over two years; but as I write, it is not clear what will come of this.

A related characteristic of the Bank is that it is inward-looking. This is an old story. I recall my first encounters with World Bank and IMF staff when I arrived as a new member of the Boards of the two institutions in 1975. My introductory meetings with the senior members of the Fund staff consisted of discussion about the international monetary and balance-of-payments situation of the time. Senior Bank staff, however, were mainly concerned with the internal politics of the Bank and the management style of the President, Bob McNamara. This characteristic has persisted. And apart from internal politics, the Bank spends a lot of time talking to itself about development issues – interestingly and intelligently, of course – and not enough on dialogue with the outside world.

One manifestation of the World Bank's self-preoccupation has been its tendency to measure its achievement, to a large extent, by the volume of its lending, and in particular the increase (or, God forbid, decrease) in its annual lending. This goes back to the McNamara years when the drive to increase the Bank's lending became the overwhelming pre-occupation of the institution, and this habit of mind has persisted. But such targets are not important to anyone outside the institution. And it is hardly necessary to stress the harm that can follow when staff feel themselves under pressure to achieve volume targets, even if this can only be done by making questionable loans of the kind I referred to in Chapter 6.

To take this point one step further, the Bank, after half a century in the business of development, seems to find it difficult to believe that it will not go on for ever. As the institution approaches its 50th birthday,[3] there is much talk about "the next 50 years". The thought that the institution might succeed sufficiently for its activities to be drastically cut back is not commonly discussed in the Bank. But the reality is that the demand from member governments for IBRD loans has been declining. In the fiscal year 1994 the IBRD planned for loan approvals of $18 billion, but found that it was able to approve only $14.2 billion. In real terms Bank lending now is no higher than it was ten years ago, and has been declining since 1990. On the other hand, IDA credits, which go to the poorest countries, have continued to rise – over the past five years they have grown from $5.5 billion a year to $6.6 billion. And, as I explained in Chapter 7, demand from the private sector for IFC financing continues to grow strongly.

The falling-off in demand for the Bank's money, which is partly due to the increased access to private capital which a number of countries now enjoy, which in turn reflects good economic performance, should be seen as heartening evidence of success; but to many in the Bank, it appears to be cause for concern. There is talk of the Bank's traditional "monopolies" being broken, in tones which imply that this is a problem. The resurgence of private flows is seen by many as unwelcome competition, forgetting that the Bank's own Articles require it to supplement rather than displace private financing.

Attitudes in the Bank do vary widely; but even now the market philosophy is not fully accepted. It is still not uncommon to hear talk of the "fashion" for private sector development and suggestions that the pendulum will (and indeed should) soon swing back to the familiar public sector way of doing things. Clearly, the more the market economy succeeds in the developing world, the more the role of institutions like the World Bank will be called into question, and Bank staff, who are no more than human, can perceive the threat to their careers. But the institution does not exist for the benefit of its staff.

Amongst the staff, a common complaint recently has been that the leadership does not provide the institution with "vision". This seems to stem largely from nostalgia for the McNamara years when the President of the Bank shook the conscience of the world into a new awareness and laid out a new agenda with the emphasis on alleviating poverty. But there can never be another episode like this, not just because McNamara was unique, but because there is no new agenda of this kind waiting to be proposed. The only important exception to this – a really new activity which the World Bank must undertake along with the IMF and the the IFC – is helping ex-Communist countries to build a market economy. This is the subject of Chapter 10.

Vision cannot, of course, be produced to order. Nevertheless, the Bank recently appointed a committee to produce a "vision" document, along the lines of the "mission statement" which has become fashionable amongst American corporations. What emerged is a bland document which contains scarcely a hint of self-criticism.[4] It propounds several principles which should govern Bank Group activity, which are neither novel nor controversial.[5] The recent downward trend in the Bank's lending, instead of being mentioned as evidence of success, is obscured by a presentation which focusses solely on the growth over the past four decades. The document speaks of the need to be flexible and client-oriented, but explains this as necessary because the Bank Group is operating in an environment which is "more *competitive* in every respect" (emphasis added) because the private sector is meeting more of the needs of borrowers who are also developing their own analytical capacities. All told, it presents a picture of an institution which is aware of the need for change but is still caught in the mesh of its institutional habits.

*   *   *

The case of the IMF is somewhat different. The Fund's institutional problems (as opposed to problems about its role, which we have discussed) would appear to be much less serious than those of the Bank. It is not so obviously overstaffed (the Fund's staff now numbers about 2400 people, compared with the Bank's 7500). Like the Bank, the Fund has been the target of much criticism, and has also not handled its public relations well. Some of these attacks are based on the naive view that the basic principles of economics should not be applied to developing countries. Some reflect the curious picture of the IMF as a dictator, imposing its will on helpless poor countries, whereas in reality the Fund can impose conditions only when a country seeks to use its resources and these conditions usually involve less hardship than the country would suffer were there no IMF, and events simply took their course.

It is a valid criticism of the IMF that it has, from time to time, shown itself insensitive to the political problems involved in implementing its recommendations. Humility is not the Fund's strongest suit. Stories abound of young, brilliant PhDs from the IMF staff arrogantly lecturing Ministers of Finance in developing countries, with little understanding of the political and social problems the government of the country is facing. In recent times the IMF has tried to improve the style and manner of its staff's behaviour.

There is also the question of the relationship between the two institutions. For many years their roles were distinct and contrasting. During the 1980s, however, each tended to move onto the other's ground. The World Bank was becoming gradually more aware of the importance of sound economic management to development and moved into "policy-based lending" with conditions relating to economic policies, mainly sectoral policies. The IMF simultaneously was becoming aware that it was frequently dealing with problems which did not arise from short term disequilibria, calling for demand-management solutions, but from underlying weaknesses, calling for structural change which could only take place over a period of time. The boundary line between the areas of responsibility of the two institutions became a subject of some controversy, the IMF arguing that the line should be between the macro-economy (the Fund's territory) and the micro, and the Bank arguing for the distinction to be between the long term (the Bank's territory) and the short term.

But we should not exaggerate these problems, as the press has often done. The degree of friction varies according to the personalities involved and the heads of the two institutions have seen it as in their interest to avoid clashes. There are guidelines for co-operation which have been updated from time to time, most recently by President Conable of the Bank and Managing Director Camdessus of the Fund in 1989. These recognise areas of responsibility for each institution and an area where responsibility overlaps and where co-operation is essential. The problems have been contained partly by the fact that the two institutions report to the same masters, namely the member governments. However, in the more powerful countries that responsibility usually rests with Ministers of Finance who have shown a tendency to take the side of the IMF in any dispute between the Fund and the Bank.

Some observers have proposed that the two institutions should be merged on the grounds that their functions are now more alike than different. This would create a colossus with a concentration of power that developing countries might well find frightening. In fact there is no convincing case for a merger – it is hard to see what benefit it would produce – and it is unlikely to happen. The fact that the boundary line between the two institutions is sometimes in dispute is a manageable problem and there are large areas of responsibility on each side which are not in dispute. A merger might threaten the expertise which has undoubtedly been built up over the years in these areas on both sides.

From the beginning there has been an unwritten agreement that the chief executive of the Bank (the President) should be an American and the chief executive of the IMF (the Managing Director) a European. But America is one country and Europe is many, so the processes by which the heads of the two institutions are chosen are very different. In the case of the Managing Director of the Fund, there is normally a competition between a number of European candidates, who are usually sponsored by their own governments, but have to gain the support of other governments to win. In the case of the President of the Bank the position is, in practice, in the gift of the White House. The process of selecting a Managing Director of the Fund tends to thrust high-quality candidates to the fore and the institution has benefited from this. The case of the Bank is more of a lottery. The White House of the time is likely to have its own agenda, usually a domestic one, unrelated to the interests of the World Bank as an institution.

The result may be beneficial for the Bank or the reverse. It was a matter of chance that brought Robert McNamara, the most innovative and dynamic President in the World Bank's history, to the position, when he resigned as Defense Secretary in the Johnson Administration. And the White House's freedom of choice is less than absolute. In 1986, when they heard that a former US Navy Secretary, Middendorf, was being considered for the position, the European governments told Don Regan, then President Reagan's Chief of Staff, they would oppose him. The White House eventually nominated Barber Conable. This was an exception because American Administrations have usually started from the mistaken assumption that, because the institution is a "bank", it should be headed by a leading banker. But the job is not a banker's job at all, in the normal sense. Heading the World Bank means being the leader of the international development movement, a task demanding high political skills, and more understanding of economic policy issues than of finance. It now also means managing a large and complex international institution, which has developed considerable problems, as I have argued. By no means all top bankers possess these qualities and some who are not bankers do.

As I write, a new President, James D. Wolfensohn is about to take over at the World Bank and hopes are high. He faces a task which is primarily one of institutional renewal. It is to adapt the institution to the changed and changing world of the market economy, a world in which private capital markets play an enormously larger role and in which the Bank's role must be different and smaller. It is to wean the institution away from some of its habits which are at odds with the market philosophy; to make it acknowledge failure where there has been failure, especially in Africa; and to adopt a humbler more self-questioning attitude to the whole business of international aid. It is to steer the institution through a period of "downsizing" – which is never easy – without allowing its morale to collapse. This is, of course, easy to say and difficult to achieve in practice. And it will not be achieved without the strong backing of the major shareholders, especially the United States.

The big questions facing the Fund, on the other hand, have more to do with role. The future role of the IMF remains undefined and perhaps cannot be defined yet. The answer to that question should determine what institutional changes are needed. It seems very likely that a substantial downsizing will be required in the case of the IMF also.

A period of history during which the multilateral institutions created at the end of World War II have played a key role in the world economy, may now be coming to an end. As the operation of market forces comes to dominate the world economy, the environment in which these two great institutions exist is profoundly different from the one in which they first came into being. There is, perhaps, a parallel between the role of the state in a national economy and the role of these institutions in the world economy. The interventionist thinking which prevailed in most developed countries, as well as developing countries, from the 1950s to the 1970s, was reflected also in international interventionism. The international aid movement was one example of this, and the traditional role of the IMF another. In a market economy, the role of the state changes – it withdraws from direct ownership, control and financing of the processes of production, but performs other important functions, some of a regulatory kind. Similarly, in a world of markets, intervention by multilateral organisations is already giving way to a different role, and this process will go further.

The future roles of the Bank and Fund remain to be fully worked out. A model of a modern international organisation might be the World Trade Organisation, which has recently replaced the General Agreement on Tariffs and Trade. It has, in fact, a regulatory function, monitoring the implementation of internationally agreed rules governing trade. In the case of the World Bank and the IMF no similar regulatory function presents itself. However, the direction of change is likely to be a gradual decline in financing activities and a greater concentration on technical assistance to member states. In the long run, over a considerable number of years, both may become centres of expertise, with no financing function.

10 The Collapse of the Second World

The Soviet decision not to join the Bretton Woods institutions at the end of World War II was one of several which drew the Second World economically into its own shell, separating it from the rest of humanity for forty-five years. When communism collapsed in eastern Europe and the Soviet Union in the years 1989–91, the rest of the world was surprised to discover how little it knew or understood about these hidden economies. It dawned on the west that, although the Soviet Union had been the first country in space and the second military power in the world, it was a relatively poor country.

Those members of the eastern bloc who had not already joined the IMF and the World Bank (Poland, Hungary and Romania had done so a few years before) showed an immediate interest in becoming members, and clearly for the purpose of borrowing. The Russians, with the mentality of a great power, paid close attention to the size of their quota in the Fund and shareholding in the Bank, their position on the two Boards and voting rights; but even they were anxious to draw on the resources of both institutions quickly.

The economic systems of these countries were so unfamiliar to western economists and statisticians that it was difficult for them to assess national incomes. Even now, the available statistics must be treated with caution. The World Bank recently estimated the 1993 income per head of Russia as $2350 a year, a little below Brazil and Malaysia and a little ahead of Turkey and Thailand. On a purchasing-power-parity basis, Russia is put at about $5200, which still ranks it a little below the border-line between the "lower-middle-income" and "upper-middle-income" groups in the World Bank's classification. The leading central European countries, Poland, Czechoslovakia and Hungary, were comparable with Russia, and the rest of the former USSR a long way behind.

Were they, therefore, to be regarded as "developing countries"? There were clearly important differences between them and the World Bank's traditional clients. But the need for international help was obvious, and the existing aid organisations were assumed to have some relevant experience and to be well placed to move into action quickly. However, very soon after the Soviet withdrawal from central Europe at the end of 1989, the French proposed the creation of an entirely new European institution to help former communist countries in the transition to market systems and to democracy. The result was the European Bank for Reconstruction and Development or EBRD, now based in London.

The motives for this move were largely political. There was a feeling that this "European" problem should not be left to organisations mainly concerned with the Third World; and a desire to create an institution which would not be dominated by the United States, as the World Bank appeared to some Europeans to be. There is no doubt that if the EBRD had not been created, it would have been necessary to endow the World Bank and the IFC with substantial new resources to do the job, and it might have been more difficult to secure such resources for them than for the new Bank. In fact, the new institution was set up with remarkable speed and opened its doors for business in April 1991, but by then the World Bank and the IFC were already involved in the new task, and have continued to be.

The EBRD was established with the European countries holding a majority of the shares but with American and Japanese participation too. It was to provide finance to both the public sector and the private, which meant that, in practice, its operations would parallel those of the World Bank and the IFC. Under US and British pressure, it was decided that 60 per cent of its outlays should be to the private sector, a point on which I commented in Chapter 7 (see p. 133). The EBRD got away to a rousing, not to say flamboyant, start with Jacques Attali, former adviser to President Mitterrand, at its head; but his management style soon made him unacceptable to the main shareholders and he resigned in July 1993 to be replaced by Jacques de Larosière, formerly Managing Director of the IMF and Governor of the Banque de France, a very strong figure who quickly built up confidence in the new Bank.

The main challenge in the former Second World was indeed significantly different from that in the Third World. The primary challenge was not to raise levels of income, but to assist in a transition to an entirely new economic system. But there were both parallels and contrasts with the Third World. The Third World was generally poorer, but nevertheless some way along the road to a market system; the ex-communist world somewhat richer than most Third World countries, but burdened with a wholly anti-market system. In some ways, the former communist countries were ahead, but in others much farther back.

As we began to understand the nature of the challenge in the former communist countries, the key differences from the Third World which emerged were that:

- educational levels in the former communist countries were much higher, both the general education of the population and the numbers trained in science and advanced technologies.

- unlike the Third World, most ex-communist countries were highly industrialised, but their industrial establishments were managed in an entirely uncommercial manner, with no knowledge of market pricing and virtually no means of identifying their own costs or their profit-or-loss position.

- industrial establishments generally provided social services – housing, education, medical services – to their workforce and the costs of these activities made it additionally difficult to assess the performance of any enterprise.

- in contrast to Third World countries, there was virtually no private sector (except small businesses and agriculture in some countries, such as Poland), and a total absence of the legal and accounting systems required for a private sector and a market economy to function.

- the planning system, based on the proposition that competition was inefficient, had created monopoly situations for most products in the Soviet Union, despite the huge size of the country.

- many of the industrial establishments were creating very serious environmental problems which would cost huge amounts to deal with.

— there was, before the collapse of communism, no serious poverty in these countries, although in the confusion after the collapse many did experience hardship.

There were also big differences amongst the former communist countries. The east-central European countries differed from the former Soviet Union, in that they had lived under communism for about 40 years, not 70, a critical difference. In the former Soviet Union memories of markets and business systems had been all but expunged, whereas in the east-central European countries it had survived to a limited extent, and some of the former owners of firms in these countries were still living (often abroad) and made their presence felt. Just as important, in central Europe communism had been an alien system imposed by the Soviet occupying power, whereas Soviet communism, despite the fact that there had been dissenters, was a home-grown product. For these historical reasons, the general direction in which Poland, Czechoslovakia and Hungary were going – towards western-style democracy and some version of the western market economy – became clear very quickly, whereas the long-run direction of Russia and other former states of the Soviet Union is likely to remain unclear for some years.

How was a market system to be built out of the ruins of communism and how could western-based international agencies help? The problem was a totally new one. No one had any experience of any similar transition, and to many it seemed bafflingly difficult. A Polish minister compared it to converting an omelette back into whole eggs. But this bafflement about how to organise the conversion arose partly from the mentality of planners who instinctively thought the whole process would have to be managed and supervised, whereas those who understood markets better realised that capitalism would grow when the soil and the climate were right.

Getting the soil and climate right, however, was by no means easy. Reforms of two kinds were needed: macro-economic reforms, designed to introduce the play of market forces while also stabilising the economy; and structural reforms, the creation of new systems and the privatisation and restructuring of enterprises. The first could be introduced either very quickly or more gradually – a point which, for a time, was debated intensely. The second type of reform would obviously take time. How long the whole process would take was also very unclear, although it was obvious that everything would be more difficult and take longer in the Soviet republics than in central Europe.

Amongst the western international agencies, it was the IMF which conducted the main discussion with the eastern governments on macro-economic issues. The World Bank, the IFC and later the EBRD, were more concerned with the structural and micro-economic problems. But of course macro-economic policies in the various countries had profound implications for the success or failure of structural and micro-economic reforms.

Leszek Balcerowicz, Finance Minister in the first non-communist government in Poland, blazed the trail for quick and radical macro-economic action in the reforms he introduced in January 1990, with support from the west to provide a foreign exchange reserve to enable him to float and stabilise the exchange rate. His courageous initiative had a considerable impact on eastern Europe. Czechoslovakia, led by Vaclav Klaus, a strong believer in the market economy, took similar steps, while Hungary moved more gradually. As the reformers fully expected, the three leading central European countries all went through a difficult period when output fell sharply and unemployment rose, and it was in about the third year that their economies began to grow again. Meanwhile structural reforms were being implemented in varying ways in the three countries.

In the case of the Soviet republics, the macro-economic issue was not handled with anything like the same decisiveness and is still, as I write, an unresolved problem in most of those countries, including Russia itself. There were plenty of voices urging the government in Moscow to introduce a macro-economic programme like the Balcerowicz reforms in Poland, but the politics of reform in Russia were vastly more complicated and difficult than anything in central Europe. Whether it might have been possible, with more effective leadership, to avoid the very high inflation which Russia has suffered, or the drastic depreciation of the rouble, is a very difficult point for an outsider to assess. However, monetary conditions were extremely lax in Russia for a time, and it was not surprising that the IMF felt that to pour money into such a situation would not only be wasteful, but would support bad policies. The Fund's conditions were later relaxed somewhat under political pressure from the US and others.

On the "structural" side of reform, much that had to be done was fairly obvious – modern corporate and commercial legislation; the introduction of western accounting systems; the modernisation of the banking system. The main debate, however, was about how to go about privatisation, a huge and daunting task.

A curious fact emerged very soon: that in all the communist countries it was unclear who owned the country's industrial firms. No laws defined who the legal owners were: in fact the question of ownership did not arise in the communist system and if they were to be "privatised", it was quite unclear who had the right to sell them. The uncertainty about this, which persisted for some time, was exploited in some cases by managers who simply assumed the right to dispose of the assets under their control, and sold them, usually to foreign buyers. This was common in Hungary in the early stages, until it was stopped by legislation which gave the central government the sole right to sell industrial assets. The paradox was that, before they could be privatised, they had first to be nationalised. And this also meant that they had to be reorganised into something like joint-stock companies, with shares as the mechanism for giving meaning to the new concept of ownership.

Surmounting this hurdle, however, was only the beginning. How was ownership then to be transferred to new private owners? Klaus of Czechoslovakia, later Prime Minister of the Czech Republic, pioneered the idea of distributing vouchers to the population to be used for the purchase of shares. He knew that the challenge of privatisation in a country emerging from communism was entirely different from the task which had been undertaken by the Thatcher government or some Latin American countries. The whole economy had to be privatised. To do this by selling off each company, case by case, after reforming it and putting it on a sound footing, would have taken at least ten, perhaps twenty years. Bureaucratic opposition and vested interests would drag the process out. There was a danger of a political backlash taking the country back to some form of socialism. Klaus wanted to move quickly to a point where the process would be irreversible. The priority was to shift ownership into private hands: the necessary reform and modernisation of the enterprises could then be undertaken by their private owners.

There was also a question of elementary justice. Under the communist system, industrial assets belonged, in principle, to the community as a whole: why then, to make them owners under the new system, should the citizenry be required to pay for them? In any case, most of the community had no savings with which to buy them. If they were sold for cash (unless they were sold to foreign investors which was likely to happen in only a minority of cases) they would pass into the ownership of the few who had accumulated money under communism, people who would not be at all welcome as the elite of the new system.

There were some practical difficulties. One was that this process meant that sales would take place before the value of the assets could be properly assessed, and buyers would have to take decisions largely in the dark. Some would be lucky, others would not. In the Czech system members of the public had to make a small payment for vouchers (probably a sound idea to make sure that the scheme was taken seriously), but fundamentally it was a scheme for free distribution of the nation's industrial assets to the public.

A second problem was that spreading share ownership amongst thousands of small holders would mean that they could not easily assert their rights as owners. In practice the management would be in control – and this would usually mean the existing management, the people who had managed the enterprises under the communist regime. For private ownership to be effective there would have to be intermediaries, such as mutual funds, which could hold substantial blocks of shares on behalf of the public, and be able to exercise influence on managements. The Czech government encouraged this – vouchers could be sold to mutual funds in exchange for shares or units in those funds. When the programme was launched in November 1991 no less than 429 investment mutual funds had registered (mergers later reduced the number sharply), which accumulated about three-quarters of the vouchers. These had emerged spontaneously and were not created by the state.

The Czech system was the most effective of the voucher systems introduced by countries in transition from communism. Over 3000 enterprises were privatised by this method. As a result the Czech Republic and Slovakia (the privatisation was carried out before the country split) are well ahead of Poland and Hungary, which have been privatising firms by conventional, case-by-case methods. By the end of 1994 Hungary had privatised 40 per cent of its state-owned firms and Poland less than a third. Poland has been planning a limited voucher system for a number of years but has not yet implemented it.

Privatisation in Russia was a different story. Anatoly Chubais was the Minister responsible for privatisation in the first Yeltsin administration, continued in this role with Gaidar as Prime Minister and subsequently under Chernomyrdin and later became Deputy Prime Minister. He had the same radical objective as Klaus – to effect a change in ownership which would be irreversible and would make it virtually impossible to put the political clock back. But Russia was not the same as Czechoslovakia. Private ownership of firms was a strange and unfamiliar idea. The danger of the political clock being put back was greater, while at the same time the powerful bosses of Russia's huge industrial complexes had asserted a good deal of independence in the confusion that followed the collapse of communism. Chubais proceeded by way of a voucher system that was biased in favour of ownership by workers and management, and seemed likely to entrench the existing managers in power.

Chubais, a quiet revolutionary who, by dogged persistence, succeeded in privatising most of the large enterprises of Russia over a period of about two years, was apparently prepared to take this risk. The risks involved in delay and the possibility of a communist backlash were greater. The first step was to "commercialise" all the firms, giving them a structure with shares owned by the state. Vouchers were issued to the whole adult population, beginning in October 1992. Each had a monetary value of 10,000 roubles and could be bought or sold until the end of July 1994, when the whole operation ended. Each firm was required to put forward proposals for privatisation for approval, and since the managers stood to gain, they were very ready to comply. Auctions were arranged all round the country, some with help from the IFC and the EBRD.

The Russian privatisation programme, with all its defects, was by far the largest ever carried out in any country. By mid-1994 some 14,000 medium and large enterprises in Russia had been privatised, and more than 60 per cent of the industrial work-force was then employed in privatised firms. But what had come into existence could not be described as a capitalist system in the western sense. There was nominal private ownership, but with the managerial barons in control and private shareholders with little effective means of asserting their rights as owners. There were as yet no stock exchanges where shares could be traded; in most cases there were no share certificates and arrangements for registration of share ownership were rudimentary. That would all come later, if at all. But if what emerged was not capitalism or a market economy, it was certainly a type of pluralism; and the economic landscape of Russia had been changed in such a way as to make a return to the old system very unlikely.

How could external agencies such as the World Bank, the IFC and the EBRD help with the process of transition to a market economy? Three types of activity seemed to be indicated: first, providing technical assistance to create the environment and the systems needed for the private sector to operate such as banking, capital markets, accounting and tax systems; secondly, assisting with privatisation; and, thirdly, helping to bring foreign investment into the country for good projects. The third of these roles was not fundamentally different from the role the IFC plays in many Third World countries, although the problems faced by incoming investors were different. The first two roles, both involving technical assistance rather than financing, were, however, very different.

The main privatisation programmes of the countries in transition were devised with little assistance from outside, particularly the Czech and Russian voucher programmes. But in Russia particularly, the IFC played a significant role in privatisation in fields other than the auctioning of large enterprises, and the story of this effort throws some light on the transition in Russia. As early as 1990, when the USSR applied to join the Bretton Woods institutions, a team of World Bank and

IFC people were sent to find ways of offering useful technical assistance. The IFC remit was privatisation. Having had some experience of small business privatisation in central Europe, we felt that this was a field where some results might be achieved quickly. The privatisation of shops and restaurants could have a quick and visible effect on the atmosphere of the cities. From Washington, however, there was no way of judging how we could be of help and whom we could work with.

The team quickly concluded that progress was not to be achieved by talking to ministries in Moscow but through city or provincial governments. These authorities were very variable in their competence and their interest in reform. In the city and province (or "oblast") of Nizhny Novgorod, an ancient Russian city on the Volga, 250 miles to the east of Moscow, known as Gorky in communist times, the IFC team found an oblast governor, Boris Nemstov, and a city mayor, Dmitri Bednyakov, who were enthusiastic about reform. Through the winter of 1991–92 three members of the team worked with the Nizhny Novgorod authorities to create a system of rules and procedures for the auctioning of the shops and restaurants of the city, which the city itself owned. The auction programme was launched in April 1992.

The value of this effort was that it created a model. The IFC itself did not have the resources to implement this programme in more than a small number of cities, although, with the financial support of the US, British and Canadian governments, it did directly assist in the privatisation of businesses in 29 cities. However, more important was the fact that the Ministry of Privatisation in Moscow asked the IFC to produce a manual describing the Nizhny Novgorod system and then recommended it to all the provinces and cities of Russia. It became the model for the privatisation of over 75,000 small businesses throughout Russia in the following two years.

There was also another attempt to create a model which could be imitated elsewhere. An IFC team spent two years working on plans for the privatisation of state farms, again using the oblast of Nizhny Novgorod as the starting point. The plan involved no cash transactions: the workers and former workers living on the farm were issued with vouchers with which they could buy land or buildings and equipment. They were encouraged to form co-operative groups which would own these assets and operate them as new farming enterprises. The first of these "sales" of farm land and equipment took place in November 1993, with the enthusiastic backing of the Moscow government. In the spring of 1994, after several more auctions had taken place, Prime Minister Victor Chernomyrdin endorsed the scheme as a model for the country as a whole. In July 1994 a decree laid down the detailed regulations for the privatisation of state farms, following the model created by the Nizhny-Novgorod/IFC team, and the scheme is now being implemented in other parts of the country. Privatisation of state farms will certainly take longer than other forms of privatisation in Russia. But the largely unsung story of the beginning of land privatisation marks a momentous break in the history of rural Russia, after centuries of serfdom and communism.

The IFC's work on privatisation in Russia was perhaps the most exciting and unusual episode in my years at the Corporation. The team which achieved these remarkable results was composed of enthusiastic young men and women from a number of countries, including many Russians. They worked frequently in conditions of hardship and sometimes danger. They were given a wide measure of freedom – they did not spend large amounts of time writing reports to Washington. The whole effort was very well managed by Roger Gale in Moscow and Tony Doran in Washington. Knowing what had happened, I did not find it altogether surprising that Yegor Gaidar, the reformist leader who was Deputy Prime Minister in the first Yeltsin Government, remarked in 1993 that the IFC had made more impact in Russia than any other international organisation.

In the longer run, the main continuing role of the international agencies in the transition in Russia and eastern Europe was always likely to consist of facilitating foreign investment. The IFC had been involved in some investments in eastern Europe before the collapse of communism, mainly in Hungary and some in Poland. When the EBRD was established, Jacques Attali and I agreed at a very early stage to exchange full information on our activities. There would be large projects where we would both be needed to raise the necessary finance, but one or the other would be in the lead; and smaller projects where the client would choose the IFC or the EBRD. It seemed to me that there would be no harm in a bit of rivalry in such cases, provided it did not consist of competing on the terms on which finance would be offered to clients. To begin with, we were concerned that the new Bank might undercut the IFC's market-based financing by offering below-market rates, but in fact the EBRD did not do so. We knew that in the long run, with their substantial resources deployed solely in this region, the EBRD's operations would be larger than the IFC's. With Ron Freeman, who had come from Salomon Brothers, in the number-two position at the EBRD, co-operation was excellent.

We all had a lot to learn about how to do business in the new member countries. The total absence of a business culture and of the information needed to analyse a company's affairs and assess its viability was at first a surprise. There were companies making technically advanced products which had no idea what their costs of production were and no means of determining what their prices should be, because these had been decided by government planners. But gradually familiarity with western accounting and management systems spread. We had to be prepared to be flexible and innovative. In Hungary the IFC, working with the EBRD, for the first time put finance into an enterprise, the national telecommunications system, while it was still government-owned, to prepare it for privatisation – which was successfully achieved. In Poland, with the World Bank's support, we arranged for the nine commercial banks of the country (each of them a former department of the Central Bank which had once been the only bank) to be "twinned" with a western bank which would give them technical assistance. In Poland, also, we established a business advisory service financed by western donors which was an immediate success.

In Russia, the rapid progress of the main privatisation programme presented a new challenge. The government wanted international organisations to invest in the newly privatised firms to enable them to modernise, but few of them could offer a real prospect of viability or profitability. Our problem at the IFC was whether we could justify using our own funds for ventures which we regarded as involving more risk than we would be prepared to accept in other parts of the world. But something had to be done.

The vast size of the country, and number of enterprises involved, meant that it made little sense to tackle the problem on a national scale. Eventually the EBRD, the IFC and the US government each established local investment banks in certain regions to search out good prospects for investment, bringing in foreign investors where possible. As I write, this effort is still getting under way, and it is too early to judge its success.

By the end of 1994, the IFC had approved financing of $994 million in the ex-communist countries to support projects totalling $9.2 billion; and the EBRD had approved $4.5 billion for private-sector projects totalling $13.9 billion. During the first four years of the 1990s the governments of the former communist countries reported commitments for foreign investment of $12.4 billion.

* * *

Looking back over the five years since the collapse of communism in eastern Europe, the extent of change seems remarkable. Poland, the Czech Republic and Hungary seem, despite occasional hiccups, to be on their way to becoming western-style democracies, with market-based economic systems and links with western Europe, as they had before World War II. Romania and Bulgaria have made less progress. The Baltic states have been more or less adopted by their Nordic neighbours and will probably make rapid economic progress.

In Russia the situation is confused and it is impossible to generalise, especially since the country is so vast and varied. The majority of Russian enterprises are now owned, in effect, by their managers and workers. This kind of ownership, as the example of Yugoslavia over most of four decades shows, is not necessarily a recipe for efficiency and progress. Almost all these enterprises need radical restructuring, but what levels of efficiency they will achieve will depend largely on whether they operate in a competitive environment. At present they do so only to a limited extent. Within the huge Russian internal market it is still possible for goods to be manufactured and traded which would be unsaleable on export markets, partly because the heavily under-valued exchange rate virtually excludes many imports. Market forces are beginning to play a more significant part in the economy, but there are many examples of the old system

continuing to function. The big industrial complexes improvise
and engage in barter deals with each other to meet their needs;
most of them are still not able to assess their profit-or-loss position
or their costs; and many of them still carry the burden of
providing social services – housing, schools, hospitals – for their
workers.

Amongst all this, a new capitalism is emerging, in which the
entrepreneurial spirit thrives and some people are making money
very fast. On the corporate scene some foreign companies are
beginning to form alliances with Russian enterprises, sometimes to
make use of their technology. In 1994 a number of funds were
established in western capital markets for investment in Russia
and an over-the-counter market, of a rather rudimentary kind,
had emerged, with share ownership recorded by entries in ledgers
rather than the issue of share certificates. Some Russian
companies, especially in the energy sector (such as Gazprom,
the largest producer of gas in the world) have made or are
planning issues of stock in western markets, and finding interest
amongst western investors. It is true that the interest which
western investors are showing in Russia stems partly from the gap
between the internal purchasing power of the rouble and its
exchange rate, which makes assets very cheap for western
investors. This can cause understandable resentment when people
see foreign companies buying Russian assets for almost nothing.
But foreign investors have also to consider whether the cheap
assets will be productive. At this stage, the answer seems most
likely to be positive in natural-resource industries producing for
export.

It is a situation in which the driving forces of change do not
come from the top. Power is highly diffused. Oblast governors and
industrial chiefs are often very powerful, but the situation varies
widely from one part of the country to another and from one
industrial plant to another. The differences between poorer and
richer areas seem likely to grow – for example, the far east around
Vladivostok shows signs of emerging as an area of capitalist
prosperity. An outsider, knowing that for centuries, under the
Communists and the Tsars alike, power was concentrated at the
centre, may wonder whether this situation will continue
indefinitely or whether a central power, in some form, will assert
itself. At the moment there seems no sign of that happening.

Instead we seem to be seeing, a confused process of change which will take a good many years, perhaps a generation, before it settles down to a recognisable pattern. The Russian scene has some obvious resemblances to "frontier" capitalism, reminding one of the United States in, say, the third quarter of the nineteenth century. Amongst the entrepreneurialism, corruption and organised crime are rife, and it is not clear whether and when these will be effectively curbed. Unlike mid-nineteenth century America, Russia is not blessed with a well-grounded legal system. This is a lack that Russia shares with China, the other large country where communism is now giving way to a form of capitalism. In Russia the legal system, heavily influenced by long years of authoritarian government, tsarist and communist, will need a great deal of development before it can play the part it should in a market economy.

It is very difficult for an outsider to judge how Russian popular attitudes towards capitalism will develop over the coming years. There must remain some doubt as to whether what emerges will look like a market economy and a democracy, as we understand those terms in the west. But there are reasons for hope. The high levels of education in the population are certainly a positive factor which seems likely to strengthen the democratic impulse in the country and assist it in building the necessary systems. However, it seems likely to be a long time, perhaps a generation, before an effective market economy and a stable democratic system are established in Russia.

As for the other republics of the former Soviet Union, Ukraine and Belorus have been experiencing economic confusion even greater than in Russia. Their future will be determined by a mixture of European and Russian influences and if there is economic and political stability in Russia, the chances of seeing it in Ukraine and Belorus will be better. But here too, it will be a number of years before the pattern emerges. In the Central Asian republics the European influence is distant, although some (especially Kazakhstan) have large Russian populations. The democratic impulse is not strong – most of these countries have emerged from the break-up of the USSR with fairly autocratic governments, and seem likely to continue so. At the same time, their shared economic history as part of the USSR makes them unlike Third World countries. They share with the rest of the former Soviet Union the major advantage of a high level of education and, given political stability (which cannot be assumed), their economic prospects are probably good. Mineral and energy resources in some of these countries are already attracting substantial amounts of foreign investment.

In the former communist countries, the basic questions about First World aid, which I raised at the beginning of this book, do not arise. The agreed purpose is to help create successful market economies, and there is no historical baggage of past aid efforts and failure. But the dangers of the misuse of aid are real in the former communist countries too. Large inflows of official money could undermine the growth of market systems and, in some circumstances, might reinforce the mentality of dependency that prevailed in a system where the state was the universal provider. There is no less need to define the purpose of aid and limit it to activities which will genuinely assist in the development of a market economy. It is also essential to see the whole task as one of limited duration. But subject to these conditions, some external assistance, properly directed and managed, may play a useful role in the republics of the former Soviet Union, including Russia itself, well into the twenty-first century. In central Europe, and particularly the three western countries of Poland, the Czech Republic and Hungary, western assistance may be superfluous before the new century is more than a few years old.

11 Where Now?

The Third World has changed dramatically in the last ten years. The shift to sound economic policies has transformed much of Asia and Latin America and set a number of countries on a track of fast growth. The axiom that economic growth in the less industrialised parts of the world was dependent on growth in the advanced countries had finally to be discarded when, in 1991–92, with the industrialised world in deep recession, there was vigorous autonomous growth in China and south-east Asia and parts of Latin America. Half way through the 1990s it is clear that a number of countries in these areas, as well as others such as India and Pakistan, are potentially on the verge of a period of high growth.

But there is still a large tract of the globe where such optimism is not in order. The changes that have affected much of the Third World have done very little yet for Africa, Bangladesh and some others. As we ponder the future of development policies and of aid in the new world environment, we are compelled to divide the Third World into at least two categories. This chapter contains some concluding thoughts about the outlook for these different groups of countries and about the relevance of international aid for them now.

First, however, we should touch on one of the most dramatic changes since the mid-1980s, one which is highly relevant here – the rise in flows of private capital to the fast-growing countries, and the integration of a number of Third World countries into the global financial system. In 1992, for the first time for a number of years, private capital flows to the developing world exceeded official capital, and by a large margin; and they did so again in 1993 and 1994. Official flows have been running level in total, with little increase or decrease, while private flows have accelerated at an extraordinary pace, especially in the early 1990s.

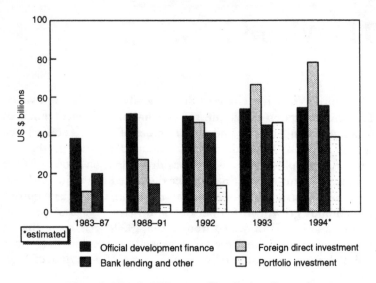

Figure 6 Capital Flows to Developing Countries

Figure 6 and Table 8 summarise what has been happening. Over the three years 1992–1994, according to the World Bank, official capital flows amounted to $159 billion and private flows of all kinds to $435 billion. The figures for the preceding three years, 1989–91, were $162 billion official and $150 billion private.

Table 8 Net Capital Flows to Developing Countries
(US $ billions, annual rates)

	1983–87	1988–91	1992	1993	1994*
1. Official development finance	38.5	51.2	50.3	53.9	54.4
2. Private capital flows	31.3	46.4	102.7	159.2	172.9
of which					
(a) Foreign direct investment	10.8	27.6	47.1	66.6	77.9
(b) Bank lending and other	20.1	14.8	41.5	45.7	55.6
(c) Portfolio investment †	0.3	4.0	14.2	46.9	39.4

* Estimated
† These figures exclude secondary market purchases, inclusion of which, according to Barings Securities Ltd, would more than double them.

Source: World Bank World Debt Tables, 1994–95.

The new private capital flows to the Third World are different not only in size but in character from the past. The private capital movements of the late 1970s and early 1980s consisted mainly of loans to governments, but now commercial bank lending plays only a minor part. What has been happening in the late 1980s and early 1990s is different – a steady build-up of private equity investment in companies in the developing countries.

Foreign direct investment has risen strongly and steadily. From about $10 billion a year in the mid-1980s it grew to about $78 billion in 1994. But most remarkable of all has been the rise in portfolio investment – purchases by foreigners of securities, including company shares and bonds of various kinds. In the mid-1980s this flow of capital was scarcely large enough to measure, but in 1993 portfolio equity investments and purchases of bonds, taken together, rose to a level which the World Bank estimates at $47 billion. If secondary market purchases by foreigners are included, the total was probably more than double that figure[1]. This flow then fell back a bit in 1994, but by the end of that year the value of foreign equity investments in the emerging markets was about $205 billion, one seventh of total foreign holdings in the stock markets of the world.[2]

The recent flow of private investment has not been evenly spread across the developing world, but concentrated, as Figure 7 and Table 9 show, in a limited number of countries in Asia and Latin America. In the poorer regions of the world, especially Africa, official capital still makes up most of the inflow. In 1991–93 private investment accounted for only 7.4 per cent of capital flows to Sub-Saharan Africa, but over 80 per cent of flows to east Asia and Latin America.

In the Latin American case, the flows have consisted partly of returning flight capital – money owned by citizens of those countries which had been moved abroad during the difficult 1980s, but began to return when the economic situation improved. In Asia, the largest recipient of private capital has been China, and a large part of that money has come from Chinese people living in Hong Kong, Taiwan, Singapore and other south-east Asian countries, responding to the opening up of the Chinese economy and the strong growth in the south and east of the country. Until recently, India has not been a major recipient, but there were significant inflows there in 1993 and 1994.

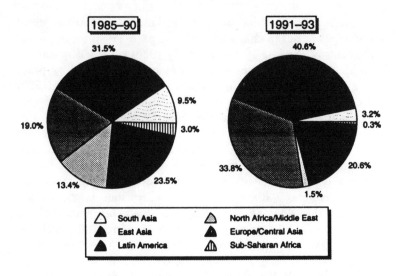

Figure 7   Private Capital Flows to Developing Countries by Region

Table 9   Net Long-term Capital Flows to Developing Countries by
Region (US $ billions, annual rates)

| | 1985–90 | | 1991–93 | |
	Official	*Private*	*Official*	*Private*
South Asia	10.1	3.2	10.5	3.5
East Asia	7.7	10.6	9.5	43.8
Latin America	7.5	6.4	5.3	36.5
Sub-Saharan Africa	12.9	1.0	16.0	0.3
North Africa and Middle East	7.1	4.5	7.3	1.6
Europe and Central Asia	2.4	7.9	10.2	22.3

Source: World Bank World Debt Tables, 1994–95.

The surge in portfolio investment, the most novel feature of the
recent flows, has been related to the growth of relatively
sophisticated stock markets in many countries in Asia and Latin
America, a phenomenon of the 1980s. The size of the markets and
the volume of trading grew steadily; the regulation of the markets
improved. In 1985 these markets were hardly known to

institutional investors in New York and London, but during the later 1980s it became common for these institutions to allocate a percentage of their resources for investment in them. The resources of the western institutional investors, who account for the largest part of cross-border equity investment, are so large that even a small percentage means significant flows of capital to developing countries.

In the early stages this investment took place mainly through funds managed by financial companies acting as intermediaries. But as time went on, an increasing number of companies in the more advanced developing countries began to raise capital directly in the international markets, usually by issuing shares.[3] Such issues have recently attracted substantial amounts of capital to developing countries – $11 billion in 1993, and even more in 1994. And in the early 1990s a substantial part of the investment has gone to newly privatised companies, especially in Latin America.

This surge of portfolio investment raises new questions for Third World countries. In some countries, the size and suddenness of the inflows has created problems of economic management, inflating the money supply and causing the exchange rate to appreciate – a novel problem in developing countries, and, it must be said, a type of problem that some ministers of finance are not sorry to have. A number of them have used the inflows to accumulate very substantial foreign exchange reserves, another new feature on the Third World scene.

But the most difficult questions concern volatility and durability. Private capital in the form of bank loans or direct investment does not readily flow out again; but capital in the form of purchases of securities on the markets may be withdrawn at short notice when sentiment changes, depressing stock, bond and exchange markets. I have argued the benefits which an efficient stock market can bring to a developing country's economy,[4] and these are real. At the same time markets can certainly be very volatile, and new, immature markets especially so. When significant amounts of foreign capital are invested in a country's markets, its vulnerability is greatly increased. The Mexican crisis at the end of 1994, to which I referred to in Chapter 9, when a loss of confidence in the currency led to large amounts of private capital being withdrawn in a few days, demonstrated the point dramatically. The power of financial markets to influence economic decision-making is a reality which the advanced countries have been living with for some time. It is a new experience for developing countries, some of which are now subject to similar pressures and Mexico, certainly, has found them painful.

But this is not necessarily bad. Markets, as investment banker Deryck Maughan put it recently, "are not politically correct"; but they are not wholly irrational either. Generally they do respond to sound policies and the discipline they impose on governments will, on the whole, favour the policies which developing countries should follow to underpin economic growth, although markets do sometimes over-react to errors or mishaps, even in countries where fundamentally sound policies are being pursued. As I argued in Chapter 9, official intervention on the scale which was required to bring the Mexican crisis to an end is not likely to be available to deal with similar crises in other countries in the future. The IMF should certainly try to improve its monitoring so as to be able to alert governments to dangers which may lead to crisis; but the remarkable fact about the Mexican crisis was that no one saw it coming. The Fund may be able to provide help in some cases, but, on the whole, developing countries which have opened up their economies will have to live with the international markets. It is, I hope, inconceivable that Third World countries will react to the gales which occasionally blow from the open ocean of world capital by crawling back into their shells, that is by re-erecting barriers to the inflow of capital. That would be to abandon the major gains which they have made in the past decade and undermine the hopes of rapid growth in the future.

As for the durability of the private capital flows, there have long been voices saying that this is a bubble of fashion which will burst. I believe this view reflects a misunderstanding of what is happening. What we are witnessing is a flow of capital seeking the best available returns; and returns are related to economic growth. The new growth in east and south Asia certainly does not have the appearance of a bubble: it is almost certainly a historic change in the economic geography of the world. In Latin America, too, the prospects for growth, while perhaps a little more open to doubt, are now rooted in sound policies. There is solid reason to believe that the countries to which capital has been flowing will grow faster than the mature industrial economies for some time to come, and so continue to offer higher returns to investors. The bubble theory would be more plausible if the investment flows were solely into stock markets, but, as we have seen, the portfolio flows have been combined with a formidable rise in direct investment, which is much less speculative.

The parallel that the scene in the 1990s bears to the situation about a hundred years ago, around the turn of the nineteenth and twentieth centuries, has often been pointed out. Before the First World War London acted as the centre of a financial world in which capital moved freely. Most of the twentieth century has been very different: from 1914 until the 1980s, with the important exception of the United States, private capital flows were restricted by governments. It is only recently that we have moved back into a world of easy mobility of private capital. In the early years of this century large amounts of private equity capital, mainly from Britain, then the most mature economy with the most developed financial markets, moved out to seek higher returns in the "emerging markets" of the time – in the Americas, North and South, and Australia. The development capital of that time was private capital. Now, once again, investors in the mature but slower-growing economies, especially institutional investors, are seeking higher returns in the newer, fast-growing economies.

With higher returns go higher risks, as a number of the investors of the late nineteenth century discovered. There will be ups and downs in the coming years. From time to time the cry of capital shortage will go up and, indeed, demand for capital will no doubt exert upward pressure on its cost periodically. But the basic factors which have led to the recent rise in private investment in the Third World seem likely to endure for some time.

So what are the prospects now for the Third World, as we come towards the beginning of a new century? And what role, if any, will there be for aid from the First World and the international agencies? The following comments focus on three areas: Asia, Latin America and Sub-Saharan Africa.

It is natural to begin with Asia. It is here that solid growth and inflows of investment seem most assured. Projections using purchasing-power-parity figures (which I referred to in Chapter 2) show China becoming the largest economy in the world. This use of PPP figures to measure the total *size* of economies has limited meaning, but the figures for income per head are a guide to the real standard of living and do generally confirm what common observation would suggest – that in most developing countries people are not quite as poor as the conventional figures indicate. If the PPP estimates are to be believed, China's income per head was about $2120 in 1993 and India's $1250. These figures seem closer to reality than the estimates based on current exchange rates of $490 and $290 respectively.[5]

I have argued that the only way that countries with large numbers of poor people can make a serious impact on these problems is a sustained period of rapid economic growth. India and China are such countries and both seem to be at a point where they may well be able to achieve this – indeed, China is already well into it. Growth will depend on sound policies being maintained (there are no miracles to be had, despite the common use of that word in this context) and of course there can be no certainty about that. However, average GNP growth rates of around 7 to 9 per cent, perhaps slightly more for China, slightly less for India, seem realistically within reach. Growth of GNP per head would be somewhat lower.

Some speculative numbers (Table 10) may illustrate what levels of income per head in PPP terms might be attainable by these two countries, with fast growth over a 20-year period from 1993 to 2013. If China's income per head were to rise at 7 per cent a year over these two decades it would reach $8200 in 2013. This would be a very substantial advance, making China's standard of living comparable with Korea or Venezuela now, both presently classified as "upper-middle income" countries. Problems of poverty, if not eliminated, would probably be much reduced.

On the other hand, if India's income per head grew by 5 per cent over the same period, it would reach $3320 in 2013. This would be similar, for example, to the standard of living today in countries such as Morocco and Jordan, or some less rich Latin American countries such as Ecuador or Paraguay, all countries which are classified by the World Bank in the "lower-middle

Table 10   Potential Growth in China and India (1993 US dollars)

	GNP per capita at current exchange rates		GNP per capita at purchasing power parity	
	1993	*2013*	*1993*	*2013*
China				
Growth at 8% p.a.	490	2280	2120	9880
Growth at 7% p.a.	490	1900	2120	8200
India				
Growth at 6% p.a.	290	930	1250	4010
Growth at 5% p.a.	290	770	1250	3320

income" group. This would amount to progress beyond anything achieved so far by India, but it would still leave it a poor country. There is no avoiding the conclusion that, for a country which starts from a base as low as India's, even 20 years at the growth rate I have assumed will not bring escape from serious poverty for at least some of its people. To achieve that will take either a longer period or still faster growth.

These hypothetical rates of growth are optimistic, but not excessively so for either country, in the light of recent performance. China has already exceeded the rates assumed for it over a number of years in the 1980s (although this was accompanied by some inflation). India has not yet achieved the rates assumed in the figures for any sustained period, but it is only beginning to gain the full benefits of its reform programme and the growth rate has been improving sharply. And of course other Asian countries, including Japan and the four Tigers, have done better still in the past.

China and India are only part of the Asian picture. In south and east Asia as a whole we may, in the next two decades, see the most significant advance in economic development since World War II, affecting very large numbers of people. Six large countries in this region – China and India, plus Pakistan, Indonesia, Thailand, and the Philippines – have a combined population of nearly 2.5 billion, nearly half the population of the world. There is still serious poverty in all these countries. World Bank figures suggest that over 40 per cent of the world's poorest people live in these six countries, a total of about 450 million people. Like China and India, the others all have some way to go before they achieve national incomes high enough to provide a reasonable standard of living for most of their people. But growth at rates which, over a couple of decades, would eliminate or drastically reduce serious poverty in these four countries is now entirely possible.

This does not mean that the countries of south and east Asia will all progress in parallel. The assumption that China will grow somewhat faster than India, combined with its higher starting base, implies that the gap in standard of living between these two in 2013 may be much greater than it is now, and there would no doubt be differences amongst the others too. But the general result in the region would be an improvement in living standards beyond anything that has been achieved over the whole period since the beginning of the development effort, except for the story of the Asian Tigers.

There is another significant point about the Asian countries: they seem to have a reasonably good chance of growing fast without great extremes of wealth and poverty, especially those in east Asia. They all have income distributions now which are more like those of Europe than of Latin America or much of Africa, and the record in the four Tigers and Japan suggests that fast growth need not change this. And twenty years' rapid growth would generate resources to enable governments, if they chose, to mount effective anti-poverty programmes and perhaps put some kind of social safety net in place. At the same time the environmental and urban problems which will come with high growth, aggravated, as I pointed out in Chapter 2, by the size and density of their populations now, will require a great deal of attention.

Will Asia need aid? Leaving aside cases such as Bangladesh, and some others which do not have the prospect of fast growth in the near future, the role of external aid will probably become increasingly marginal over the next two decades. The aid agencies will have to adapt themselves and what they offer to an environment of rapid or fairly rapid growth under market conditions. Technical assistance in the development of market-economy systems, and to help governments cope with social and environmental problems, may be more important than lending to governments.

However, in all the main Asian countries, huge amounts of investment will be needed to sustain high growth. Savings rates are typically high in the Asian countries and much the largest part of the investment needed to fuel growth, private and public, will come from within the countries themselves. But external capital will be needed, the largest part of it for investments by the private sector, which is already leading the expansion, and for infrastructure. Capital from abroad, whether for use in the public or private sector, should come mainly from private rather than official sources. The international aid effort should be concentrated on facilitating this. Selective support from aid agencies for sound private investments and investments in infrastructure may make a valuable contribution in Asia for a good many years. Further development of the region's capital markets, some of which are already quite far advanced, will enable them to play a growing role both in mobilising local capital and in channelling foreign investment into the countries.

The Latin American scene bears some resemblance to Asia, but there are important differences. In a number of the main countries of the region, there is now good reason to expect that the next decade will see strong growth: Argentina and Chile are already well on their way and as Mexico becomes part of the North American economic area, the medium-term prospects seem good. The election of a reforming President in Brazil gives reason to hope that that country will also achieve economic stability and embark on another period of rapid growth. Other countries such as Colombia and Peru also have a chance of doing well.

Latin America's history as a developing region is very different from Asia's. A century ago these countries were, from a European viewpoint, in the category which we now call emerging markets: today they are still viewed in that way. The failure of Latin America to "emerge" decisively through the 20th century is an historical puzzle, to be answered mainly in political terms – the depredations of Peronism in Argentina, which had achieved something like a European standard of living at the beginning of the century; and the decades of state management of the economy under the PRI in Mexico. Political factors may still deny the Latin countries the fast growth they could achieve, but the prospects seem better now.

Latin America has the greatest extremes of wealth and poverty of any region in the world, and despite their relatively high average GNP per head, serious poverty still exists in a number of countries. However, research by Pfeffermann and Webb at the World Bank showed that during the period of rapid growth in Brazil from 1967 to 1973, the poor benefited substantially.[6] Another period of rapid growth could benefit the whole population. But growth will not be enough and Latin American governments, especially in Brazil, will have to address the question of poverty seriously.

In terms of growth, there are reasons for suspecting that even the best performers in Latin America may not do as well as the leaders in Asia. The type of economic activity we are now seeing in Asia may be building a stronger base for sustainable growth. In the fast-growing Asian countries, with their high savings rates, whole new industries, many with an export orientation, are emerging every year. There are fewer signs of this in Latin America and capital flows into the region have been concentrated more on privatisation and infrastructure.

On the other hand, the Latin Americans are already far ahead in terms of GNP per head – an average of $2700 in 1992 compared with $470 for east and south Asia, excluding Japan and the four Tigers.[7] And there are some good reasons for optimism. Latin America has strong private companies – those who survived the 1980s had to be resourceful. The opening up of the Latin economies, the creation of free trade areas, especially Mexico's membership of NAFTA, which will integrate its economy much more with that of the United States, have created a much more competitive environment. The inflow of investment capital and the region's growing access to world financial markets will assist growth. And perhaps the most significant positive factor is the general improvement in macro-economic management in the past few years. On the other hand, there is always the possibility, given the volatile politics of the region, of reversals in economic management, as happened in Venezuela in 1994.

So, while the progress of "development" in Latin America in the coming years cannot be predicted with confidence, the potential is great. The existence of a reasonably well developed private sector in the region means that good macro-economic policies are likely to be rewarded with vigorous supply responses –

as Peru's strong growth after only a short period of sound policies under President Fujimori witnesses. The larger and richer countries of the region, particularly Mexico, Argentina, Chile and possibly Brazil, are at a point where a decade of economic success would effectively take them out of the category of developing countries.

In these countries, assuming reasonable success, the role of external development agencies seems likely to fade gradually during the coming decade. But, as in Asia, sustained growth will call for very large amounts of investment, mainly by the private sector, and conditions are still such that agencies like the IFC may be able to play an important facilitating role for a time. As in Asia, too, infrastructure investments, in which the public and private sectors will both participate, will probably grow fast and here also the external agencies may have a useful role for a number of years.

* * *

Without doubt the most formidable development challenge facing the world now is in Sub-Saharan Africa. I have touched earlier on the record in Africa – the huge aid effort (and the volume of aid continues to rise); progress in terms of life expectancy, child mortality and literacy statistics; but, with populations growing fast, income per person falling for a decade and a half. War and civil strife have played their part, but even in countries which have been peaceful, standards of living are apparently no better than they were when the colonial powers withdrew in the late 1950s and early 1960s. The collapse of Soviet communism means that Africa is no longer a cockpit for cold-war conflict, but the fact that this has not brought stability to the region suggests that Africa's troubles are, and always were, more indigenous than imported. Meanwhile, the efforts of most providers of aid are being increasingly focussed on Sub-Saharan Africa.

I can suggest no comprehensive answer to the problem of development in Africa. But the record makes it clear that a new approach is needed – the answer cannot simply be more of the same, the same type of aid in ever larger quantities. Indeed, the *quantity* of aid may already be part of the problem.

Should the approach to development be different in Africa than elsewhere, and, if so, why? In any part of the world, economic development must be rooted in sound economics. If the market economy is the best basis for growth in the rest of the world, this must be true in Africa too. There can be no other rational position, and, indeed, Africa itself offers dramatic evidence, in countries like Tanzania and Zambia, of the foolishness and irresponsibility of basing "development" on non-market policies. It is absolutely no service to Africa to argue that the standard IMF prescriptions of sound fiscal and monetary policies are not appropriate here.

The opposition in some quarters to "structural adjustment" – the jargon term for reform programmes which shift an economy towards market principles and eliminate or reduce distortions – also comes from people who question whether normal, mainstream economics are relevant in Africa. There has been much research in the aid industry on the question whether structural adjustment "works" in Africa, leading to mixed conclusions. The basic reality to be faced, however, is twofold. First, structural adjustment succeeds by creating the conditions for private-sector-led growth, and in countries where there is hardly any private sector at the start of the process, the "supply response" is bound to be slower than in countries which already have a substantial number of private companies. Secondly, the idea that there is a choice is illusory – no alternative means of achieving rapid growth is on offer. But part of the problem in Africa is that there is so little record of adjustment programmes being implemented effectively. The World Bank has estimated in 1994 that out of 29 African countries which were ostensibly engaged in "adjustment" programmes, only six had achieved decisive improvements in macro-economic policies and about a third continued to combine poor macro-economic policies with extensive interventionism.[8]

Amongst the obstacles to be overcome is a problem of attitudes, amongst both African governments and foreign aid donors. There is a lingering tendency to assume that Africa must be forever a commodity exporter. The vision of an Africa where there are modern, manufacturing industries, exporting to the world, is far from the minds of most people involved in "development" in the region. But without this, the growth that will provide jobs for the rapidly growing population and raise standards of living will not be achieved. If the building of a modern private-sector-led economy in Sub-Saharan Africa is simply an unrealistic goal, as some would argue, we are driven back to the despairing conclusion that the best that the rest of the world can do for Africa is to provide a kind of safety net, in practice continuous subsidy – and pauperisation.

If it is to be effective, the development effort must be led by Africans, though it can usefully be influenced by dialogue with others. But in much of Africa, development activities appear to be dominated by outsiders, promoting plans and programmes which, whether they are good for Africa or not, are not African. Insensitivity on the part of aid providers is part of the problem; but it is also true that Africans have not always been good at articulating positions on development issues, and when specifically African ideas have been articulated, they have not always been successful – again Nyerere's Tanzania comes to mind. But Africans are as capable as anyone else of learning from experience.

Against this background, it is appropriate to consider an agenda for a new dialogue between Africans and the external agencies who remain eager to provide aid to Africa. The discussion should be addressed primarily to the problem of developing a successful market economy in African countries.

The first question is how *official aid to governments* can be used more efficiently. Some countries in Africa are almost certainly suffering from too much aid. Most donors now concentrate heavily on Africa and the data (Table 7 in Chapter 2 shows that many African countries have become dependent on external aid, mainly in grant form, for a significant part of their GNP. In the early 1980s concessional aid amounted, on average, to 4 per cent of African countries' GNP. Since then it has risen steadily to 13.4 per cent in 1992, a disturbingly high figure. In many individual cases the percentages are higher (leaving aside special cases such as Somalia which has needed huge amounts of disaster relief); and projections indicate that it will continue to rise. Clearly, the reaction of donors to the failures of the past, which became increasingly evident during the 1980s, was to pour in more aid. The tendency, which I mentioned earlier, for some institutions to be driven by a wish to achieve pre-set targets for lending has contributed to this trend.[9]

The objective of development, for countries as for individuals, must be economic self-reliance, not dependence. Not enough attention is paid to the danger of creating a debilitating dependency in African countries. This danger cannot be simply a function of the volume of aid which a country receives as a percentage of its GNP, but as the percentage rises, the danger must increase, and 10 per cent is a very high figure. One would suppose that in countries with high savings rates the level at which aid tends to result in pauperisation will be higher, but African savings rates are by far the lowest of all regions in the developing world. The form of the aid must be a factor too – straight subsidies involve the greatest danger of creating dependency, and investments in market-based enterprises, the least. Nowadays many donors, including the UK, for understandable reasons provide aid to Africa mainly in the form of grants. As I argued in Chapter 6, the use of grants, although it seems logical for countries which have great difficulty in servicing debt, tends to weaken the rigour with which aid projects are appraised. And common sense must make one question whether African governments and bureaucracies can use resources on the present scale efficiently, especially when the money comes from many different donors, each with their own ideas and priorities, all demanding time and attention from governments which have only a thin layer of competent personnel.

More discipline is needed in the processes of providing grant aid to African governments. One way to do this, shocking as it might seem to the practitioners, might be to ration aid by setting ceilings, agreed amongst donors, for each country. Thoughts of this kind would not be worth considering were it not obvious that resources have been used inefficiently – and in some cases harmfully – in Africa, so that it is not to be assumed that an overall reduction in aid would do harm. On the contrary, if at the same time systems were introduced to subject aid proposals to much stricter examination, the key test being the contribution they would make to the growth of a market economy and to rising incomes, the effect should be beneficial. A rationing process would itself ensure that each aid proposal was subjected to tough questioning.

Setting country ceilings would not be popular in the aid fraternity, nor would they be easy to administer. The desire to be seen to be pouring money into Africa to help the very poor is such that some donors would probably refuse to join in. It would only be possible if the larger donors, and especially the World Bank, took the lead, but the Bank itself would clearly have to abandon quantity as an objective in favour of total concentration on the quality and effectiveness of aid.

The criteria suggested in Chapter 6 for aid to governments are particularly important and relevant in Africa, where the tendency for the heart to rule the head has been most marked. Subject to these criteria, agencies providing aid to governments should focus attention specifically on the range of things which governments need to do to create a stimulating environment for the private sector, including carefully selected investments in infrastructure, education and training.

The second item for the agenda should be a major shift in the development effort towards promoting a strong *private sector* to lead economic growth. But here too we must beware of eagerness to do good – the dangers of nurse-maiding the private sector by flooding it with easy money, which I discussed in Chapter 7, are at their greatest in Africa, where there are so many donors with little understanding of the private sector and so many people in governments who cannot refuse whatever is offered. In the interests of the African private sector of the future, whatever is done must be wholly business-like.

Africa starts a long way back, compared with Asia or Latin America, with very little private sector in most countries, and this does make the development task different. The private companies of the future will have to emerge (a) from new businesses and (b) from foreign investment. Both will require (c) a modern, market-based financial sector. These three points suggest a framework for a programme to promote a private sector in Africa.

There are a few successful programmes for *promoting new businesses* which could be enlarged and made more effective. One such, which could be taken as a model, is the Africa Project Development Facility, created and managed by the IFC and co-sponsored by the United Nations Development Programme and the African Development Bank and funded by them and a number of donor governments. It provides technical advice and guidance to small and medium businesses and helps them to raise funding for investment. The APDF, launched in 1986, has been highly successful, but for an operation aimed at helping the private sector in a continent of 540 million people, it is tiny. For the first five years, the APDF operated from just two offices, at Abidjan in west Africa and Nairobi in the east. In the second five year period a third office was opened in Harare, the capital of Zimbabwe. The organisation's total professional staff at the end of 1993 was only about 20 people, and there is no other comparable organisation at work in Sub-Saharan Africa (although a similar operation is now being mounted in South Africa). Over eight years the APDF has advised and secured financing for 183 companies, but the number of firms and entrepreneurs who have applied for its help over this period is very much larger – about 2400. The effort illustrated what we already knew from other evidence: that Africa is not short of budding entrepreneurs.

How was this effort viewed by the donors to Africa? For the first five years of the APDF's operations, the sponsors and donors together contributed a total of $18.3 million. For the second period, when it was enlarged, a total of $45 million was raised with considerable difficulty. When these figures are placed in the context of the total aid being provided to Africa – $17.9 billion in 1990 – they tell us something about donors' priorities. The effort to promote private-sector development was seen by donors as marginal to their main effort through governments. If donors are serious about the market economy – and that is the only way of being serious about economic growth in Africa – a major shift in priorities is needed. The APDF might well be increased ten-fold, or other similar efforts might be mounted.

This is one example. Every aid agency and government in Africa should be looking for effective ways of promoting successful African businesses. Micro-lending for very small, informal businesses, which has been developed successfully in Bangladesh, Venezuela and elsewhere, should be tried. Schemes which would provide seed capital to entrepreneurs to start new businesses on the basis that they can buy the business over time out of the proceeds of success should be explored too. The whole field simply needs more attention and creativity.

The second way of building a private sector in Africa is to attract a renewed inflow of *foreign private investment*. As I have remarked before, for more than two decades foreign investment has played a very small part in economic development in Sub-

Saharan Africa. There has been a few large investments in oil, gas and minerals in a small number of countries, but foreign investment in manufacturing enterprises, which did take place in the 1960s, has since then been almost wholly lacking. The loss to development in Africa has been great. Foreign investment could not only bring in capital, management skills and technology, provide employment and contribute to national output, including production for export, but could indirectly promote the growth of local businesses to supply them. A renewed inflow of foreign investment could make an important contribution to the development of a market economy in Africa. South African companies, with their experience of operating on the continent, are showing some interest in investing elsewhere in Africa, and could help to attract other investors too.

A much stronger and more sustained assault on this problem than anything done so far is needed, by African states acting together, and with technical assistance and advice from aid organisations. To achieve results will take some time. The image of Africa for investors in Europe, North America and Japan remains unappealing, aggravated by war and upheaval in some countries (and the inability of some investors to distinguish between one country and another on the continent). The answer does not lie in special subsidies or inducements offered by governments either in Africa or in the capital-exporting countries, but in creating conditions which will convince investors that they will be able to operate in a stable economic environment (sound macro-economic policies are as important here as elsewhere), free from undue government interference and excessive taxation. The Foreign Investment Advisory Service, established by the IFC, has done much useful work in advising African governments on this subject, but clearly there is still a long way to go.

Thirdly, Africa needs a stronger *financial sector* in each country to mobilise savings and allocate them efficiently to productive use, and to provide financial services to companies. In this area, most of Africa lags well behind the rest of the developing world, although Zimbabwe is an exception. An important part of the development task consists of creating the legal and regulatory systems for the financial markets to work well and of promoting sound private financial companies, as the IFC has been doing. More good banking, venture capital and leasing companies will sustain the growth of a local private sector. Skills and capital from South Africa could play a useful part here too.

Indeed, what happens in Sub-Saharan Africa as a whole will be influenced by what happens in South Africa, a special case, where a First World economy is mixed with a Third World economy. But the impact that South Africa can have on the rest of the continent should not be exaggerated, given the enormous problems of its own that it has to cope with. South Africa may be on the verge of a period of rapid growth which will significantly improve the lot of its black people. It has strong companies, although they are somewhat ingrown as a result of years of isolation, and they are anxious to expand. But steady growth will require political stability. In the transition from apartheid, the country has been blessed with outstanding political leadership, both black and white, but the ingredients of social unrest are obviously present and the future is uncertain at this stage.

＊　　＊　　＊

The late 1980s and early 1990s seem to have been a turning point in world economic history and also in relations between the First and Third Worlds. The relationship we have today seems more mature, with a healthy component of realism. The artificiality of the "North-South dialogue", the demands for a New International Economic Order, the confrontational debates in UNCTAD and elsewhere now seem remote. They have been replaced by a new belief in markets, itself to some extent the consequence of crisis, especially in the Latin American case. As the leaders of a number of Third World countries, from Indonesia and India to Argentina and Chile, take a grip on their own affairs and begin to experience the benefits which follow from sound macro-economic management, they also experience an accession of confidence which is new in the Third World. The world of "dependency" has gone. Fernando Henrique Cardoso, one of the early proponents of the dependency theory in Latin America, has assumed office as President of Brazil with a very different philosophy of openness and co-operation. The new generation of Third World leaders is a very different lot from those who met at Bandung to launch the Non-Aligned Movement. One good example: I recall listening with relish as Mohamed Barrada, then Finance Minster of Morocco, speaking as the 1992 Chairman of the Annual Meetings of the IMF and World Bank, admonishing the assembled finance minsters of the industrial world for failing to maintain proper fiscal discipline, pointing out that Morocco's budget deficit was a mere one per cent of GDP, and demanding open markets rather than aid.

In the new First World–Third World relationship, the concept of aid as we have come to know it begins to look dated. The relationship of donor to recipient, benefactor to beneficiary, rich to poor, almost inevitably also takes on a tone of superior to inferior. In this respect, the move towards development through markets rather than official aid is an advance to maturity. The market relationship is one between equals, with no flavour of superior or inferior. Africa has not reached there yet, but the dealings of the older industrial countries with much of Asia and Latin America are becoming a market relationship rather than an aid relationship, and much healthier for being so.

What part will aid play in the future? The main initiator of the international aid effort soon after World War II was the United States, but over time the American mood has changed radically. In recent years, the US has been the lowest contributor amongst the industrial countries in terms of its own GNP. Disillusionment and hostility towards foreign aid have been growing steadily. The Republican Congress elected at the end of 1994 may make drastic reductions and there has even been talk of ending US aid altogether. On the other hand, in Europe and Japan, although aid is under budgetary pressure, there are no signs that it will be abandoned or cut drastically – indeed some smaller European countries are still providing relatively large percentages of their GNP in aid, with popular support.

Indeed, a considerable difference in attitudes to aid has opened up between the United States and Europe. They seem to reflect two ways in which Europeans and Americans see the world differently. One is a difference in attitudes towards the welfare state and the use of taxation to support the disadvantaged. "Welfare" is viewed with hostility in the United States but generally accepted in Europe. In the United States, a very high value is placed on personal independence, whereas in Europe the responsibility of the state to support the disadvantaged is taken for granted, except by the extreme right. Similarly, Europeans seem to have accepted international aid as part of the natural order of things, whereas Americans have not.

The other difference is one of expectations. Americans, having launched the international aid movement in a spirit of generosity, expected results. The fact that they are still being asked to contribute to aid through taxation seems to most Americans to prove that aid has failed, and that no more money should be wasted on it. European countries, on the other hand, some with historical connections with the Third World through the empires of the past, are more inclined to accept that the Third World and its poor are always with us. The American view may seem naive to Europeans, but perhaps Europeans have something to learn from the American impatience with an effort which after forty-five years seems to have achieved so little.

A radical cut in US aid, which now seems possible, would emphasise this difference even more. It would not directly affect other countries' bilateral programmes, but could have consider-able implications for international organisations. Those organisa-tions which depend on capital contributions, such as the IBRD and the IFC within the World Bank Group, and the various regional development banks, would be able to go on operating on the basis of their existing capital and callable capital. The IBRD's capacity for new lending now substantially exceeds demand, so that it may never need a further injection of capital. However, there would be a major impact on the International Development Association (IDA) the soft-aid arm of the World Bank, created as a result of an American initiative in 1960, which is replenished with contributions from governments every three years. The reaction of other countries to a withdrawal or drastic cut by the US would probably be to scale down their own contributions proportionately, possibly shifting some resources to their bilateral programmes. The world aid effort would almost certainly be reduced, and the American share of it would be smaller still.

What would this mean for the Third World? The question suggests a larger and entirely hypothetical one which it may be salutary to ask at this stage. What would be the impact on developing countries if, at this point in history, all aid programmes were cancelled? This does not seem in any way likely to happen, but of course the underlying question is: how important is international aid to the Third World now? I think the answer falls into two parts.

First, we should acknowledge that the impact even of a total close-down of aid on the main Asian and Latin American countries at this stage would be limited – larger than zero, but not critical to their continued economic progress. Despite their poverty, these countries now enjoy good access to international capital markets, and would probably keep up reasonably fast growth even without further official aid. This is not to say that aid does no good in these countries – the right kind of aid can assist and accelerate the process of building a sound market economy and raise more resources for investment – but most of Asia will probably progress vigorously with or without aid and most of Latin America too.

Secondly, however, the loss of aid would undoubtedly come as a severe blow to the very poor countries, especially in Sub-Saharan Africa and Bangladesh, through the loss both of IDA funding and of much bilateral assistance, mainly from Europe. But this again is partly an indication of how dependent some poor countries have become on external aid, and as I have argued, radically new thinking is needed about that. Total and abrupt cancellation of aid would certainly do damage; but a judicious reduction in aid to Africa, combined with a redirection of the effort and a more selective use of the available resources, would probably be beneficial in the long run.

Whether the reader agrees with these comments or not, there is no denying that the international aid movement is in crisis. It is under assault from many different angles; but fundamentally the crisis is about effectiveness. The questions about the impact of nearly half a century of the aid effort, which I have discussed in this book, cannot easily be disposed of. The professionals of the business tend to avoid the hardest questions, and many of them assume that the old answers will still do. What we need now is for outsiders, serious people in public life, in the press, in academic institutions, commerce and finance, to insist that the important issues are not ignored. I would like to see this discussion led by people who sympathise with the basic aims of the aid enterprise, but are prepared to be objective about the record and the lessons to be learned from it.

The aid movement has lost its way and needs to be led into change. In the coming decades the global aid effort will and should be smaller and more concentrated. Whether it will be more effective remains to be seen; but I believe it will be so only if methods and priorities change significantly, re-orienting the effort towards realistic ways of supporting market economies in the developing countries. This must include a major shift in the balance of aid away from providing finance to governments and towards support for the private sector.

So far, the poor are still with us; but the phrase "the Third World", invented as it was to describe the condition of our planet at the mid-point of the twentieth century, has already become an anachronism. I excuse myself for using it in the title of this book, and often in the text, on the grounds that I have been speaking mainly about a half century when it was apt. But before the new century is far advanced it will be meaningless and the passing of the Third World should surely not be cause for regret.

12 Twenty-one Propositions about Development and Aid

1. There is a strong moral and political case for the rich countries of the world to try to help the poor countries achieve higher standards of living and reduce poverty. But the key question, after 40 years of effort, is whether, and if so how, they can do so effectively in practice.
2. The basic test of development success must be economic growth as measured by the change in GNP per person. Although there are also other valid measures of development, a rising level of incomes is basic because it widens the choices available to people in shaping their communal and individual lives.
3. By this test, the overall results of the international development effort over the past four decades have been disappointing. Although a few countries in the far east have done very well, there are still large numbers of very poor people even in countries which have made some progress (much of Asia); and in Sub-Saharan Africa, where standards of living have been falling for long periods of time, despite huge quantities of aid, there has clearly been failure.
4. A significant improvement in GNP per person in poor countries can be achieved only through a sustained period of rapid economic growth, usually lasting at least two decades.
5. The statist approach to economic development is one of the main reasons why economic growth has been slower than it could have been in most of the Third World. Aid agencies bear some of the responsibility for this because they supported policies involving government planning, controls and public ownership. Aid also strengthened the role of the state in Third World countries, simply by channelling large amounts of money to governments.

6. There is now sufficient experience to put it beyond doubt that the only effective route to fast economic growth is the market economy. The widespread acceptance of the market philosophy holds out new hope that poor countries will be able to achieve a significant improvement in their standards of living. The basic aim of international aid should now be to help developing countries to run successful market economies.

7. Efficiency and fairness in a market economy require the role of the state to be well defined and competently performed. While keeping out of decisions which should be left to the markets, the state must provide the framework within which the market economy can work, including infrastructure and essential services, legal and regulatory systems and a sound macro-economic policy.

8. The unfettered play of market forces can cause social problems which are more difficult to deal with in poor countries. Before a country can afford unemployment pay, the only effective answer to the problem of unemployment is to achieve a momentum of growth in which new jobs are created as old jobs are lost.

9. Rapid growth does not necessarily mean greater inequality of incomes, as is commonly supposed. But where they occur, extremes of wealth and poverty are socially damaging and governments should seek to reduce poverty by increasing the productivity of the poor rather than by subsidy. Reducing poverty is more important than equalising incomes.

10. The market philosophy requires that the intellectual basis of aid activity be re-examined. The doctrinaire view that any kind of aid is inconsistent with market principles is wrong; but misguided forms of aid can retard the development of a market economy. Aid can be harmful and is not validated simply by good intentions.

11. Aid can do harm if it supports bad economic policies in recipient countries, such as anti-market policies involving state ownership and control.

12. Aid can also do harm if it continues for long periods in large amounts by creating a mentality of dependency or pauperisation, as appears to be happening in much of Africa now.

13. The creation of modern financial systems and capital markets is critically important to building a market economy. But the wrong kind of aid, such as large inflows of funds on non-market terms, can stifle and discourage the growth of financial markets.
14. As a general rule, all aid (apart from disaster relief) should take the form of investment, designed to increase productive capacity and contribute to faster growth. Investments in the public sector, which cannot be put to a market test, need to be appraised with particular rigour to make sure they will earn a proper return for the country. The danger of insufficient rigour is particularly great when aid comes in the form of grants and when donors pursue volume targets for their aid.
15. There is a valid role for aid to governments, provided it supports the growth of a market economy, and is highly selective. As a rule such aid should support only activities which the private sector will not or cannot do, or where there are compelling reasons why the state should undertake them.
16. Aid provided directly to the private sector can be justified by the fact that markets often work badly in Third World countries. But it must also be subject to strict criteria to ensure that it does not displace private finance. Such aid is best provided on market terms, and subject to market risk, and should be used to mobilise funding from private sources to the greatest extent possible.
17. The present balance between aid to governments and aid to the private sector, which is still heavily skewed in favour of the former, needs to be changed substantially.
18. A number of countries in Asia and Latin America now seem poised for a period of rapid growth which could reduce poverty substantially, especially in Asia. Aid will play a diminishing role in these countries in future, but should focus on facilitating inward investment and on technical assistance to support an efficient market economy.
19. Private capital seems sure to play a much larger part in the development of these countries in the future, including investments in infrastructure, relieving governments and aid agencies of much of the burden.

20. In Africa and some other countries where the development effort has had little success, a radically new approach is needed. The quantity of official aid, and the dependency it creates, appears to be part of the problem. More discipline needs to be introduced in aid provided to governments, and the balance of the aid effort needs to be shifted to programmes to promote private sector development.
21. The aid business, now 45 years old, must not be seen as never-ending. If governments follow the right policies, with the support of aid agencies, standards of living can be raised substantially and poverty drastically reduced.

Notes and References

1 International Development, 1949–94

1. It is interesting to compare the Third World aid numbers with the Marshall Plan. Over the four years from mid-1948 to mid-1952, US aid to Europe under the Marshall Plan totalled about $70 billion in terms of 1987 dollars, a remarkable 1.1 per cent of US GNP over those years, considerably exceeding American aid to the Third World at any stage. On the other hand, it was a four-year burst rather than a prolonged effort.
2. J. M. Burniaux and J. Waelbroek: "The Impact of the Common Agricultural Policy on Developing Countries: A General Equilibrium Analysis", in Stevens and Verloren van Themaat: The EEC and the Third World: (London, Holden & Stoughton, 1985).
3. *The Effect of Industrial Countries' Trade, Agricultural and Industrial Policies on Developing Countries.* Paper prepared for the Development Committee by the staffs of the World Bank and International Monetary Fund. (Washington, DC, April 1991).
4. *Crisis or Transition in Foreign Aid*, ed Adrian Hewitt, (London: Overseas Development Institute, 1994).
5. P. T. Bauer, *Equality, the Third World and Eonomic Delusion* (Harvard University Press 1981).

2 Success or Failure?

1. *United Nations Development Programme: Human Development Report 1994* (Oxford University Press 1994).
2. This is a case where dollar figures based on market exchange rates are particularly misleading, because of a significant real depreciation of the Chinese currency during the decade.
3. People living in "absolute poverty" are defined as those who subsist on incomes of less than one dollar of 1985 value a day, at purchasing power parity, a severe definition indeed.

223

4. *Report of the Independent Consultants' Study on Aid-Effectiveness to the Development Committee's Task Force on Concessional Flows* (Washington, DC: World Bank 1985).
5. See, for example Peter Boone, London School of Economics: "The Impact of Foreign Aid on Savings and Growth", June 1994.
6. Tony Killick: "Conditionality and the Adjustment-Development Connection". Paper delivered at the conference on the Future of the IMF and the World Bank, Madrid, September 1994.

4 The Market Revolution

1. See p. 19 in Chapter 1.
2. For an interesting discussion of the influences leading to economic reform, see *The Political Economy of Policy Reform*, edited by John Williamson, Institute for International Economics, Washington, DC, 1994.
3. *The East Asian Miracle* (Washington, DC: World Bank September 1993), pp.43–6.
4. John Williamson, "In Search of a Manual for Technopols", in *The Political Economy of Policy Reform*, *q.v.* note 2.
5. Killick, "Conditionality and the Adjustment-Development Connection", *q.v.* Chapter 3, note 6.

5 Is Capitalism Right for the Third World?

1. Moises Naim, *Latin America's Journey to the Market* (Panama City: International Center for Economic Growth, 1995).
2. See George Psacharopoulos in *World Development*, vol. 22, No. 9, (1994).
3. *World Development Report, 1994*, Table 30 (Washington, DC: World Bank, 1994).
4. Simon Kuznets, *Towards a Theory of Economic Growth* (New York: Doubleday, 1956.)
5. Nancy Birdsall and Richard Sabot: "Inequality, Exports and Human Capital in East Asia: Lessons for Latin America", in *Redefining the State in Latin America* (Paris: OECD, 1994).
6. Peter L. Berger, *The Capitalist Revolution* (Basic Books, 1986), p. 74.
7. Berger, *q.v.*, p. 76.

6 Re-inventing Aid

1. Bauer, *q.v.* Chapter 1, note 5.
2. A flavour of Bauer's style of argument may be gleaned from a quotation from his book p. 111: "Official aid", he says, "does not go to poor people, to the skeletal figures of aid propaganda. It goes instead to their rulers whose spending policies are determined by their own personal and political interests, among which the position of the poorest has very low priority." The "skeletal figures" must be taken as a reference to the publicity efforts of non-governmental organisations – as a rule, official agencies do not appeal to the public in this way – and NGO money does not go to rulers. The implication that official aid agencies have no control over the use of aid money is also wrong. Official aid has in fact been used to support successful poverty-reduction programmes in a number of countries and a serious critique of aid must recognise successes as well as failures, rather than attacking every aspect of international development as pernicious.
3. *The World Bank's Guarantees* (Washington, DC: World Bank, October 1994).

7 Aid to the Private Sector

1. Chapter 8 contains a personal account of my period as head of the IFC.
2. *Financing Infrastructure Projects* (Washington, DC: IFC, 1994).
3. The Deutsche Investitions und Entwicklungsgesellschaft (DEG) in Germany; the Caisse Française de Développement (CFD) and its subsidiary, Proparco, in France; the Commonwealth Development Corporation (CDC) in Britain; the Nederlandse Financierings-Maatschappij voor Ontwikelingslanden (FMO) in the Netherlands; the Overseas Economic Co-operation Fund (OECF) in Japan; and similar agencies in Sweden, Denmark and Finland.

8 The International Finance Corporation, 1984–93

1. *Bretton Woods: Looking to the Future*, Report of the Bretton Woods Commission, Washington, DC, July 1994.

9 What Future for the World Bank and IMF?

1. The point is made effectively by Rosemary Righter in her book *Utopia Lost*: (New York, Twentieth Century Fund, 1995).
2. *Bretton Woods: Looking to the Future, q.v.* Chapter 8, note 1.
3. The Bank and Fund were effectively established at a conference in Savannah, Georgia in 1946, a follow up to the Bretton Woods conference of two years earlier.
4. *The World Bank Group: Learning from the Past, Embracing the Future* (Washington, DC: World Bank, July 1994).
5. One example: "Selectivity – identifying, particularly at the country level, the strategic actions through which the Bank Group can help catalyse the maximum potential of its partners as well as maximise its own impact."

11 Where Now?

1. The figures for secondary market purchases and total equity holdings come from Baring Securities Ltd, London.
2. Guy Pfeffermann and Richard Webb, "Poverty and Income Distribution in Brazil", *Review of Income and Wealth* (Washington, DC: World Bank, June 1983).
3. See Chapter 8, p. 152.
4. See Chapter 3, p. 64 and Chapter 7, pp. 128–9.
5. For comparison, the PPP estimates put Mexico's income at $7100 per head, Malaysia's at $8630, Britain's at $17,750 and the United States' at $24,750.
6. Pfeffermann and Webb, "Poverty and Income Distribution in Brazil", *q.v.* note 2.
7. Or, on a PPP basis, $5900 for Latin America and $2000 for Asia.
8. *Adjustment in Africa* (Washington, DC: World Bank, 1994), p. 3.
9. The World Bank itself, in the report referred to in Chapter 3 (see p. 66), acknowledged that Tanzania could have been better off with less Bank lending, and that the Bank was influenced by the need to meet lending targets.

Index

227